Quilted New York

Celebrate the City with Fabric and Color

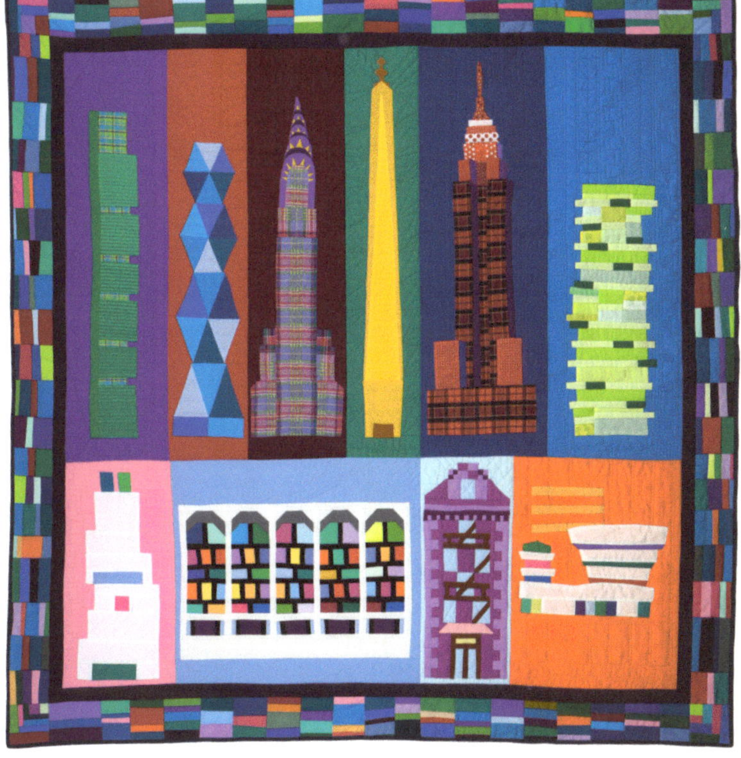

Above, Color Block New York
Right, New York Condensed

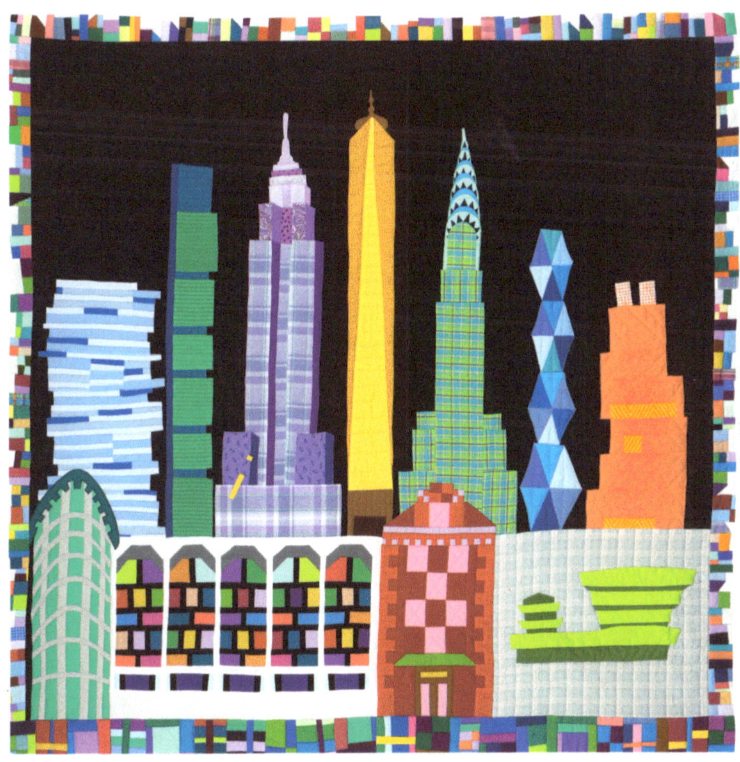

Cathy Perlmutter

ISBN-10: 0-9799932-4-5
ISBN-13: 978-0-9799932-4-4
LCCN
Published by: Uncommon Page Press
1129 Stratford Avenue
South Pasadena CA
Printed in the United States of America

Questions? Comments? Suggestions? Want to buy more copies? Did you make something from this book? I would love to hear from you!
email: cathy.perlmutter@gmail.com
WEBSITE: cathyperlmutter.com
BLOG: gefiltequilt.com
ETSY SHOP: https://www.etsy.com/shop/CathyPStudio
FACEBOOK: Cathy Perlmutter
INSTAGRAM: @cathy.perlmutter

A significant portion of the proceeds from this book will go to organizations that benefit New York City's homeless.

This is not a licensed product. I am not affiliated or associated with any buildings that inspired the artwork in this book.

Profound gratitude to the pattern testers for their time, patience, thought, creativity and rigor!
Cathy Alexander, Donna Bresnick Babchuck, Flora Cohen, Saraj Cory, Barbara Fritz-Elliot, Cecelia Goodman Ellis, Jane Holbrook, Marilyn Knepp, Vivian Lewis, Glenda Graci Parks, Michele Pusateri, Gail Solomon, Sue Warshell, Crissi Wells
Copy Editing: Vivian Lewis
All remaining errors are my own. Find errata on my cathyperlmutter.com webpage.
Special thanks to Eleanor Levie for convincing me to try, and to Richard Lewis, for his wise counsel and wife's time!
Dedicated to the kind and helpful New Yorkers I have known and loved, including my husband, my daughter/artistic advisor Riva, my son Eli and daughter-in-law Liz, my new grandson Abe, and a random dude who went out of his way to accompany me and my young kids on the NYC subway when we were lost, ensuring that we reached the right station. I love New York.

BISAC
CRAFTS & HOBBIES/Quilts & Quilting CRA031000
CRAFTS & HOBBIES/Patchwork CRA026000
ARCHITECTURE / Buildings/Landmarks & Monuments ARC024010
ARCHITECTURE / Design, Drafting, Drawing & Presentation ARC004000
TRAVEL / United States / Northeast / Middle Atlantic (NJ, NY, PA) TRV025050

CONTENTS

PART 1: How This Works

PART 2: Inspiration Buildings

PART 3: The Quilts

"Every iteration of the New York skyline is an abomination to one generation and an inspiration to the next."
    – Justin Davidson, *Magnetic City: A Walking Companion to New York*

Introduction

I'm a city girl, born in New York, raised near Boston, and lived in Washington D.C., Tokyo, and for the past 30 years, Los Angeles.

Walking around cities (or, in the case of LA, driving), while gaping at the architecture was always one of my great joys, and even more so after I started quilting in 1991. Every interesting building asks the same question: "How would you translate me into fabric?"

New York City is the ultimate city, and the closest thing my family has to an American homeland. My Dad, Phil Perlmutter, was raised in a Williamsburg tenement, a bridge away from Manhattan. He dropped out of high school at 17, lied about his age to join the Army, and was in combat in WWII. Afterwards, he attended college and graduate school at NYU and Columbia University, tuition paid by the GI Bill. He became a community leader, and authored books about our country's ugly history of anti-immigrant prejudice. My mother, Rosanne, came to New York from Poland after surviving the death camps, where she lost most of her family. A few years later, she earned a bachelor's degree from NYC's Hunter College. She became a teacher and psychologist. Both my children have lived in NYC, and one still does; my son and daughter-in-law are raising my shiny new grandson there. Whenever I visit, it feels like coming home.

So here is my "thank you," with an occasional "What the heck?" (but a stronger word), to the city that gave my family and the world so much, and continues to do so, with the thrilling diversity of its people and structures – the extravagant, overwhelming, fascinating, iconic, eccentric, controversial, highly-litigated, and always over-the-top buildings.

Fabric

Buildings: No rules! Mine are mostly solids, for a modern look. Plaids are great for complicated buildings. If your quilt shop doesn't have plaids, check out men's shirts. Any print can be great fun, especially geometrics. Or, for a watercolor look, choose batiks.

For most buildings, you need only a fat-quarter or quarter-yard, plus smaller amounts for windows. A few require more. You may have most of what you need in your stash.

Background(s): You're more likely to need to shop for these – the two yards required for the sky in 'Condensed New York' (p. 71); or the large background rectangles in 'Color Block New York' (p. 76).

Supplies

▶ **The Usual** – Zigzag sewing machine + Rotary cutter, ruler & mat + iron + seam ripper + scissors.

▶ **Temporary school glue sticks** or **stitchers' glue pens** – Either is fine, pens are less messy.

▶ **Sharp awl** – For machine appliqué, to tuck flaps under. (A pointy seam ripper can do this too.)

▶ **Paper-backed fusible web** – Total 10" square for three spires (Chrysler, Empire State, World Trade). Plus two more 8.5" x 10" pieces for Flatiron.

▶ **Appliqué press sheet** or **parchment paper** – Keeps board clean when working with fusible.

▶ **Open-toe sewing foot** – For machine appliqué.

▶ **Invisible monofilament thread** – For appliqué. (Or, thread matching each building's color.)

▶ **Freezer paper** – Just a little, to shape curved pieces in the Guggenheim and Chrysler.

▶ **Tear-away stabilizer** – Optional - see p. 6. Or use clean lightweight paper, like newsprint.

The Basic Idea: Piece First, Place It Anywhere

The eleven buildings in this book are mostly pieced, using my technique for turning outside edges to the back *during* piecing. A few buildings also require fused raw edge appliqué for small or curved details. Finally, each is pieced or appliquéd to a background.

Why Turn Edges as We Build?

As soon as I started piecing buildings, I realized I had a problem: Most have uneven edges, like my version of NYC's New Museum here.

Imagine you sewed these rectangles together the traditional way. The outside edges would all wind up raw. Then, to prepare to appliqué it to a background, you would want to turn each outside edge back 1/4". That would require ripping stitches at every inside corner (where arrows point), weakening seams, and making threads more likely to show. (Plus it's boring.)

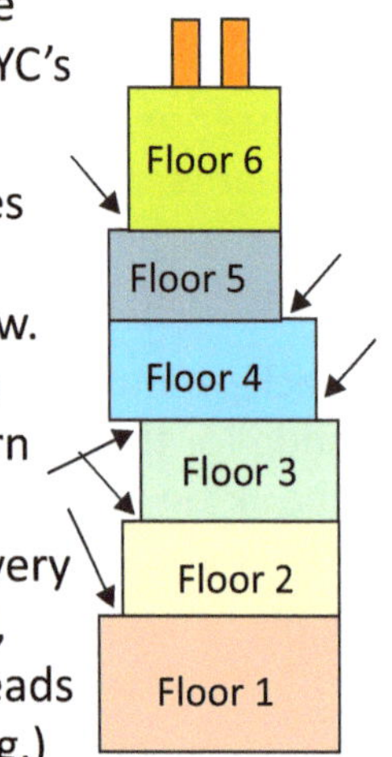

But I love the look and durability of turned-edge appliqué, and I was determined to find a way to turn edges without ripping seam ends.

I developed a system for fastening edges back during piecing. Turned flaps are secured with backstitching, which also hides pesky thread ends that would otherwise poke out from seam ends.

My trick is fully illustrated in each chapter. An example is below: joining the bottom two floors of the New Museum above. First press floor 2's left edge back 1/4". Flip it down onto the first floor. Pull up threads at **a**; backstitch the flap shut, to **b**; sew off the end at **c** – no need to backstitch there because there's no flap and edges are even. When you open floor 2, its left raw edge will be neatly pressed backward; the seam end at **b** will be strong, and the thread tails will be hidden far back from the edge, at **a**.

This will make more sense as you work your way through the directions – it's fully illustrated almost every time.

By the end of each chapter, the building is just about ready to be appliquéd to a pillow, wallhanging, or a larger quilt, like 'Condensed New York' (p. 71); or 'Color Block New York,' (p. 76). Because most edges are turned, you can decide to sew that building anywhere – and then easily change your mind! Wherever you put it, hand or machine appliqué goes faster when the edges are turned back in advance.

Sew This First

I suggest you start with the New Museum or One Madison, or at least read those chapters first. They were the easiest for me. Structures are generally more challenging as you move through the book, but the detailed directions should make it all doable. I find fusible appliqué with satin stitching more challenging than piecing, but you may feel the opposite! In that case, the last building (Flatiron) may be the easiest for you!

On Improv

I'm an improviser at heart. I do as little measuring as I can get away with. Use my measurements, or just take them as general guidelines and build it your way!

Pick Your Palette

Realism can be a problem. Most American city buildings are not very colorful. And if you put a bunch of brown and grey buildings next to each other they may weld into an amorphous blob. That's why I often go fanciful! I give each building a dominant color, different from buildings that might adjoin it. But you should do it your way!

Appliqué: When, Where and How

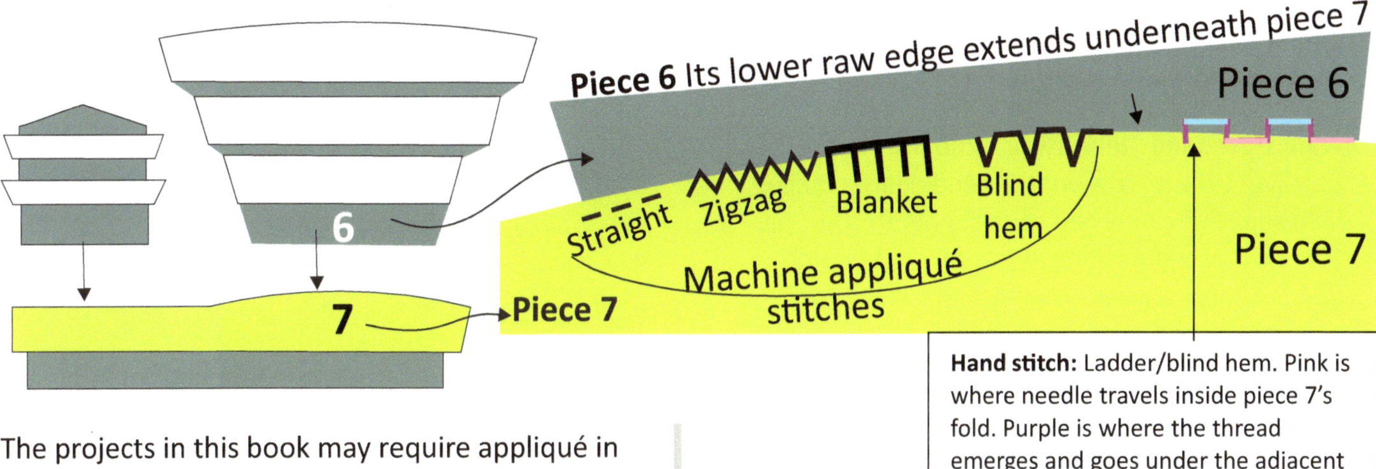

The projects in this book may require appliqué in three situations:

► **Inside some buildings.** Four buildings require a little appliqué. These include the Guggenheim, above, which needs appliqué to secure piece 7's upper curved, turned edge atop the bottom raw edge of piece 6.

► **On spires and other small and/or curved raw-edge details.** In four buildings, I suggest fusible web and a tight zigzag to cover raw edges.

► **Around every building.** To fasten its mostly-turned edges to the background.

Hand vs. Machine

You decide. Choices are:

Hand appliqué Disadvantage: It's slow. Advantage: Slow means it's easy to tuck flaps under as you go.

Machine appliqué Advantage: Much faster – but that's a disadvantage too. Once underway, it's more challenging to tuck flaps under and trim protrusions. Suggestions below will help.

Machine Appliqué Tips

► **Clean up the building** Turn back, trim and/or glue back every protruding flap and thread in advance, so they can't be seen from the front. It's much easier to fix things before the building goes into the machine, than when the problem area is approaching the presser foot.

► **Do a tension test** Do it before you start, and whenever you change thread, fabric, or stitch. You don't want bobbin thread to show; you may find that stabilizer helps. Make a test sample with the same layers you plan to sew. (More about this is on the next page.)

► **Try to love "invisible" monofilament thread** It's a time-saver for multicolor buildings. But if you don't like invisible thread, match the building's color with both top and bobbin threads.

► **Good visibility is crucial** Use an open-toe foot for appliqué . I also wear magnifying headgear.

Which Stitches?

Above is the same area of the building as on the left. Piece 7 's folded top edge is atop 6, making 7 "the appliqué" and piece 6 "background." Options:

By hand:

► Blind hem, blanket, ladder, or a running stitch.

By Machine:

► **Zigzag** My favorite, usually medium wide (1.5), medium tight (1.25), with most of the stitch laying on the appliqué (piece 7). This is the stitch I use for most turned edges, with invisible or matching thread. But for raw-edge fusible-backed details, like spires, I go to a wider, tighter zigzag, close to a satin stitch, with thread color matching the appliqué.

► **Machine hem or blanket stitch** Medium-width, for turned edges. Its straight stitches go in the "background" (piece 6); then the needle swings intermittently into the higher appliqué (7).

For any machine appliqué stitches, I start and end with a few tiny back-and-forth straight stitches.

(continued)

Consider Stabilizer

Machine embroiderers use stabilizer to prevent fabric from distorting or collapsing when covered with hundreds of stitches. But stabilizers can also help quilters with machine appliqué. It's especially helpful if your fabrics are very lightweight. (If you're doing hand-appliqué you don't need this section.)

Sewing stores sell "tear-away" stabilizer – it's not expensive. When I run out, or need a large piece, I use a sheet of clean newsprint; a lifetime supply cost me $6 at the packing store. Any lightweight paper is a third choice, as long as it's clean (no ink to smear) and tears out easily. I've used copy paper when desperate, but test it first, as described below.

Make a sample (right), with the same fabrics and layers as the area you wish to appliqué. If there's fusible on those pieces, apply fusible to your test sample, too.

If the edges you plan to sew are folded under, fold all the edges of your building fabric sample.

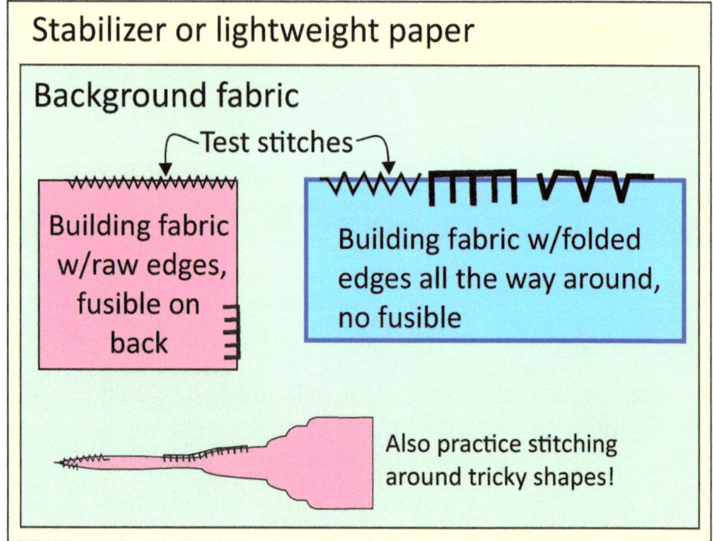

Then go around it with different stitches, widths, lengths, and if there's an issue, tensions.

Try it without stabilizer first. You'll know immediately if your stitches look good! If they don't, put stabilizer on back to see if it helps.

There's one more hurdle: Rip away the stabilizer in your sample. If it rips out stitches along with it, don't use it – you need lighter-weight paper. If you have some tracing paper on hand, try that; it's brittle and rips easily.

Sewing With Stabilizer on Back

Once I see that stabilizer is helpful and ripping it out won't tear stitches, I cut a piece big enough to cover the area that needs stitching, and pin it underneath.

Occasionally, stabilizer is needed behind an entire building's outline. Yes, it's awkward to sew with this big sheet on the back, but you get used to it! If your stabilizer isn't big enough to cover the outline, add pieces as you go – just be diligent about checking the back often, so you know when you're about to sew into a no-stabilizer zone!

The New Museum of Contemporary Art

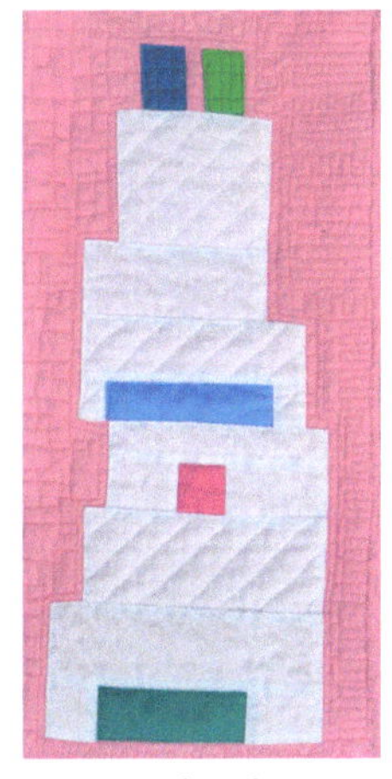

Mostly white

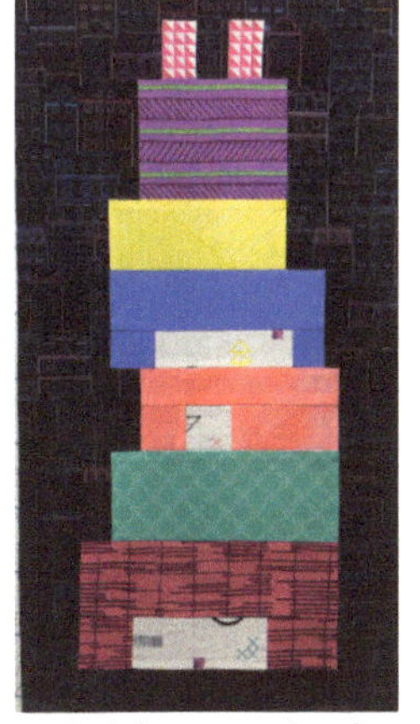

Rainbow version by
Marilyn Knepp

Cutting Diagram

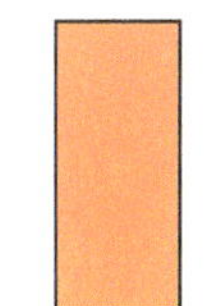

Two pieces
Cut each
1.25" x 2"

Floor 6
Cut 5.25" x 4"

Floor 5
Cut 6.25" x 2.75"

Floor 4, top unit
Cut 7.5" x 2.5"

Cut
2" x 1.75"

Floor 4, bottom unit
Cut 5" x 1.75"

Cut
1.5" x 1.75"

Floor 3, top unit
Cut 7.25" x 1.75"

Cut
1.75" x 2"

**Cut
2" x 2"**

Cut 4.5" x 2"

Floor 3, bottom unit

Floor 2
Cut 8" x 3.5"

Floor 1, top unit
Cut 9" x 3"

Floor 1, bottom unit

Cut
2.25" x 2.25"

Cut
5" x 2.25"

Cut
2.75" x 2.25"

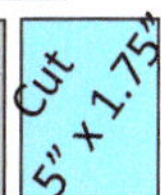

The 2007 New Museum of Contemporary Art building looks like a tower of birthday presents stacked by a child. In reality, the offsets are more than whimsy – they allow for roof skylights, to help light up gallery levels that lack windows. The 4th floor and up are cantilevered over the lower floors – just hanging beyond them, with no obvious support. This is both an architectural and a piecing challenge! I'll take you through my technique for meeting it.

The building's color scheme is stark white. The third and fourth floor have doors and windows in front, but in daylight, they're almost invisible. Lit up at night, they can be seen clearly. In my white version above, I splashed bright colors in those spots, and in the entrance.

Or you could make each level a different color. I did that in these diagrams just to help you keep track of floors. But one of my testers, quilt artist Marilyn Knepp, did it in fabric with her fun version above. Makes sense to me – after all, this is an ART museum!

Inspired by the New Museum

Finished building size: approx. 20.5" x 8.5"

Fabric

Main building A fat-quarter or quarter-yard.

Windows and doors A few scraps.

Background for the "Color Block" quilt. 10.5" x 22". A fat-quarter, 1/3 yard or 1/2 yard.

This is not a licensed product. I am not affiliated or associated with any of the buildings depicted in these quilts.

(continued)

1 Cut out the pieces in the cutting diagram on p. 7.

2 Assemble the three two-part floors: 1, 3 and 4. For example, in Floor 1, bottom section, start by sewing the "doorway" (the grey rectangle) to the two pieces next to it. Press seam allowances outward. Sew that strip to Floor 1's top rectangle. Press seam allowance up. Repeat with floors 3 and 4.

3 Arrange floors on your work surface in order. You may want to pin a label on each or mark the floor number on the back.

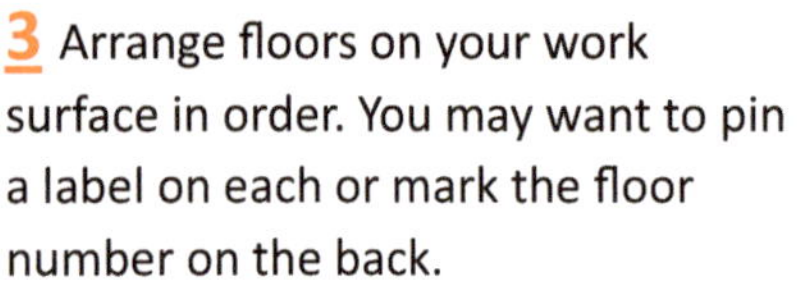
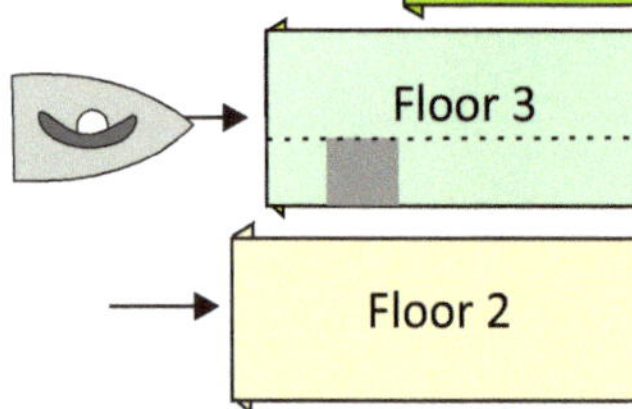

4 Press left edges of pieces 2, 3, and 6 to the back 1/4".

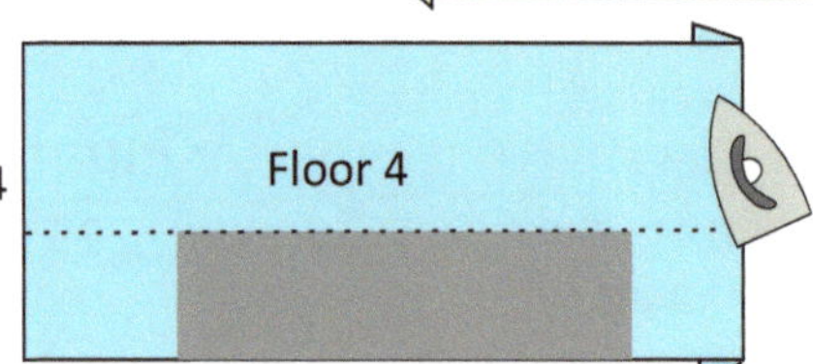

5 Press only the right edge of Floor 4 inward 1/4".

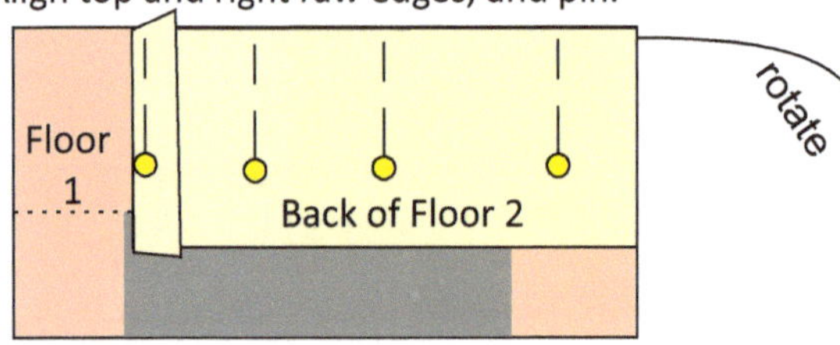

6 Flip Floor 2, good side down, on top of Floor 1, good side up. Align top and right raw edges, and pin.

7 Rotate it all clockwise, moving the pinned edge to the right. Now comes the trick you'll find throughout this book, which turns raw edges back, keeps seams tight, and prevents thread tails from poking out, because they're hidden far underneath.

8 Pull up threads just below the flap (at the red dot by **a**). Backstitch to the dot by the **b**, which is JUST below the fold. (If you oversew a bit onto Floor 1, you probably won't have to take it out! Decide later – 99% of the time, a few extra stitches are no problem.) You've sealed that flap shut.

Sew straight from **b** to **c**. There's no need to backstitch at **c** because there's no flap there, the top and bottom ends are even, and that entire straight edge will be turned under together later (in step 14), which also hides the thread ends at **c**.

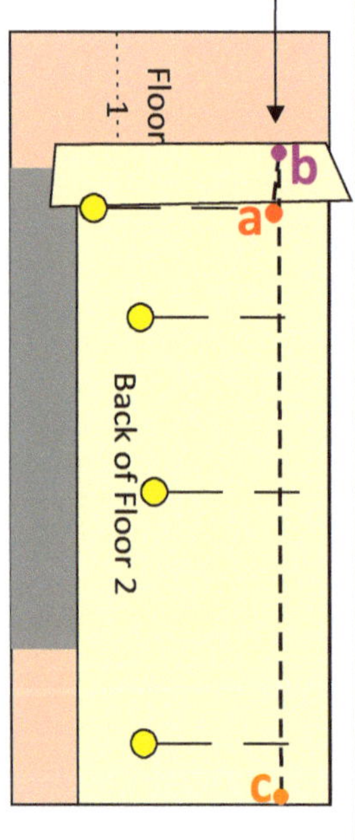

9 Press seam allowance down toward the wider level, Floor 1. Also, beyond Floor 2, on the left, press the extended seam allowance flap down neatly 1/4" to the back. (If you oversewed there in step 8, you can probably hide those stitches behind the fold.)

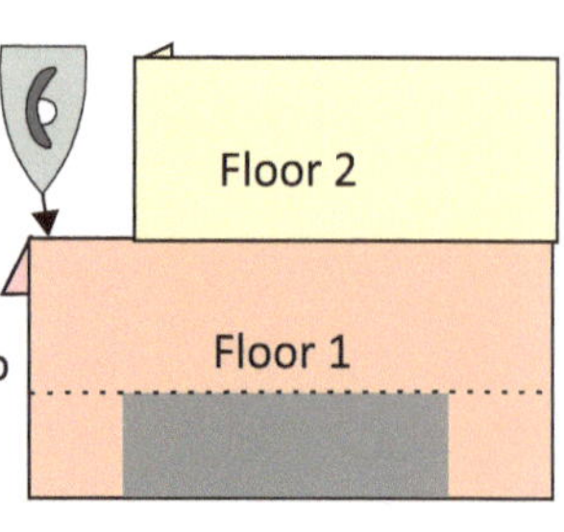

10 Flip to the back and fold the far right vertical edge of Floor 1 to the back, 1/4". A little glue helps. Angle the corner slightly down (smush a tiny crease in the flap).

Don't do anything to the lower right corner yet (circled).

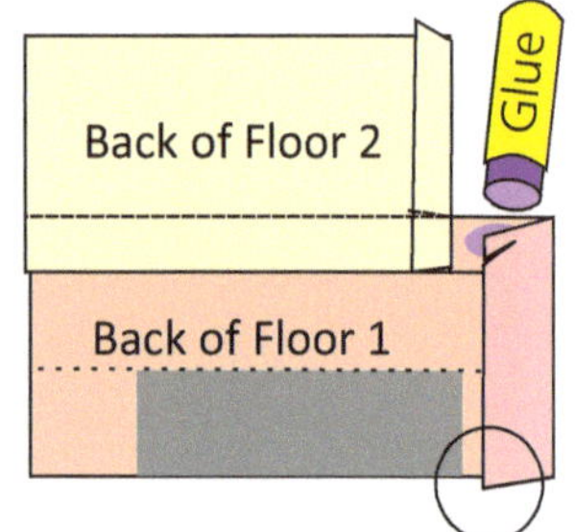

11 Place Floor 3 face down on the upper right corner of Floor 2 (which is face up), matching top and right raw edges. Pin.

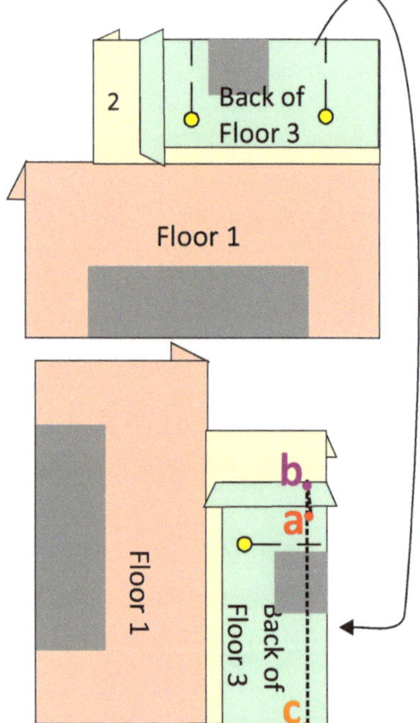

12 Rotate pinned edge to the right. Sew as in step 8, starting at **a**, backstitching to **b**, and sewing to the end at **c**.

13 Unfold Floor 3. Press seam allowance down. Beyond Floor 3 on the left, press extended seam allowance flap of Floor 2 down 1/4".

Notice that right edges of 3, 4, and 5 are in a straight line. That's why we didn't press those edges inward separately. When edges align, we can press them to the back together, after they're joined.

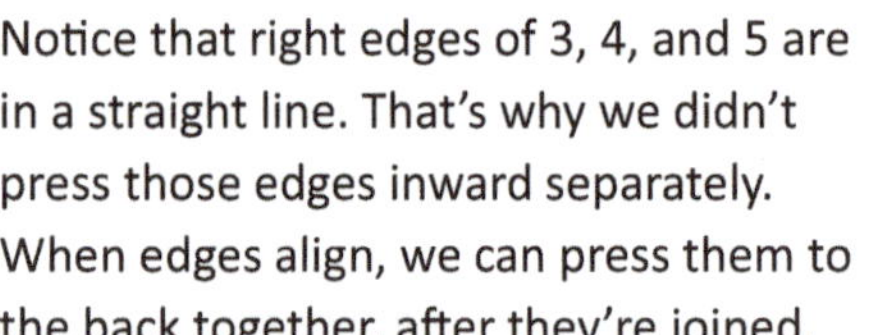

14 So let's do that now. Flip unit to the back and press the joined left edge of the unit (pieces 1, 2, and 3 together) 1/4" inward toward the back.

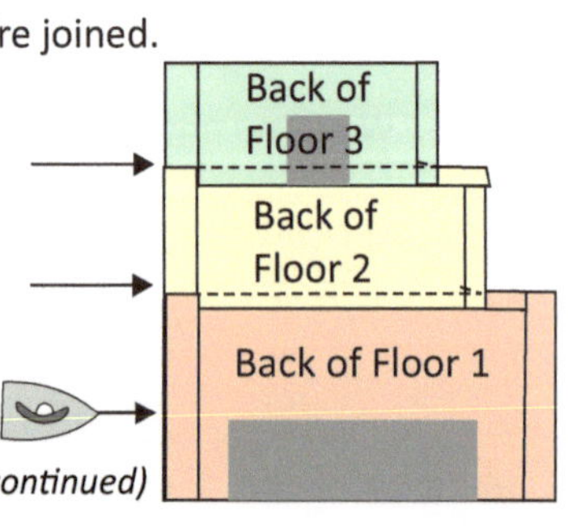

(continued)

15 Set that bottom half of the building aside. Now we'll create the top half.

16 You already pressed Floor 6's left edge to the back (in step 4). Flip Floor 6, good side down, on top of it, matching the top and right raw edges with Floor 5.

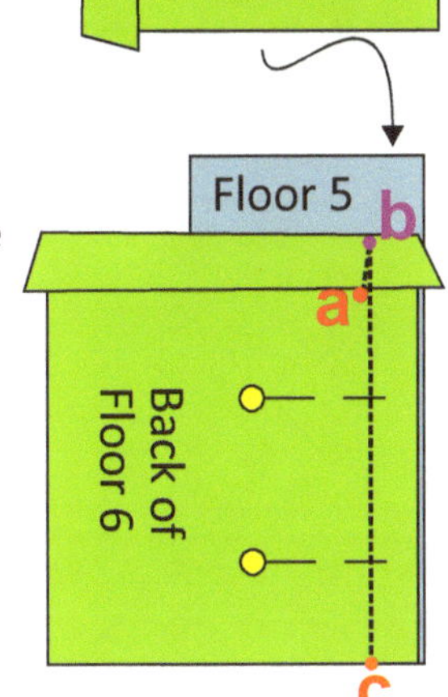

17 Rotate the pinned edge to the right. Pull up threads at **a**, backstitch to **b**, then stitch down to **c**.

18 Press seam allowance down toward the wider level, which is Floor 5. Also, press down the extended seam allowance on top of Floor 5.

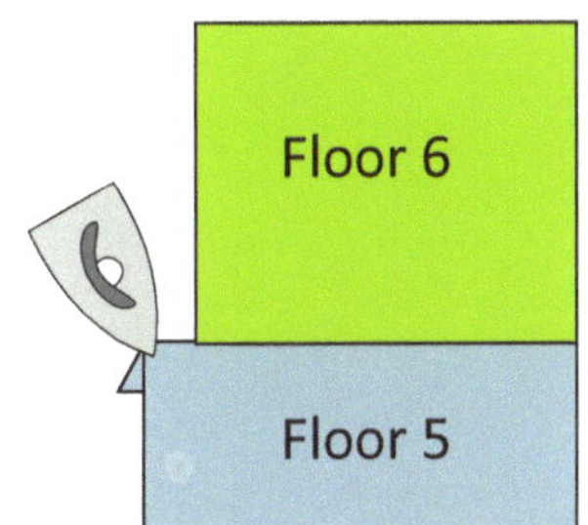

19 Flip unit to back. Press the combined raw edge of pieces 5 + 6 (now on the left), to the back 1/4".

Both sides of Floor 6 are pressed in, and only one side edge of Floor 5 is pressed in.

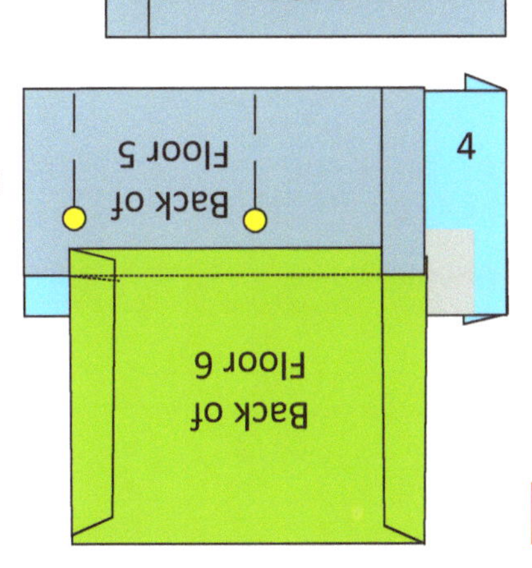

20 Place Floor 4 good side up. (Its far right edge is pressed to the back). Flip pieces 5+6 face down on top. Align the raw upper left corners and top edges. Pin.

21 Rotate pinned edge to the right. Start sewing at **a**. No backstitching is needed here. Sew to **b**; backstitch and cut threads at **c**. As the presser foot approaches the bottom flap, a sharp awl or other tool will help persuade the flap to go under it, staying shut.

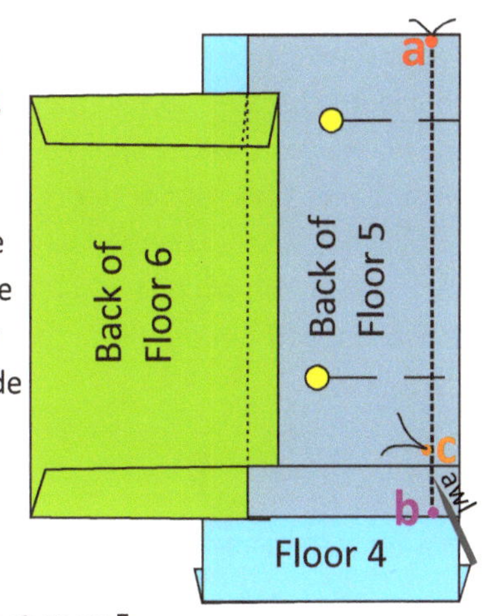

Press the seam allowance between 5 and 4 down under 4. Also press downward piece 4's extended seam allowance flap, on its upper right.

22 Time to bring together the halves, between Floors 3 and 4. What makes this seam different: Floor 4 extends beyond 3 on the left side; but Floor 3 extends beyond 4 on the right.

This means there are no corners to match – you must guesstimate! Also, you will have to press this seam OPEN, to prevent raw edges from sticking out into the overhangs.

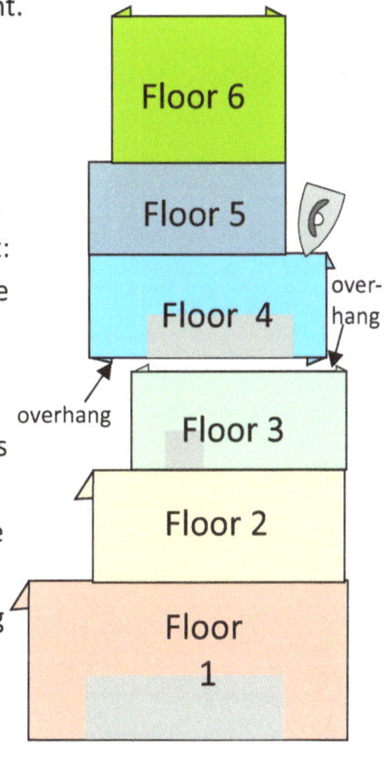

23 Flip the back of unit 4 + 5 + 6, good side down, on top of the front of pieces 1+2+3. Align Floor 4's bottom raw edge with Floor 3's top raw edge. These measurements don't have to be precise!

Floor 4 sticks out approx. 1" beyond the left folded edge of Floor 3 underneath.

Match raw edges along the tops of 3 and 4.

The good side of Floor 3 peeks out, approx. 3/4" beyond the right fold of 4.

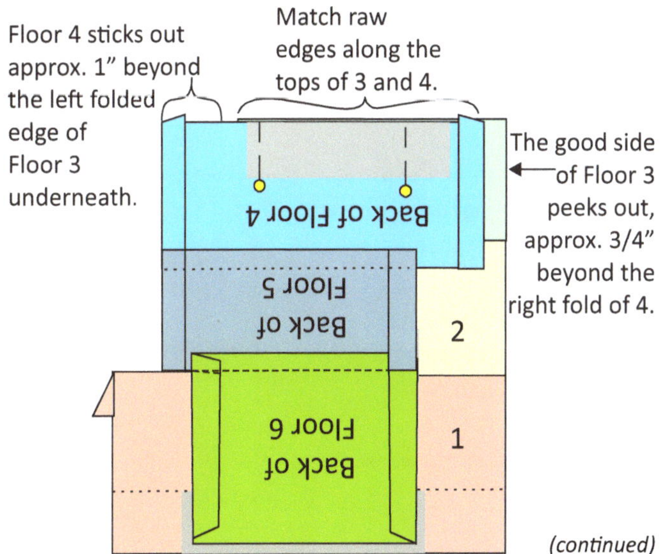

(continued)

24 Pin and rotate pinned edge down the right side. Mark two dots on the back of Floor 4 (they may be on its window). Mark one where you can feel and see that the underlying flap of piece 3 ends (the red dot next to the **a**). Mark another dot 1/4" higher, where you can feel or see piece 3's fold directly underneath (the dot by the **b**). No need to mark the **c** or the **d**, because you can see these spots (where the flap starts, and the fold ends.)

Bring up thread at **a**, backstitch to **b**, sew straight down to **c**, where the fold on Floor 4 ends; backstitch to **d**. Cut threads.

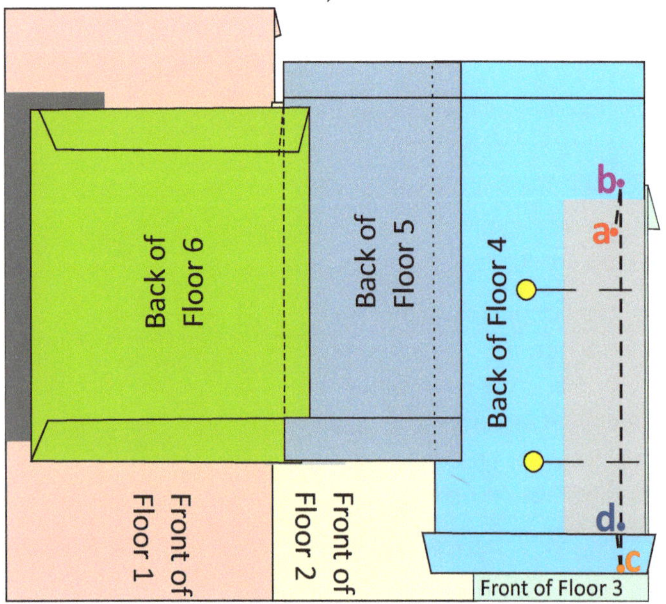

25 You must press this seam open, to hide the top flap behind the upper section, and the bottom flap behind the lower section.

26 Press in three sides of the two roof pieces, leaving each bottom edge raw.

27 Center them on the 6th floor with about an inch between them. Pin. Sew the bottom, starting at the **a** dot, backstitching to **b**, sewing down to **c**, and backing up to **d**. Cut threads and do the next one.
Press seam allowances down, under Floor 6.

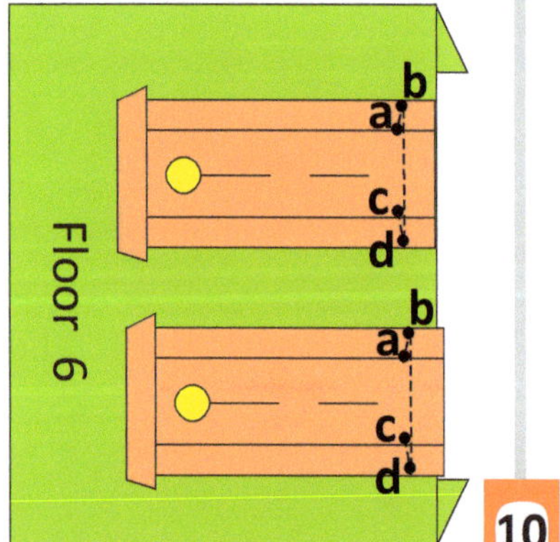

For 'Condensed' quilt: No need to press the bottom edge of the building up. See next steps on p. 71.

For 'Color Block' quilt: Press bottom raw edge of building up 1/4". Audition backgrounds. In the sample quilt, it's pink. Cut background to 10.5" x 22". Eventually, you will place the building's bottom folded edge 3/4" above the bottom raw edge of the background. This information and next steps are in the quilt directions that start on p. 76.

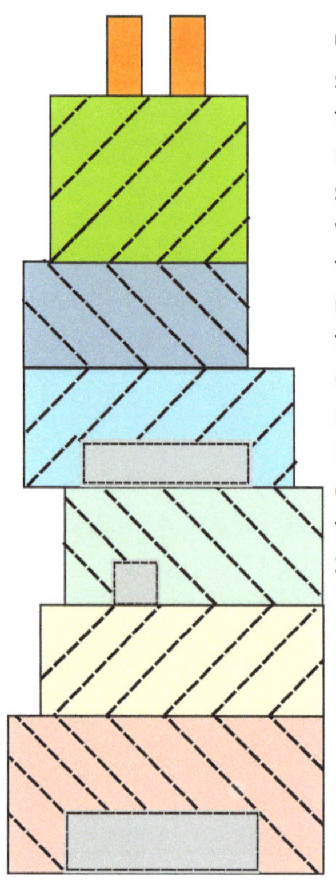

Quilting Ideas: Along with stitching around the outside of the building, I ditch-stitched next to the main horizontal seams. I also stitched just inside windows and doors, to push them lower. In real life, the museum is covered with a high-tech diagonal mesh, so I quilted (one-way) diagonal lines on mine, about an inch apart. In the Color Block quilt, I quilted designs into the background that suggest more buildings. See those on p. 79.

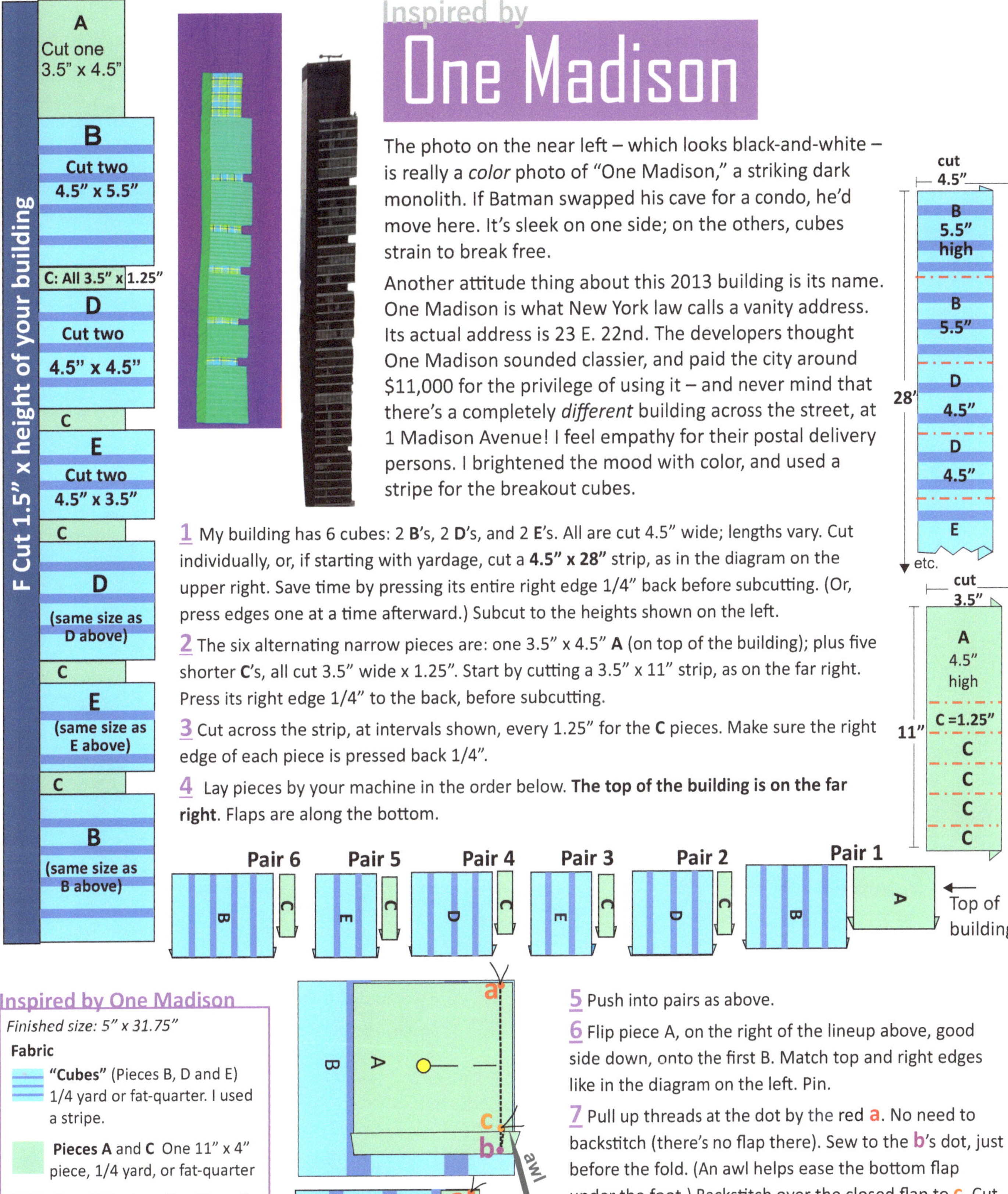

One Madison

The photo on the near left – which looks black-and-white – is really a *color* photo of "One Madison," a striking dark monolith. If Batman swapped his cave for a condo, he'd move here. It's sleek on one side; on the others, cubes strain to break free.

Another attitude thing about this 2013 building is its name. One Madison is what New York law calls a vanity address. Its actual address is 23 E. 22nd. The developers thought One Madison sounded classier, and paid the city around $11,000 for the privilege of using it – and never mind that there's a completely *different* building across the street, at 1 Madison Avenue! I feel empathy for their postal delivery persons. I brightened the mood with color, and used a stripe for the breakout cubes.

1 My building has 6 cubes: 2 **B**'s, 2 **D**'s, and 2 **E**'s. All are cut 4.5" wide; lengths vary. Cut individually, or, if starting with yardage, cut a **4.5" x 28"** strip, as in the diagram on the upper right. Save time by pressing its entire right edge 1/4" back before subcutting. (Or, press edges one at a time afterward.) Subcut to the heights shown on the left.

2 The six alternating narrow pieces are: one 3.5" x 4.5" **A** (on top of the building); plus five shorter **C**'s, all cut 3.5" wide x 1.25". Start by cutting a 3.5" x 11" strip, as on the far right. Press its right edge 1/4" to the back, before subcutting.

3 Cut across the strip, at intervals shown, every 1.25" for the **C** pieces. Make sure the right edge of each piece is pressed back 1/4".

4 Lay pieces by your machine in the order below. **The top of the building is on the far right**. Flaps are along the bottom.

Inspired by One Madison

Finished size: 5" x 31.75"

Fabric

"Cubes" (Pieces B, D and E) 1/4 yard or fat-quarter. I used a stripe.

Pieces A and **C** One 11" x 4" piece, 1/4 yard, or fat-quarter

Piece F The long "backbone". It's approx. 32" x 1.5".

Background for "Color Block" quilt only, p. 76. 10.5" x 39.5". A third- to a half-yard.

This is not a licensed product. I am not affiliated or associated with any buildings depicted in these quilts.

5 Push into pairs as above.

6 Flip piece A, on the right of the lineup above, good side down, onto the first B. Match top and right edges like in the diagram on the left. Pin.

7 Pull up threads at the dot by the red **a**. No need to backstitch (there's no flap there). Sew to the **b**'s dot, just before the fold. (An awl helps ease the bottom flap under the foot.) Backstitch over the closed flap to **c**. Cut threads. If you oversew a bit onto the underlying piece, don't worry, you probably won't have to take it out!

8 Pull out pair 1, cut threads, and put it back in the lineup. Flip piece C-1 good side down onto D-1. Sew as in step 7: Start at **a**, sew down to **b** (sealing the flap), backstitch to **c**, and cut threads. Repeat for all pairs.

(continued)

9 Press each pair's seam allowance down toward the wider pieces, also pressing the extension of the seam allowances neatly 1/4" down on the B, D, and E pieces. They may fight you and want to go crooked! The printed stripes can help you press them straight – and remember: a little wonkiness is charming!

10 Cut threads and lay each piece out in order again, but this time, place the top of the building on the far left, with flaps along the uppermost edge.

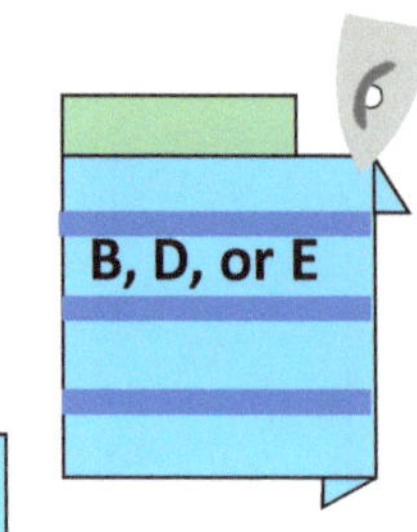

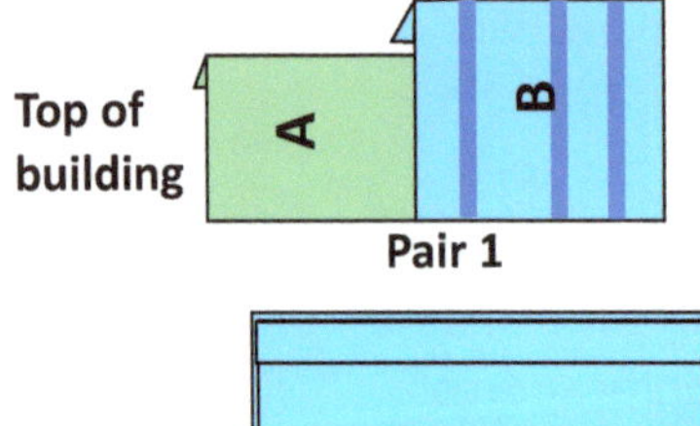
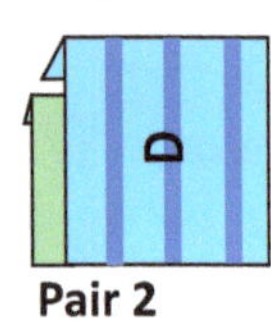
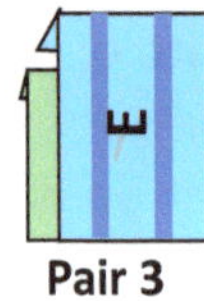
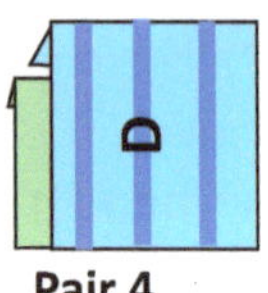
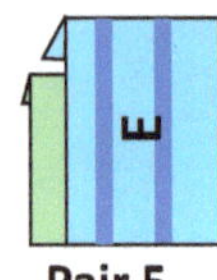
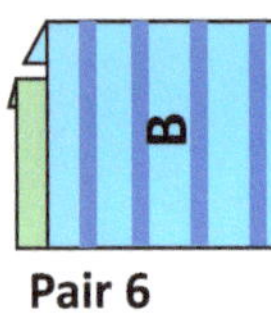

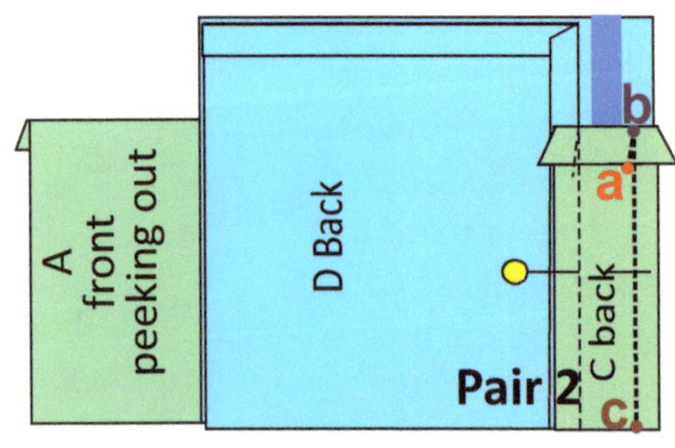

11 Flip pair 2, good side down, onto pair 1, good side up. Line up their far right and lowest edges; pin the right edge.

12 The flap goes through the machine first. Pull up threads at **a**, just below the flap. Backstitch to **b**, sealing the flap shut. Stop just below the fold. Sew straight down to **c**. No need to backstitch there. Press seam allowance down to the wider level.

13 You just made quartet 1. Put it back in the lineup as below. Now flip pair 4, good side down, onto pair 3, good side up; stitch the same way as step 12. Press to the wider level. Add pair 6 to the bottom edge of pair 5. Press. Put the three quartets back in order, with the top of the building again on the far left. The lineup looks like this:

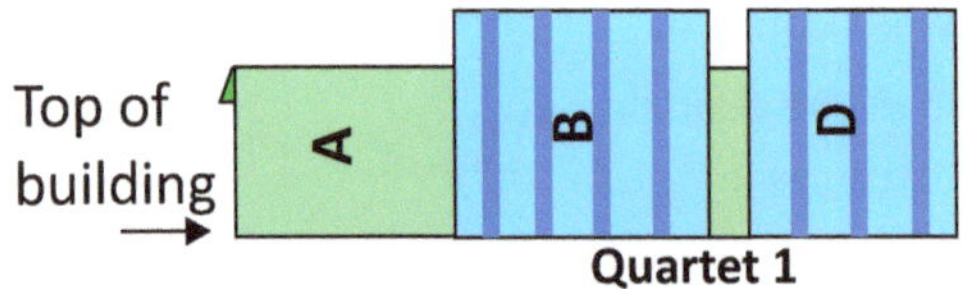
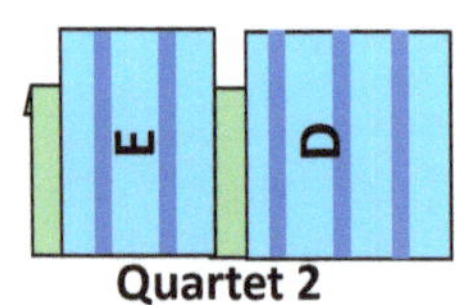
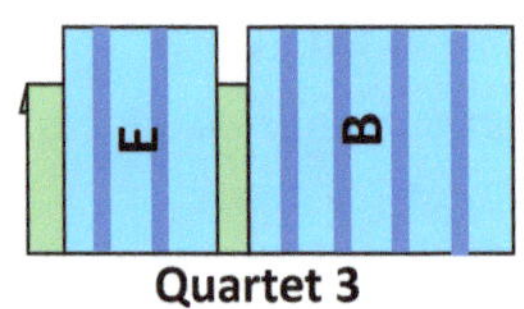

14 Flip quartet 2 onto the far right lower edge of quartet 1, and sew down the back right edge of C-2 (it will look like the drawing in Step 11.). Finally, flip quartet 3 onto the bottom edge of quartet 2, and sew. Press new seam allowances toward the wider level, so all C pieces' seam allowances point outward.

15 Measure height of the completed unit. It should be around 31". Cut strip F 1.5" wide x that height. Sew it along the straight left edge of the building. I sew from the back of the pieced area, to make sure seam allowances remain turned correctly. When you're done sewing it, press the left edge of piece F firmly to the back 1/4".

16 If you didn't do it earlier, press right edges of each B, D and E piece back 1/4". Press down the top edge 1/4".

For 'Condensed' quilt: No need to press the bottom edge of the building up. See next steps on p. 71.

For 'Color Block' quilt: Press bottom edge up 1/4". Audition backgrounds. In the sample quilt, it's purple. Cut it 10.5" x 39.5". Eventually, you will place the building's bottom folded edge 3/4" above the bottom raw edge of its background. This information and next steps are in the quilt directions that start on p. 76.

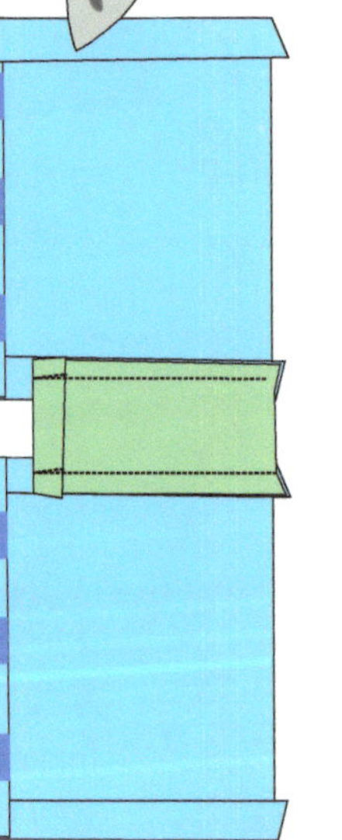

Quilting ideas: I ditch-stitched just inside all the small C pieces. Dotted lines on the right show the rest of my quilting on the C's: lines next to main printed verticals. I quilted a grid on the top large A piece. On the cubes, I quilted next to every other horizontal stripe (This came out to about 1" apart). On the F piece, I quilted diagonals, to represent window rows in perspective.

In the Color Block quilt, I quilted designs into the background that suggest more buildings. See some of them on p. 79.

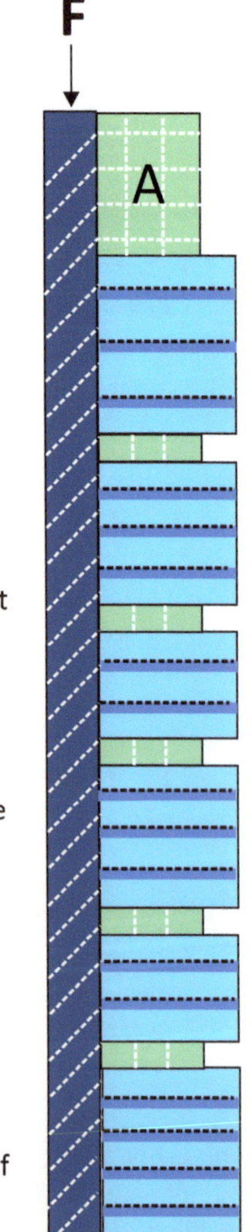

56 Leonard St., aka Jenga™ Building

The first time I saw this building, in daytime, it astounded me – the windows melded with the sky, leaving thin white rods floating in mid-air – what IS that? The effect prompted New Yorkers to nickname it after the Jenga(™) game, in which you remove long pieces from a block tower, hoping not to bring it down. (The "rods" here are slender balconies.) The architects conceived it as a stack of individual houses, each slightly offset.

Those offset ends are a challenge for quilters as well as architects. That's a LOT of edges to turn under. So we'll use my technique for turning strip ends back *during* piecing, instead of having to rip seams to turn all of them afterwards.

Strategy Overview:

► First, we'll cut all the darkest **S** pieces, and some **F** and **M** pieces. The rest will be cut as we go.

► Sew together the three "special groups", top, middle, and bottom (marked in red on the left), cutting **A** pieces, and more **F** and **M**'s, for them.

► Finally, sew everything together.

Read through the directions before you embark, to see how this works.

(continued)

Cutting diagram
Read directions before cutting

Penthouse

M Cut 7.25" x 1.75"	
A-2 Cut 5.25" x 1.25"	**A-1** Cut 2.5" x 1.25"

F Cut 2.25" x 1.25" — **Cut** 2.5" x 1.25" — **F** Cut 4.25" x 1.25" — Floor Divider

A-1 Cut 7.25" x 1.75"

F Cut 5.5" x 1.25" — **Cut** 2.5" x 1.25" — **F** Cut 2" x 1.25" — Floor Divider

Highest Special Group

A-3 Cut 2.25" x 1.5" — **A-2** Cut 3" x 2.25" — **M** Cut 3.25" x 1.25"

F Cut 3.25" x 1.25" — **F** Cut 2.25" x 1.25" ← Broken Floor dividers

Cut 2.5" x 1.25" — **F** Cut 3" x 1.25" — **A-3** Cut 2" x 2"

A-2 Cut 2.5" x 1.75" — **A-1** Cut 3" x 1.75" — **Cut** 2.5" x 1.25"

F Cut 2" x 1.25" — **Cut** 2.5" x 1.25" — **F** Cut 5.5" x 1.25" — Floor Divider

M Cut 7.25" x 1.75"

F Cut 4.25" x 1.25" — **Cut** 2.5" x 1.25" — **F** Cut 2.25" x 1.25" — Floor Divider

M Cut 7.25" x 1.75"

Cut 2.5" x 1.25" — **F** Cut 6.5" x 1.25 — Floor Divider

Middle Special Group

A-3 Cut 3.25" x 1.25" — **M** Cut 3" x 2.75" — **A-2** Cut 3" x 2"

F Cut 3" x 1.25" — **F** Cut 3.25" x 1.25" Broken Floor dividers

A-1 Cut 3" x 2.25" — **F** Cut 3" x 1.25" — **A-3** Cut 3" x 3.25"

A-2 Cut 3.75" x 2.25" — **A-1** Cut 3" x 2.5"

F Cut 2" x 1.25" — **Cut** 2.5" x 1.25" — **F** Cut 5.5" x 1.25" — Floor Divider

M Cut 7.25" x 1.75"

F Cut 4.25" x 1.25" — **Cut** 2.5" x 1.25" — **F** Cut 2.25" x 1.25" — Floor Divider

A-1 Cut 7.25" x 1.75"

Cut 2.5" x 1.25" — **F** Cut 6.5" x 1.25" — Floor Divider

M Cut 7.25" x 1.75"

F Cut 6.5" x 1.25 — **Cut** 2.5" x 1.25" — Floor Divider

Bottom special Group

A-3 Cut 2.75" x 1.75" — **M** Cut 5.5" x 2"

F Cut 3" x 1.25" — **F** Cut 6.5" x 1.25" — Broken Floor dividers

A-2 Cut 2.75" x 2.5" — **A-1** Cut 6" x 2.25"

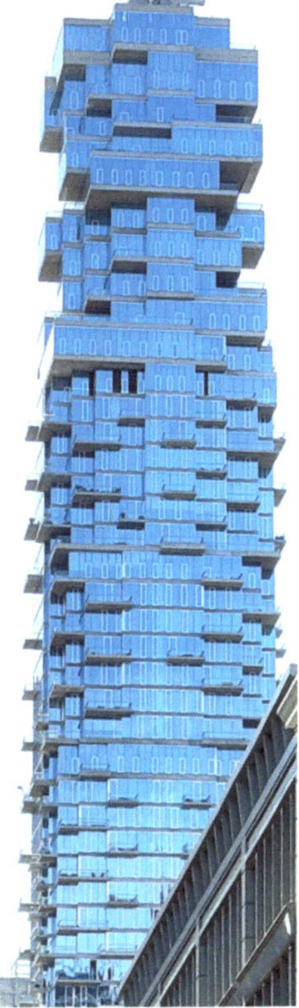

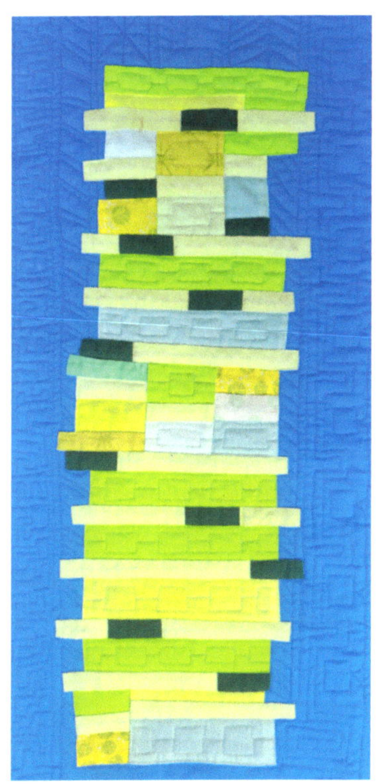

Finished size: Approx. 9.5" x 24.75"
Fabric
Letters refer to the diagram on the previous page.

S = Shadows, under balconies. Fat-eighth, fat-quarter or 1/4 yard. Choose very dark fabric (navy in diagrams). Cut a total of 30" x 1.25" wide, which will be subcut into 2.5" lengths.

F = Floor dividers. Lightest fabric (white in diagrams). Start with 1/4 yard or a fat-quarter.

M = Main windows. 1/4 yard or a fat-quarter. Choose fairly light fabric, darker than **F** pieces. Cut 50" x 1.75" wide. The 50" need not be continuous - it will be subcut into shorter segments (usually 7.25").

A = Assorted windows (A-1, A-2 and **A-3).** Darker shades of the **M** color. In diagrams, they are a variety of greys. I cut **A** pieces as needed. Most will be 2.75" - 8" across and no more than 3" high.

Background for "Color Block" quilt only, p .76; 13.25" x 39.5". A third to a half-yard.

Improv Versions

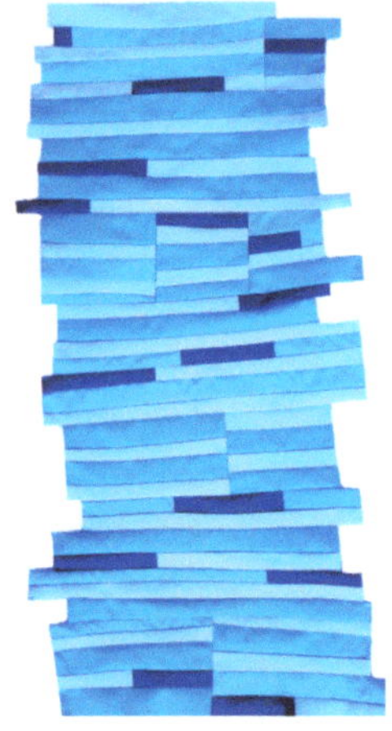
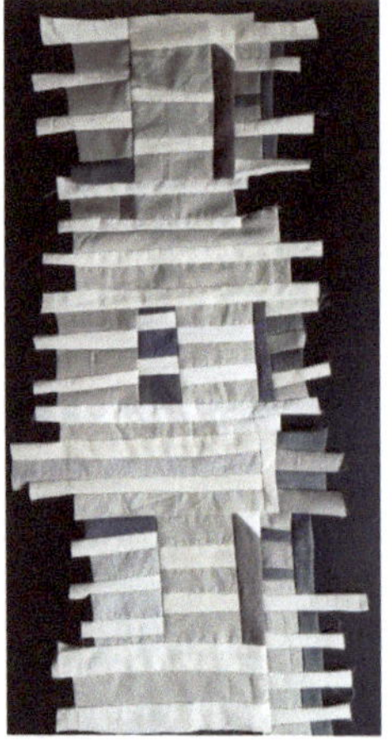

I had a blast making these two improv version. I cut a bunch of strips to widths from 1"-2", and then did minimal measuring – mostly I chopped off pieces and sewed them together!

By contrast, the green version presented in this chapter was made with the measurements on the previous page.

Go either way, or do a hybrid – cut strips to approximate widths suggested, but build each row with improv cutting and sewing.

This is not a licensed product. I am not affiliated or associated with any buildings depicted in these quilts.

Make Floor Divider Rows

1 Floor divider rows all contain shadow **(S)** pieces. **S** lengths are all the same *(unless you're improvising)*. Start with about 30" x 1.5" strip. From that, cut eleven pieces, each 2.5" x 1.25". (You'll use nine in this section – the remaining two will be sewn in place later.

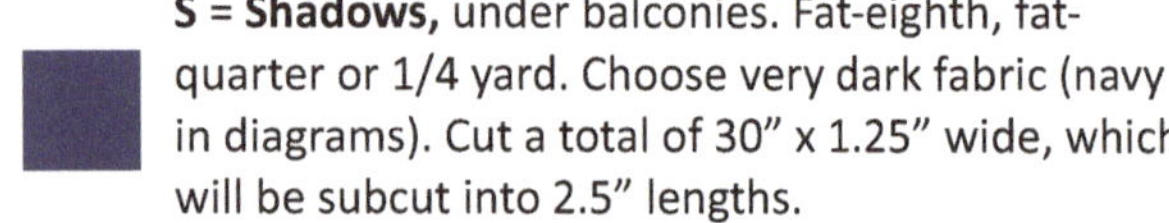

x 11
2.5" x 1.25"

2 Cut floor divider fabric, the lightest **F** pieces, white in the diagram on p. 11, into long 1.25" wide strips. Length should add up to about 100". The 100" needn't be continuous, we're about to chop pieces off as needed.

3 Cut four **F** pieces to 6.5" x 1.25". Sew three units like this.

| F   Cut 6.5" x 1.25" | | **x 3** |

2.5" x 1.25"

When you place them in the building, you can flip them around so the shadows end up on the right or the left.

4 Cut and sew three like this.

| Cut 2.25" x 1.25" | | Cut 4.25" x 1.25" | **x 3** |

2.5" x 1.25"

5 Cut and sew the last three like this:

| Cut 2" x 1.25" | | Cut 5.5"x 1.25" | **x 3** |

2.5" x 1.25"

We'll cut more F fabric to different sizes later. *Improvisors: no need to follow these exact measurements. Just try to keep the total length of the floor divider rows 9" or less.*

Cut Main and Longest Windows

6 From **M** fabric, cut five strips to 7.25" x 1.75". (Don't put the M fabric back in your stash yet – we'll cut smaller pieces for "special groups" later.)

7 Press sides of four of the five 7.25" pieces to the back 1/4". Set aside the fifth strip to serve as the top of the building.

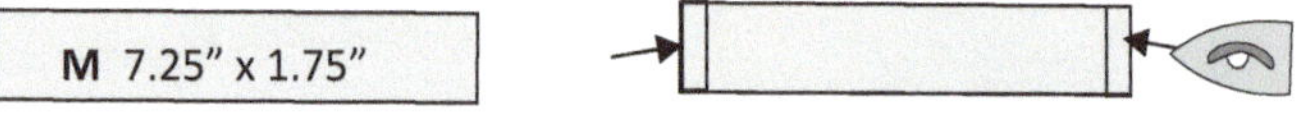

8 From **A-1** fabric: Cut **two** rectangles the same size as the M's, 7.25" x 1.75". Set remaining A-1 fabric aside, we'll cut smaller pieces from it later. Press short edges of **both A-1** pieces inward.

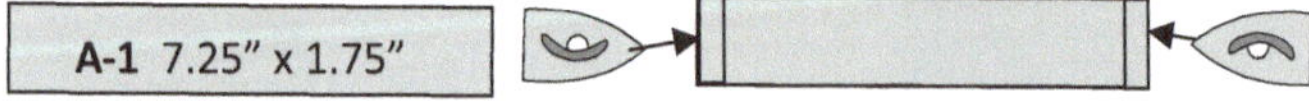

9 Lay out the pieces you've cut (so far) on the design surface, in approximate position (following the diagram on p. 13).

(continued)

Arrange the Penthouse and Floors Just Below

10 Follow the measurements in the p. 13 diagram. For the top piece, use the **M** strip whose edges you didn't press inward in step 7. Cut an **A-2** fabric to 5.25" x 1.25", and an **A-1** to 2.5" x 1.25". Sew the **A-2** next to the **M**, then sew **M** on top. That's the penthouse. Place a floor divider strip under it. Cut an A-1 piece to 7.25" x 1.75". Place it in position. Put a different floor divider strip under that. Don't sew these pieces together yet.

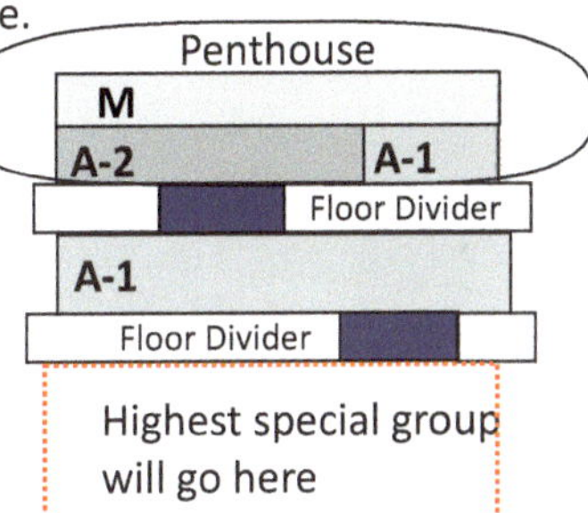

Make the Highest Special Group

The central **F** is on a different level than the **F**'s on its left and right. Whether you follow measurements or improvise, place the central **F** higher **or** lower than those on the sides.

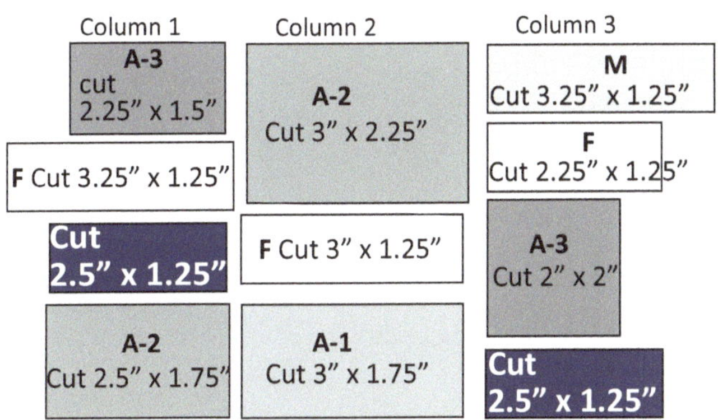

11 Cut and lay out all the pieces. You already cut the **S**'s. Now cut three **F**'s; one **A-1**; two **A-2**'s; and two **A-3**'s.

12 Arrange in three vertical columns as above. All column 2 pieces are the same width, inside the building, so start there. Sew **A-2** to the top of the **F** and sew an **A-1** on bottom.

13 Column 3: Press all their right edges to the back 1/4".

14 Flip the **F** piece, face down, onto the lower edge of the **M** above it. Lower left corners should align. Pin with F's flap closed.

15 Rotate the pinned edge to the right side. Bring up threads at **a**. Backspace to **b** (sealing the flap). Stitch down to **c**. No need to backstitch at **c**, because there's no flap there. (The backstitching between **a** and **b** secures the flap tight and hides thread ends at **a**, well underneath the piece.)

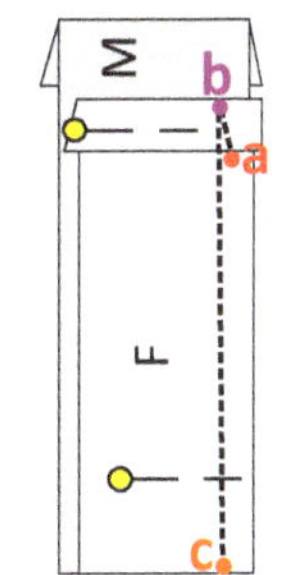

16 Press seam allowances (sa) up to the longer **M** level, including the extended seam allowance on the lower right of piece M.

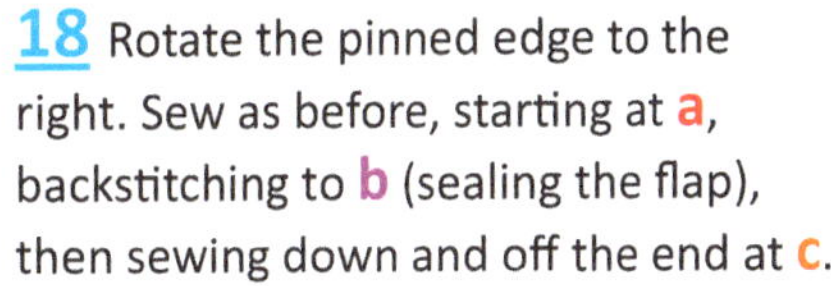

17 Flip the **A-3**, face down, onto the bottom left corner of the F. Pin.

18 Rotate the pinned edge to the right. Sew as before, starting at **a**, backstitching to **b** (sealing the flap), then sewing down and off the end at **c**.

19 Press sa up, toward the longer (white) level F. Also press the extended sa on the bottom right end of piece **F** upward 1/4".

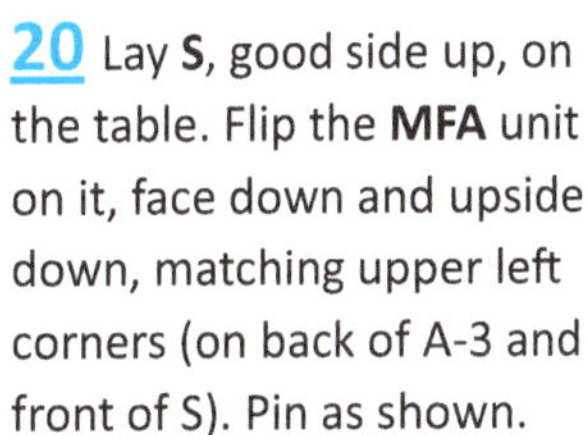

20 Lay **S**, good side up, on the table. Flip the **MFA** unit on it, face down and upside down, matching upper left corners (on back of A-3 and front of S). Pin as shown.

21 Rotate pinned seam to the right. Start sewing at **a** - no flap means no backstitching. Sew to **b**, just before the fold. Backstitch to **c** and cut threads. An awl will help you tuck the flap under the presser foot as it approaches.

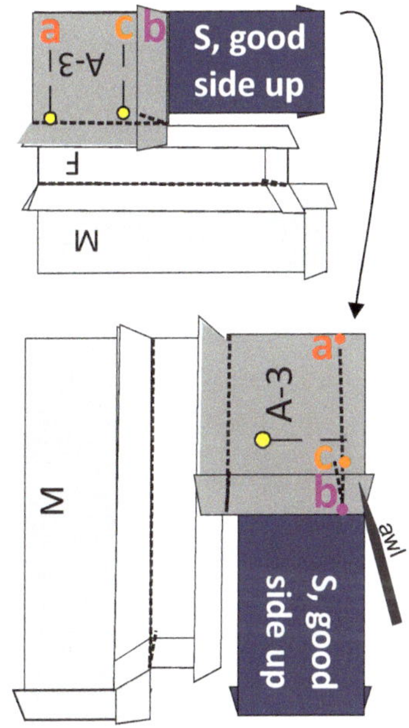

22 Open the **S** piece. Press seam allowance down to the longer level. Press the extended area of the seam allowance, on the top right of the bottom strip, neatly down 1/4".

23 Sew the left column to the central one, the traditional way, top to bottom, no backstitching. Press seam allowances left, under the central column. We'll do this on both sides to create the illusion that this central section juts forward.

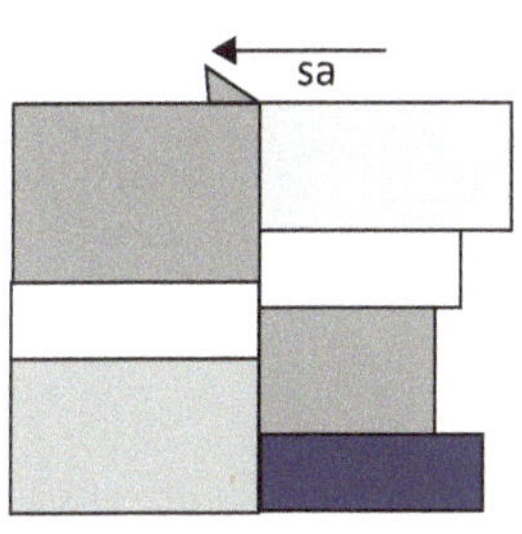

(continued)

24 For column 1, press the furthest left-edge of pieces **A-3** and **F** inward 1/4".

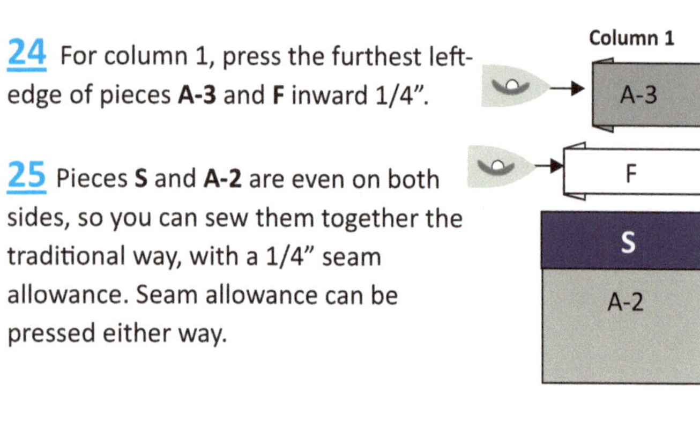

25 Pieces **S** and **A-2** are even on both sides, so you can sew them together the traditional way, with a 1/4" seam allowance. Seam allowance can be pressed either way.

26 Press the joint edge of **S** and **A-2** 1/4" to the back.

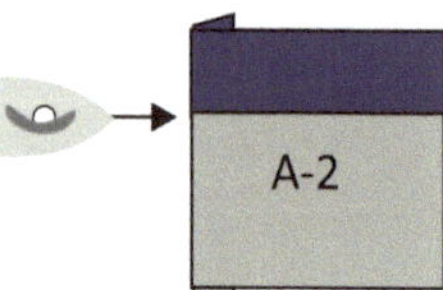

27 Place **F** on the table, good side up, flap on the left. Flip **A-3**, good side down, onto **F**. Match upper and right edges, and pin.

28 Rotate and sew the pinned side, starting at **a**, backstitching to **b**, and sewing down to the end at **c**.

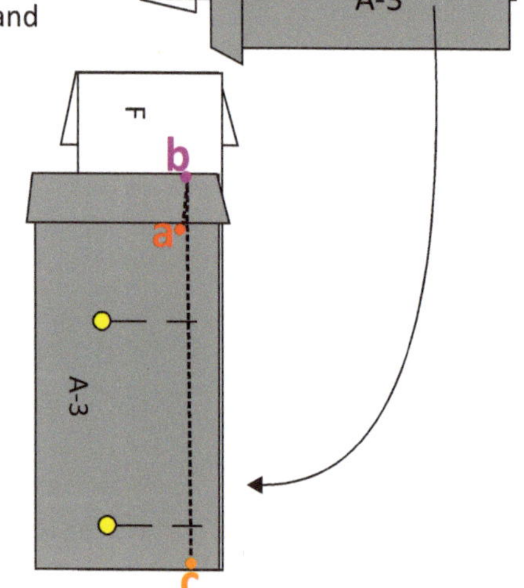

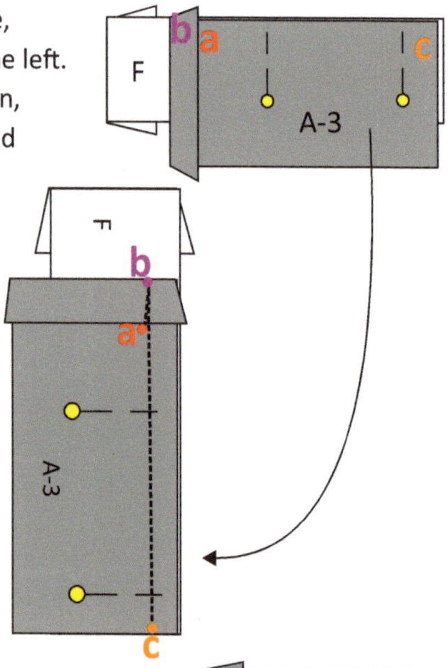

29 Press seam allowance down to the wider level, including the flap on the top left of **F**.

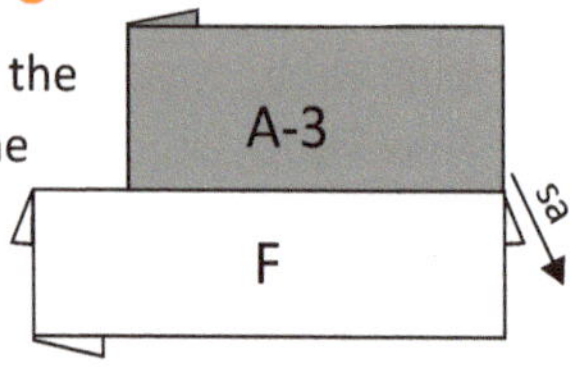

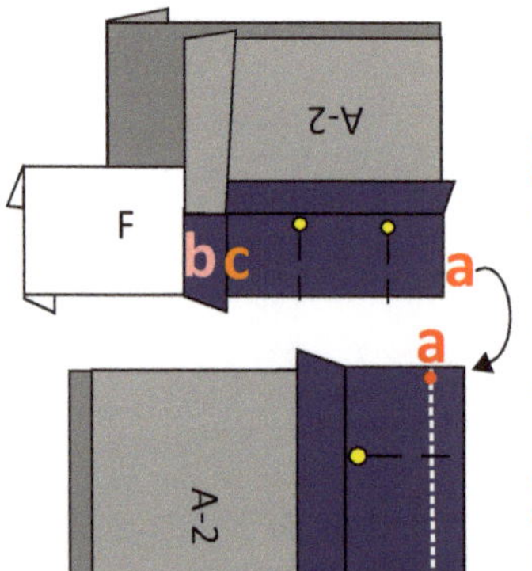

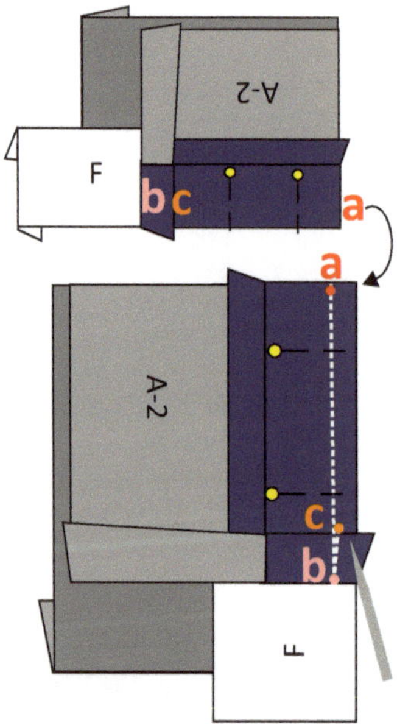

30 Flip the bottom unit face down onto the lower right edges of the upper half, right sides together. Pin along the bottom.

31 Rotate the pinned edge to the right. Start sewing at **a**. Sew to **b**, stopping right before the fold. Backstitch to **c** and cut threads. An awl can help ensure the flap stays closed under the presser foot.

32 Press the new sa up under the longer level.

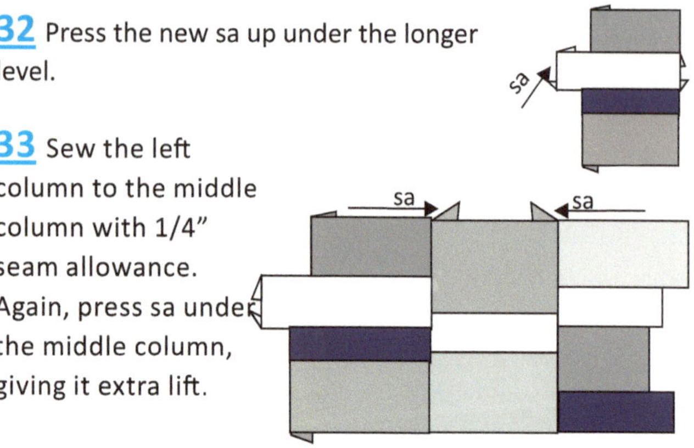

33 Sew the left column to the middle column with 1/4" seam allowance. Again, press sa under the middle column, giving it extra lift.

34 Put this special group back in the lineup. In my version, it's the highest, but you could eventually switch it with the middle group, or put it anywhere you like!

Make the Middle Special Group

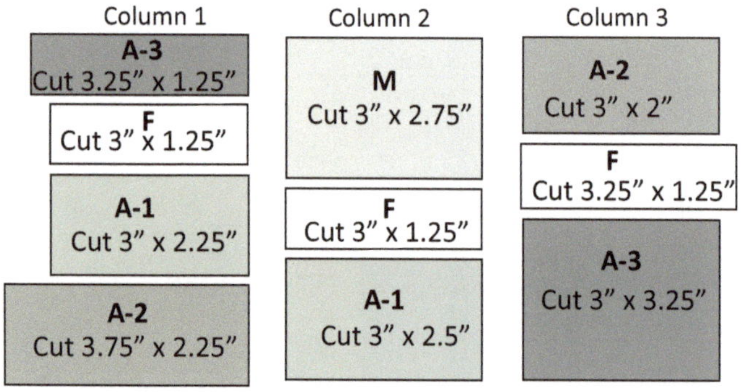

Column 1	Column 2	Column 3
A-3 Cut 3.25" x 1.25"	**M** Cut 3" x 2.75"	**A-2** Cut 3" x 2"
F Cut 3" x 1.25"		**F** Cut 3.25" x 1.25"
A-1 Cut 3" x 2.25"	**F** Cut 3" x 1.25"	**A-3** Cut 3" x 3.25"
A-2 Cut 3.75" x 2.25"	**A-1** Cut 3" x 2.5"	

35 Cut the pieces. Sew with principles from the first set:
► Join column 2 the traditional way. They're all the same width and inside the building, so there's no backstitching or flaps.
► In column 3, press **A-2** and **A-3**'s right edges back 1/4", before sewing each to the **F**.
► For column 1, sew the **F** on top of **A-1** first; then press their mutual left edge in 1/4". Add **A-3** on top, and **A-2** on bottom.
► Last, press in the left edges of the **A-3** and **A-2** in column 1, and in column 3, the right edge of **F**.

Assemble the Bottom Special Group

This group has only two columns.

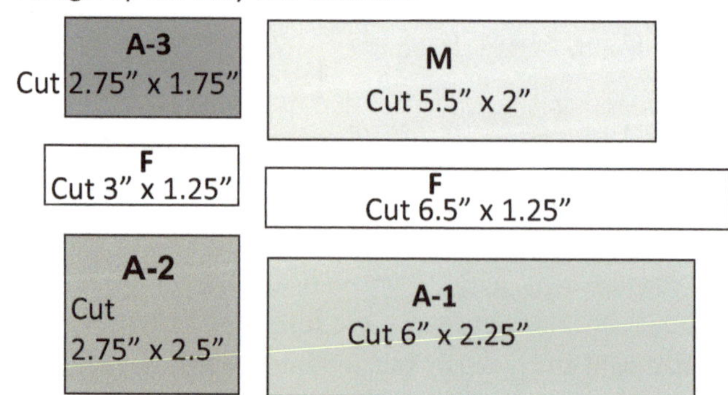

A-3 Cut 2.75" x 1.75"	**M** Cut 5.5" x 2"
F Cut 3" x 1.25"	**F** Cut 6.5" x 1.25"
A-2 Cut 2.75" x 2.5"	**A-1** Cut 6" x 2.25"

(continued)

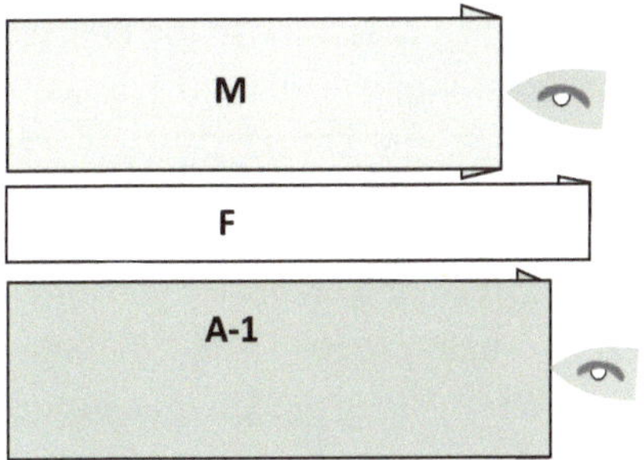

36 In column 2, press all far right edges inwards 1/4".

37 Flip **A-1**, face down, onto the bottom edge of **F**, and stitch together.

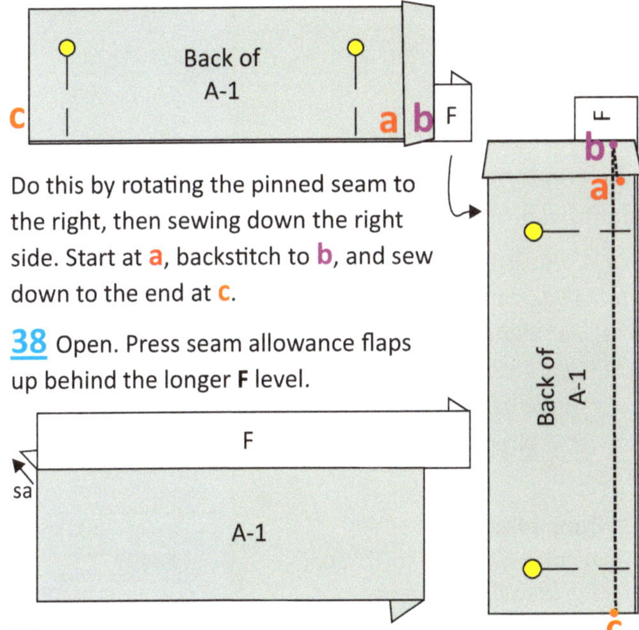

Do this by rotating the pinned seam to the right, then sewing down the right side. Start at **a**, backstitch to **b**, and sew down to the end at **c**.

38 Open. Press seam allowance flaps up behind the longer **F** level.

39 Flip piece **M** face down on the upper edge of the **FA** unit. Pin the top edge.

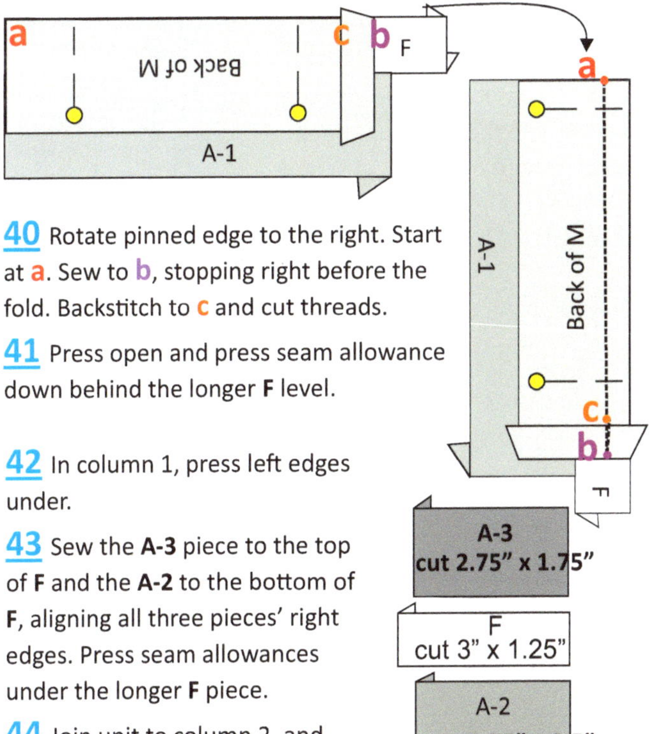

40 Rotate pinned edge to the right. Start at **a**. Sew to **b**, stopping right before the fold. Backstitch to **c** and cut threads.

41 Press open and press seam allowance down behind the longer **F** level.

42 In column 1, press left edges under.

43 Sew the **A-3** piece to the top of **F** and the **A-2** to the bottom of **F**, aligning all three pieces' right edges. Press seam allowances under the longer **F** piece.

44 Join unit to column 2, and press seam allowances under column 2.

Prepare the Lineup and Sew

45 Place everything you've cut and/or sewn in position on your design surface. The two **A-1**'s; four of the **M**'s cut and pressed in steps 6-9; the three special groups; and a bunch of floor dividers.

46 One by one, press each floor divider's ends to the back 1/4". Swipe a bit of glue under flaps to hold them.

Smush carefully, so their top and bottom corners can't be seen from the front. Press to dry glue.

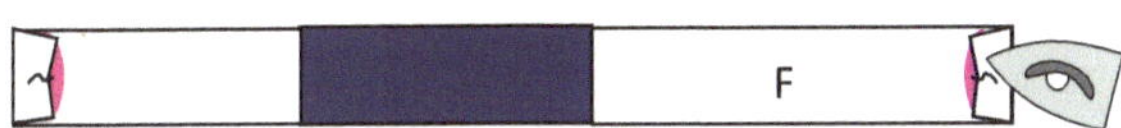

Place dividers back where they belong in the layout.

47 Sew each divider to its upstairs and downstairs neighbors. Usually, the neighbor will be narrower in length; sew these from the narrowest strips' backs. For example, below is a floor divider, with a narrower A-1 under it. All 4 ends of the two should be turned under.

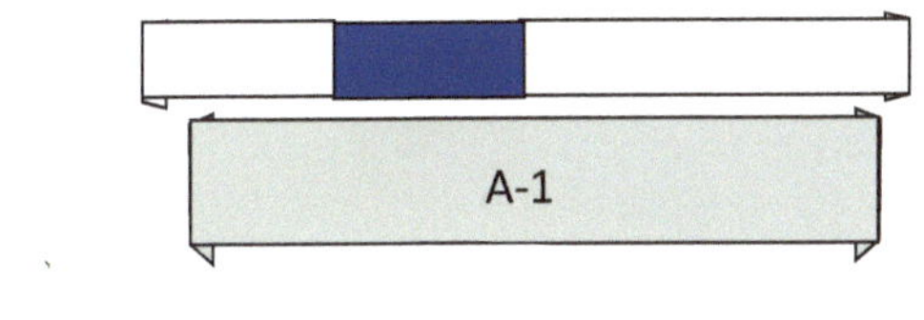

48 Flip A-1, good side down, on the bottom edge of the floor divider, good side up. Pin lower edge.

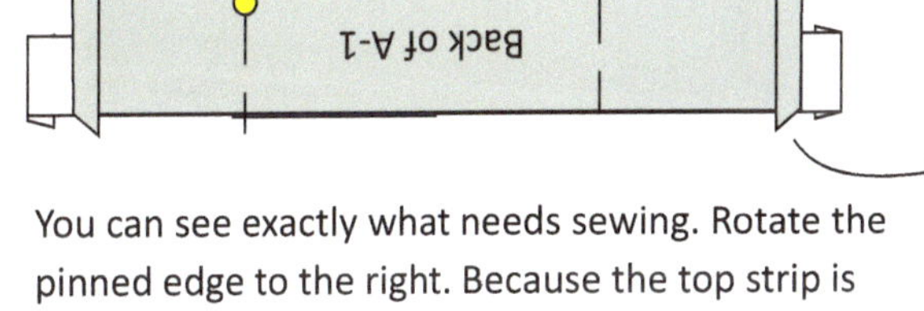

You can see exactly what needs sewing. Rotate the pinned edge to the right. Because the top strip is shorter at both ends, you'll have to backstitch at the beginning AND end (**a** to **b** to **c** to **d**).

49 Chain-sew a bunch of pairs like this - then bring them, still attached by threads, to be pressed (usually pressing seam allowances under the floor dividers). Cut apart threads and replace in your lineup. Sew pairs into larger groups the same way.

50 What if you improvised a pair like this – with a neighbor longer than the floor divider?

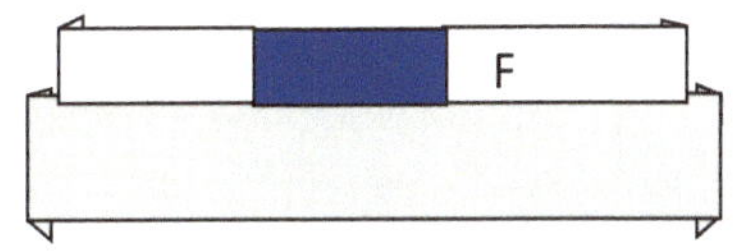

In this case, sew from the back of the narrower F level, where you can see both its end flaps and keep them turned in.

(continued)

 The trickiest situation is when the same piece is offset differently on the right and left. If you did lots of improvising, you will face a situation like this:

The F strip is longer on the left, but shorter on the right.

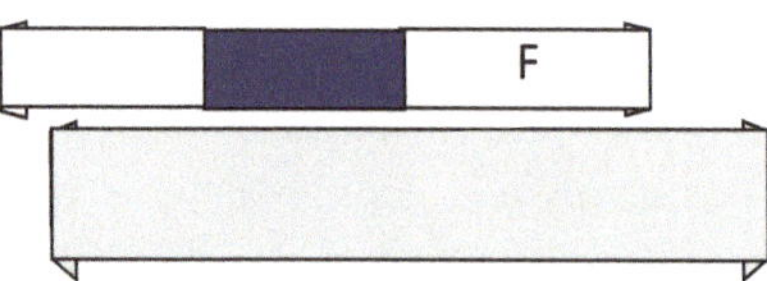

In this case, whichever side you sew from, you will only see one of the side flaps you're sealing. Let's say we flip the A-1 face down onto the bottom of the F piece:

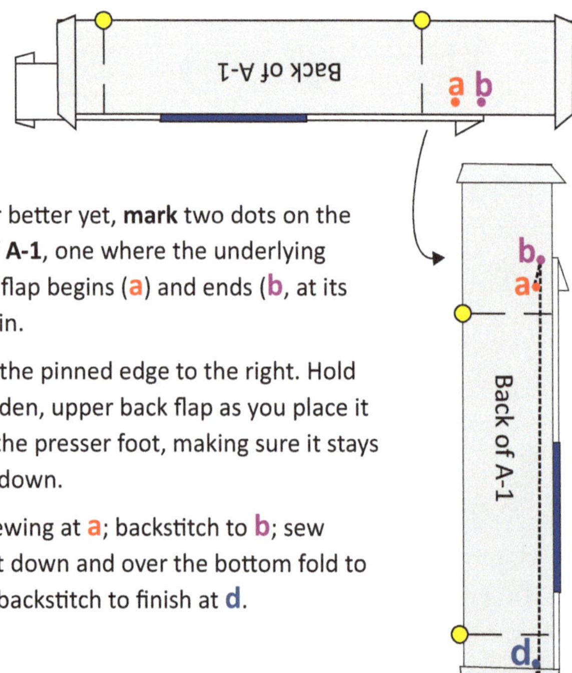

Feel, or better yet, **mark** two dots on the back of **A-1**, one where the underlying piece's flap begins (**a**) and ends (**b**, at its fold). Pin.

Rotate the pinned edge to the right. Hold the hidden, upper back flap as you place it under the presser foot, making sure it stays folded down.

Start sewing at **a**; backstitch to **b**; sew straight down and over the bottom fold to **c**; and backstitch to finish at **d**.

Clean Up and Prepare for Appliqué

52 Flip to the back and neaten. Trim threads, press seam allowances correctly, and, especially if you're planning to do machine appliqué, glue under protrusions. (If you'll do hand-appliqué, you don't have to be as diligent - it's easier to tuck things under as you hand-sew.)
Strips that stick out beyond their neighbors – especially floor dividers – need extra attention. Once joined, long seam allowance flaps are usually pressed inward. (Their good sides are grey in the next four diagrams).

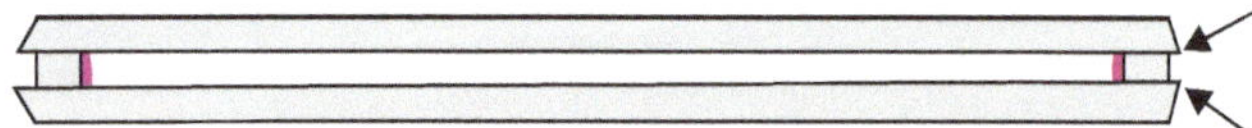

At the ends, the flaps' 4 corners will want to poke out and be seen from the front side. (Arrows above point to two disobedient corners). To hide, dab a bit more glue under them (on top of the short vertical flaps)....

.... and then press-smush the long flaps' corners back from the edges into hiding. Do this on both ends.

Or, if that's not working for you, turn the long flaps' corners back on themselves, gluing and pressing in position. The long horizontal flaps turned back on themselves are dark orange below. (Again, you may not have to do this if you'll be hand-appliquéing.) Find more appliqué tips on p. 5.

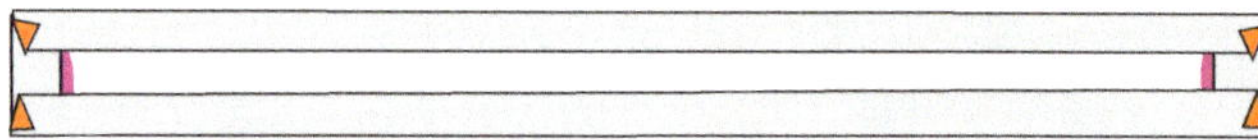

53 Turn top edge down 1/4".

For 'Condensed' quilt: No need to press the bottom edge of the building up. See next steps on p. 71.

For 'Color Block' quilt: Press bottom raw edge of building up 1/4". Audition backgrounds. In the sample quilt it's sky blue. Cut background to 13.25" x 39.5". You will place the building's bottom folded edge 2.5" above the bottom raw edge of the background. This information and next steps are in the directions that start on p. 76.

Quilting Ideas

Ditch-stitch back and forth along the horizontal seam lines. I also quilted rectangular windows into some of the widest strips, which you can see in the photo on bottom right of p. 13. In this diagram, they're the black dotted lines.

In the Color Block quilt, I quilted designs into the background that suggest more buildings. See some of them on p. 79.

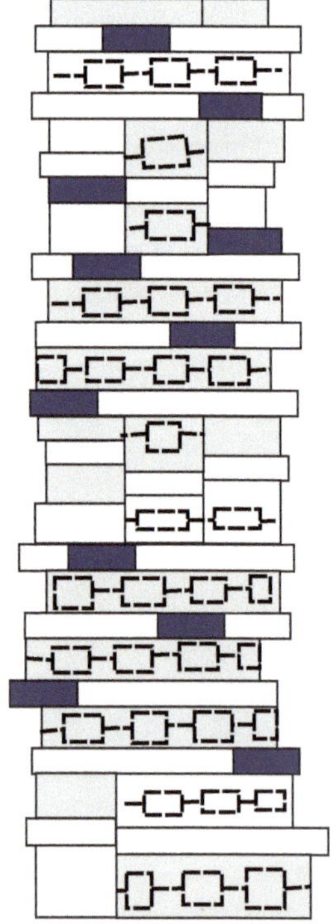

The Empire State Building

This 1931 Art Deco tower held the title of world's tallest for 42 years, until the World Trade Towers were built. Buildings from this era feature "wedding cake" setbacks on top, mandated by 1916 NYC law, to prevent them from blocking light – access to sunshine was considered a major public health issue. And speaking of light, when my husband and I recently stayed in a midtown hotel four blocks away, we could lie in bed and watch the spire's colorful LED light show! I'm sure the 4 million tourists who visit it each year, plus millions more on the streets, feel a similar affection for this familiar landmark.

Nonetheless, when I started making fabric buildings, this was the first one I swore off – I wasn't interested in sewing endless identical windows. But eventually it came to me: this building could be an opportunity to play with plaids, which offer complexity on a tiny scale that can't be approached with piecing!

My version is built in the units on the lower left. The long body is unit A; it's topped by units B, C, T, and a spire. At the bottom, it widens, with D and E. The spire (above the T level) is raw-edge fusible appliqué. In all the other sections, edges are turned under 1/4" as you piece.

I fancied this building up with perspective, the deep purples on the far right. We'll use some piecing tricks to create the angled tops, which will pop your building into the third dimension!

(continued)

There's no piece C-2

All D and E fabrics are repeats from above.

Inspired by the Empire State

Finished Size: Approx. 11" x 36.25"

Fabric

In my example the fabric gets lighter as you move up (mostly). Reasons: At night, the top is lit up. In day, the sun's most likely to hit the top. Have fun following or disobeying these rules!

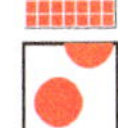

Main color. Collect ~8 pieces. The largest will be a fat-quarter or half-yard of one plaid or geometric for sections A and E. Plus approx. 7 more strips, scraps, etc. of lighter and darker fabrics, solids and prints. Small pieces go in sections B, C, T, D and the spire, and can be repeated in different areas.

Dark side, small amounts. On the far right of sections A, B, C and D. I used three purple solids - but you could get away with two. In Section A, it must be long enough to cut two 1.25" x 21" strips (start with a 2.5" x 44" strip, or a fat-quarter). For sections B, C, and D, small pieces are needed.

Background, for "Color Block" quilt only, p. 76. A third to a half-yard. Cut it to 13.5" x 39.5".

Also needed:

► A small piece of paper-backed fusible web for the spire, approx. 3" x 7".

19 This is not a licensed product. I am not affiliated or associated with any of the buildings depicted in these quilts.

Cutting Diagram

This diagram is for reference. Read through the directions before you cut. I prefer to cut when I reach that section, rather than doing it in advance and potentially mixing up the pieces (especially if the cat gets to them.)

Arrows indicate that two pieces are cut to the same size, from the same fabric. Be sure to read step 26 before cutting geometrics or plaids.

***** On levels A and B, where you see asterisks, it's **optional** to make the piece 3's from the same fabric as pieces 1 and 4.

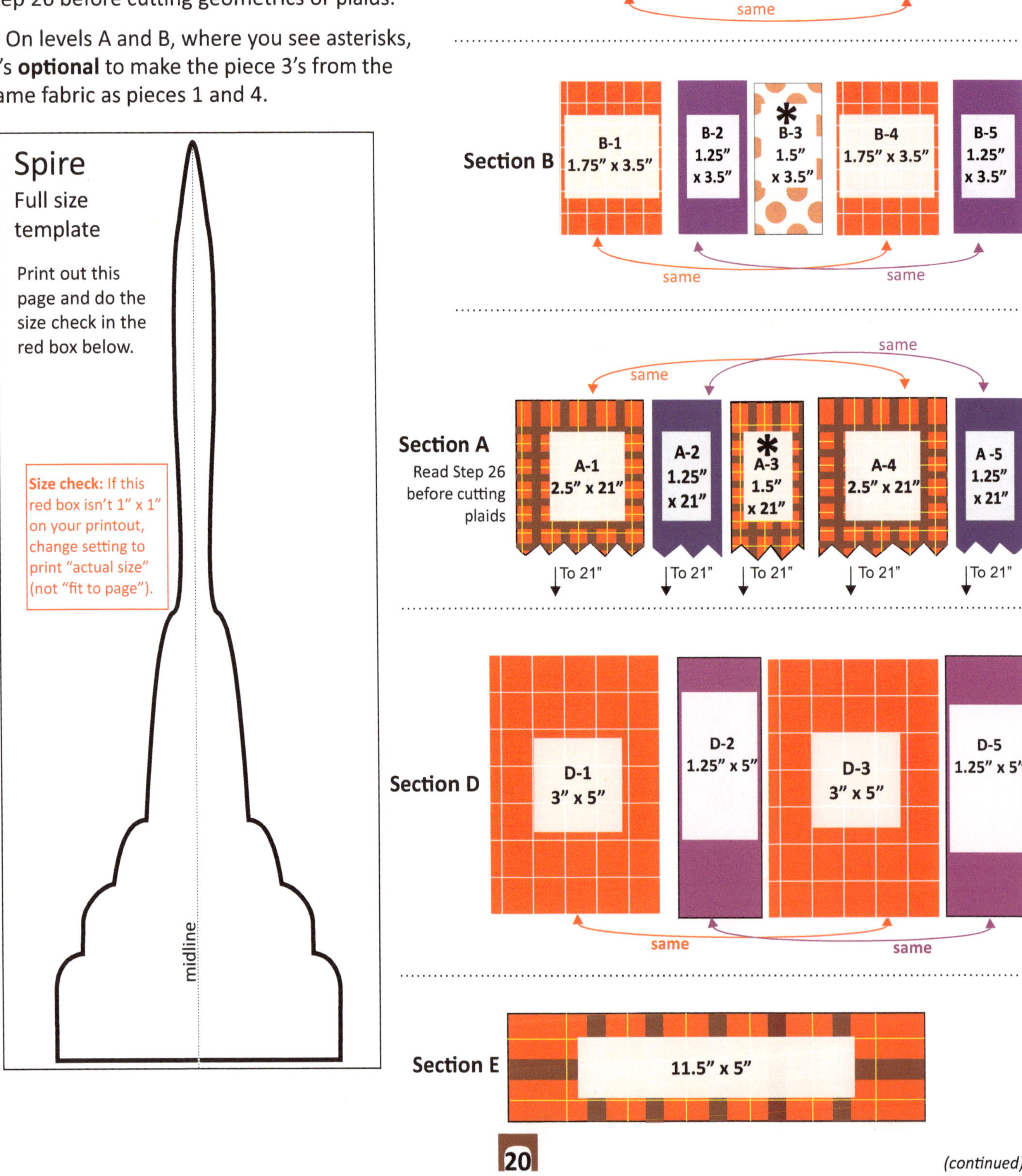

(continued)

We'll start with Unit B. It's pieced the same way as A, but Unit A is more confusing because its strips are so long! So doing B below will prepare you for A.

Overview of finished level. All B pieces will be cut to the same height, 3.5". The photo shows how they'll look when done. 1, 3, and 4 will have folds straight across their tops. Pieces 2 and 5's tops will have angled folds. That's because 1,3, and 4 are flat (looking straight at the building); and pieces 2 and 5 show the building's right side in perspective. All bottom edges will wind up raw. (They will eventually be covered by the folded tops of level A.)

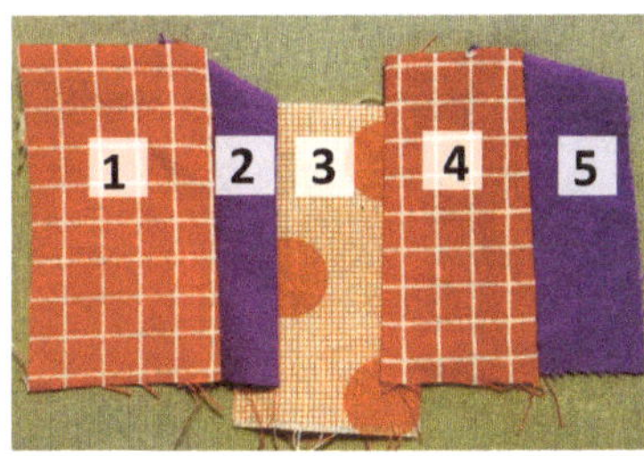

1 Cut the five B pieces to the measurements in the cutting diagram on p. 20. Use the same or a different fabric for B-3 as for B-1 and B-4. If you use a geometric print, read the box on p. 22.

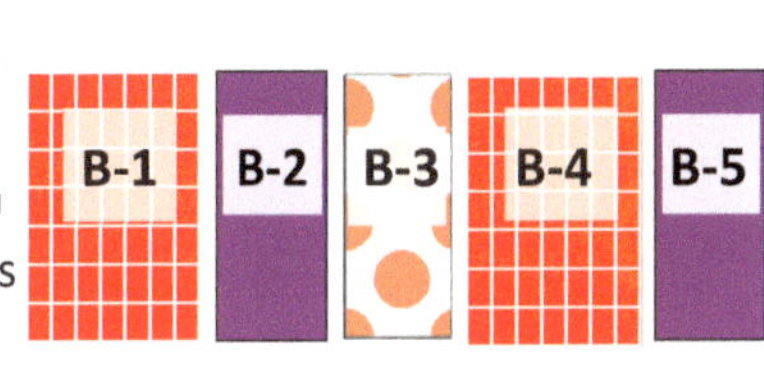

2 On pieces 1, 3, and 4 (the "flat" pieces): Press top edge 1/4" to the back. Don't do anything to pieces 2 and 5.

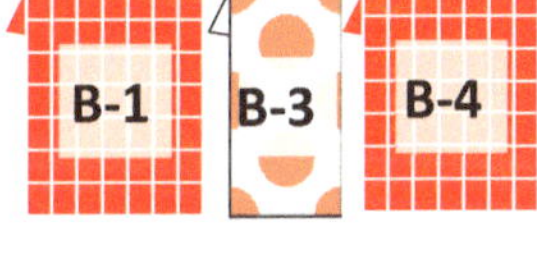

3 Flip B-1, good side down, on top of B-2, matching left and bottom edges.

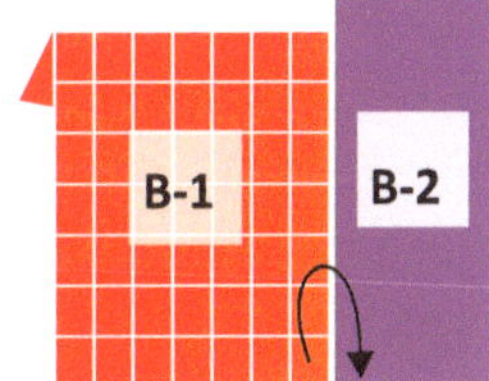

4 Pin the pair. On the back of B-1, let's name the lower left corner **x**.

We want to sew between **x**'s dot on bottom, and **y**'s dot at the top – but we can't start sewing at **y**! The seam is not along the right edge, the way we usually machine-sew!

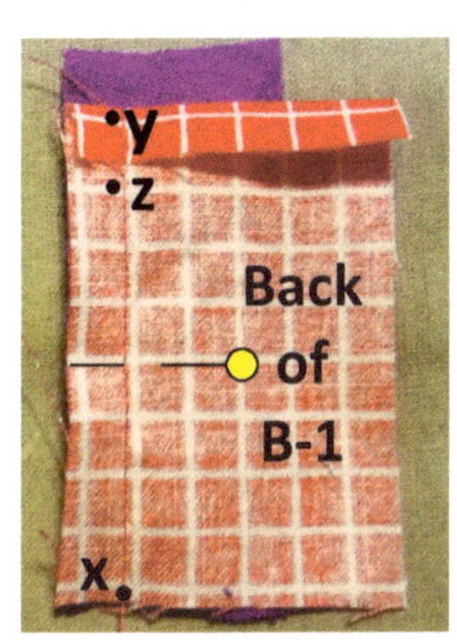

So **rotate** everything a full 180 degrees, with the back of B-1 still looking up at you. You're moving the pinned seam to the right (NOT flipping the pieces over). **X** is now on the upper right where we want it!

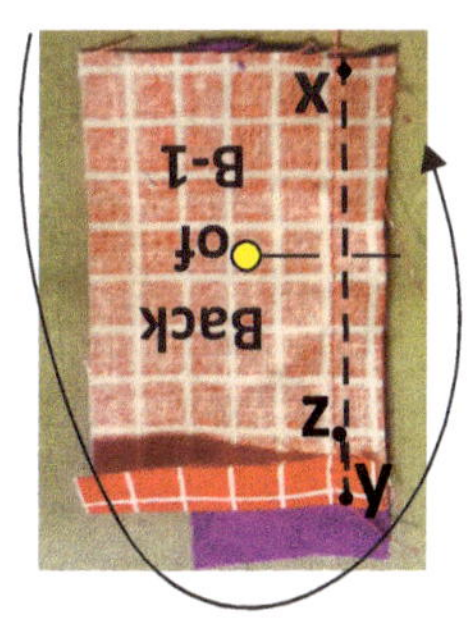

5 Start sewing at **x**. No need to backstitch here because there's no flap; just hold threads back. Sew towards **y**. **When you reach the flap, travel over it, so it's folded down permanently!** An awl will help you tuck it under the foot. Sew to **y**, stopping a thread or two before the fold. Backstitch to **z**, just before the flap. Cut threads at **z**.

If you overshoot a little onto piece 2, don't worry about it, you probably won't have to take it out!

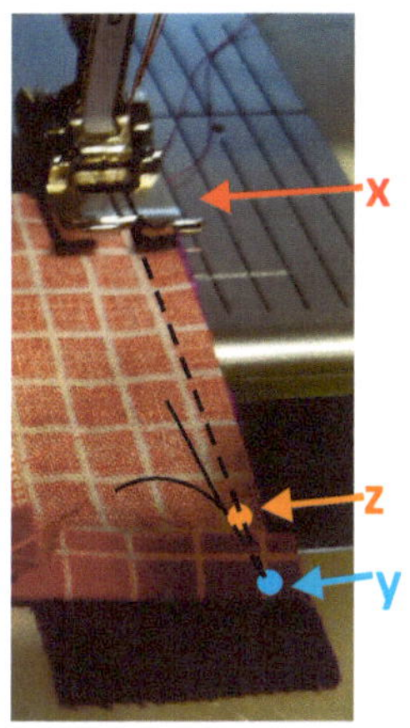

6 Unfold and press seam allowance **left**, under piece 1. Here's how it looks now, good side up. Only the top of B-1 is folded back.

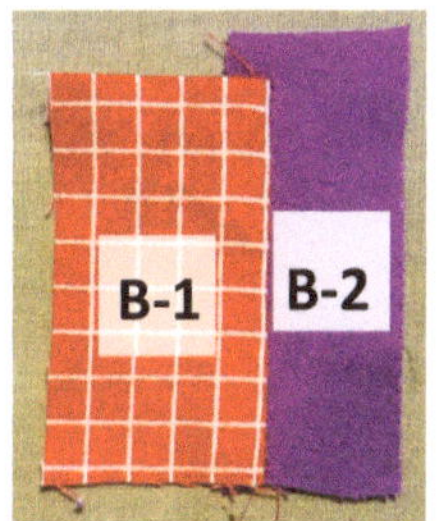

7 Add piece 3. We want the fold on top of 3 to be 1/2" lower than the top raw edge of 2. (This also means piece 3's top will be 1/4" lower than the fold on top of 1.)

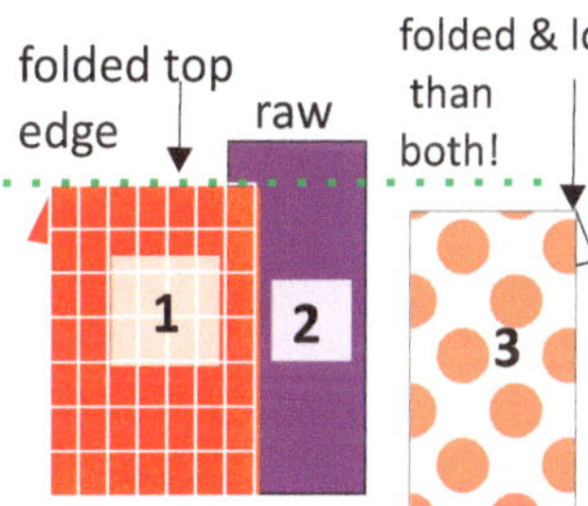

8 Flip piece 3 down on the lower right edge of 2. Start sewing at the dot by the **a,** bringing up threads. Backstitch over the flap, sealing it down. Stop at the **b** dot, just below the fold. Stitch forward, to **c**. (No flap there, so no need to backstitch). Although piece 2 underneath ends 1/4" shy of the end, you don't have to stop precisely there – nothing bad will happen if you sew off the end.

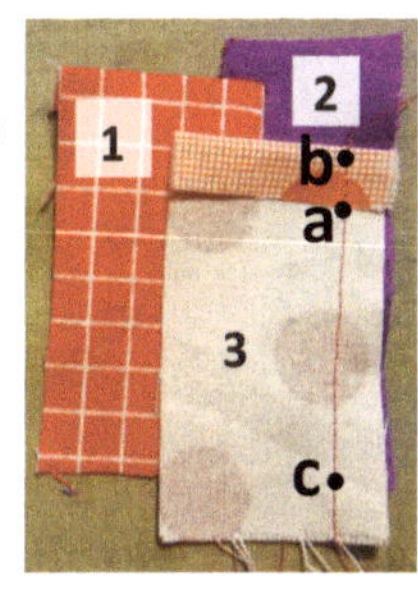

9 Press open. Press seam allowance left, under piece 2. Yes, the top raw edge of that purple piece is sticking up. We'll deal with it soon.

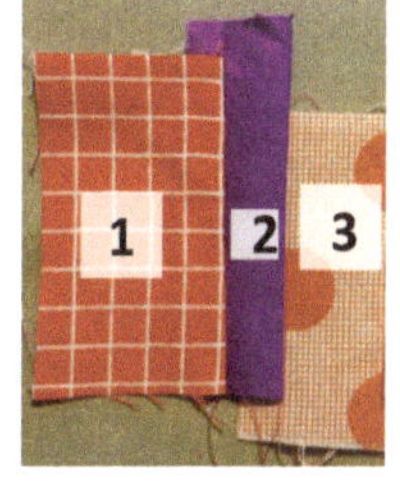

(continued)

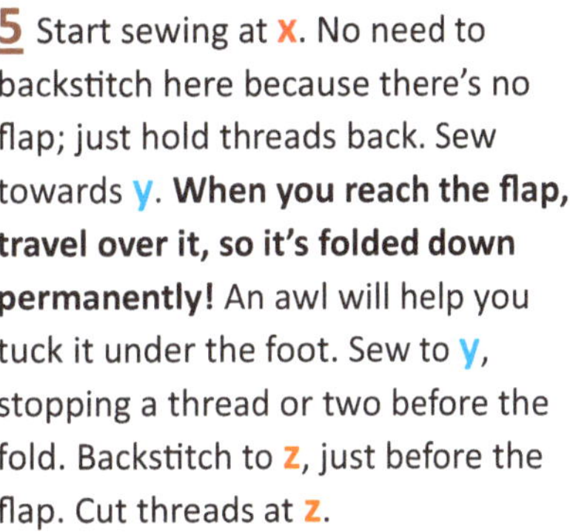

10 Place piece 4 on the table, good side up, folded edge at the top.

11 Flip unit 123 face down on 4, with left edge of 3 wrong side up, meeting the left edge of piece 4. **There are no corners to match**. You want to see the folded top of 4 peeking out 1/4" above 3's top fold. Piece 4's top fold should be at the same level as 1's (at the green line). Pin.

12 Rotate (with the backs of 123 still looking up at you), putting the **x** on top. Feed the **x** corner into the machine. Bring up thread and try to start where piece 4 underneath starts (but this needn't be precise). No need to backstitch. Stitch down to the dot by the **y**, sealing the flap. Backstitch to **z** and cut threads.

13 Open, and press seam allowance between 3 and 4 **right**, under piece 4.

14 Piece 5 needs its raw top edge 1/4" ABOVE the top fold of piece 4 - and the same height as the top raw edge of 2.

So flip the 1234 unit, good side down, on 5, good side up. Align left and bottom edges. Corners match at **x**. Pin as shown.

15 Rotate, putting **x** on the upper right. Stitch from **x**, down to **y**, sealing the flap, then backstitch to **z**.

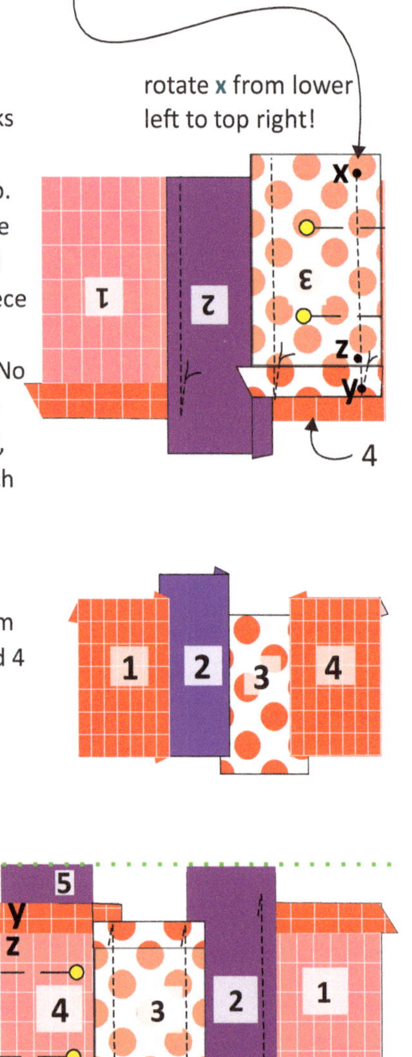

16 Fold tops of 2 and 5 back on an angle, shown by blue lines. Fold piece 2 from upper right corner of 1, down to the upper left corner of 3. With 5, guesstimate a similar angle. Press. Glue helps.

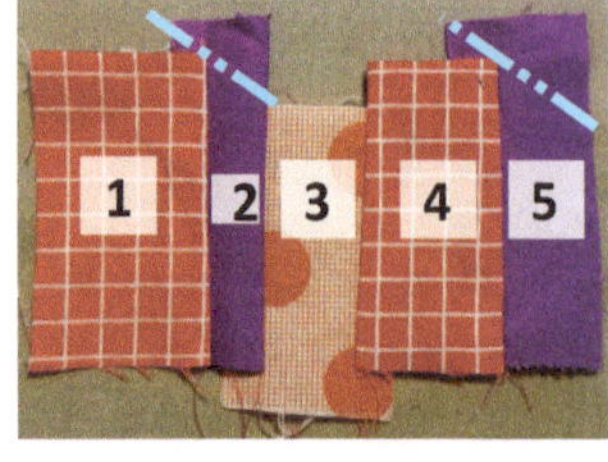

17 Tiny triangles of pieces 2 and 5 will peep out on top of piece 1 and 4. Press back at the base of each, using a bit of glue.

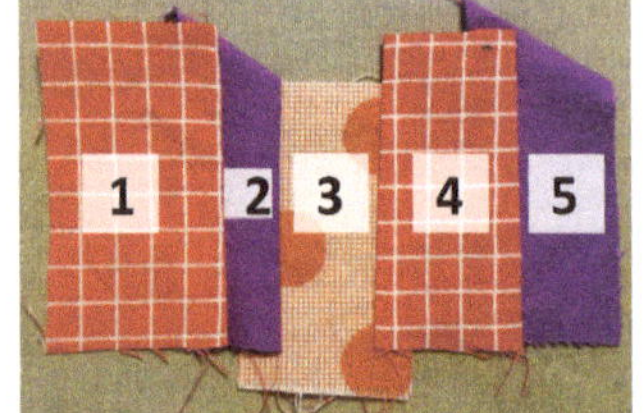

18 Fold the two vertical outside edges - far left of piece 1 and the far right of piece 5 - to the back 1/4". Press with glue. Section B is finished.

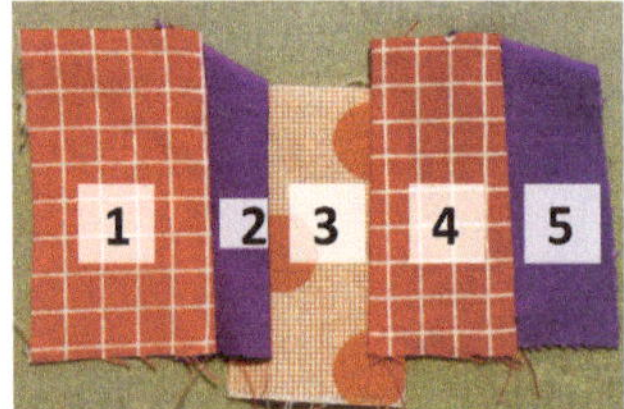

When to Misalign

In section A, B, or C if you're using the same plaid or print for piece 3 as for 1 and 4, be sure to *misalign* piece 3.

Piece 3 represents part of the building pushed back to a different plane than 1 and 4. With perspective, its horizontal lines should *not* line up with those on 1 and 4.

When 3 is misaligned, differentiating sections is easier. But piece 1 and 4's horizontal lines SHOULD line up with each other.

If you cut all three pieces at an identical level, as in step 26, the three pieces should automatically misalign.

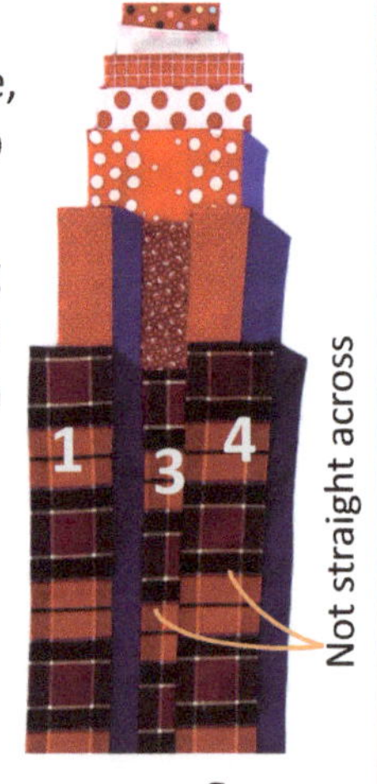

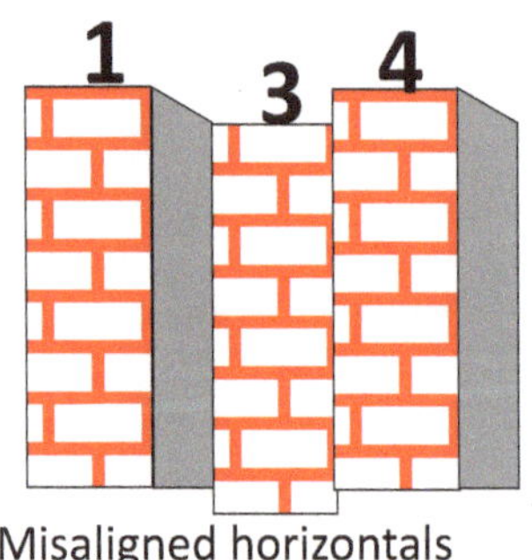

Misaligned horizontals help differentiate piece 3

Alignment of 3 & 4 weakens the illusion

(continued)

Here's what Unit C looks like finished. It's less complicated than A and B, with only four pieces (1-5, but no piece 2).

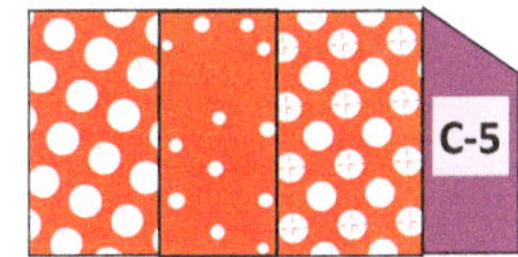

All pieces will be level on bottom. The first three are at the same level on top – only 5's top edge is folded at an angle.

19 Cut out pieces 1, 3 and 4, and sew together the traditional way, in order, with 1/4" seam allowances.

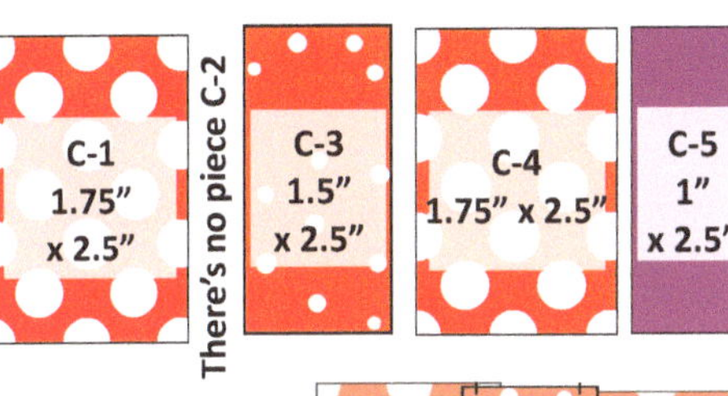

20 Press seam allowances outward from piece C-3.

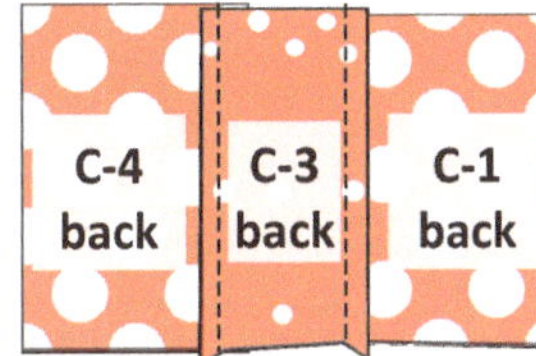

21 Press down the long top edge of unit 123 as one, 1/4" to the back.

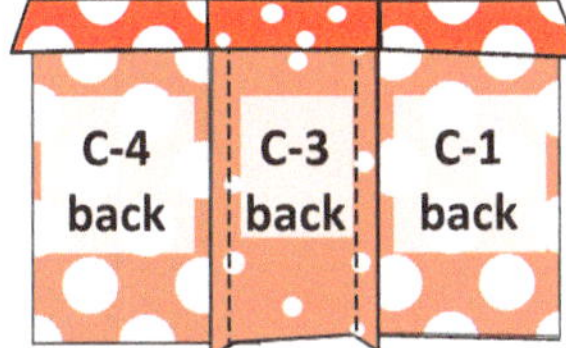

22 Place the good side of piece 5, facing up, on the table. Flip unit 134 to its back, and line up lower left corners and the vertical left edge. Pin.

23 Rotate 180 degrees so corner **x** is on the upper right, but the back side of 123 still faces you. Start sewing at **x**. Sew down to **y**. Backstitch to **z**.

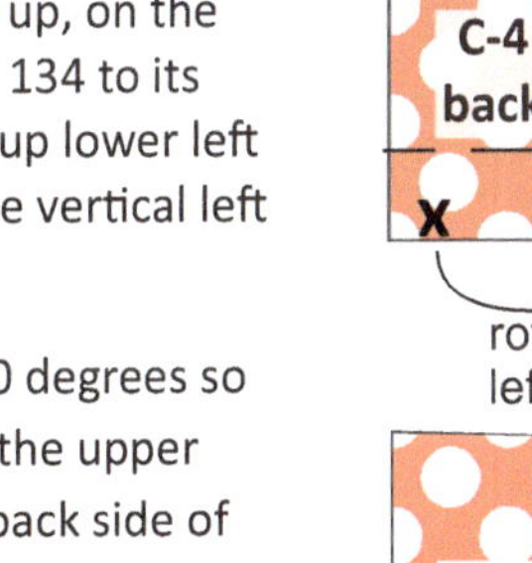

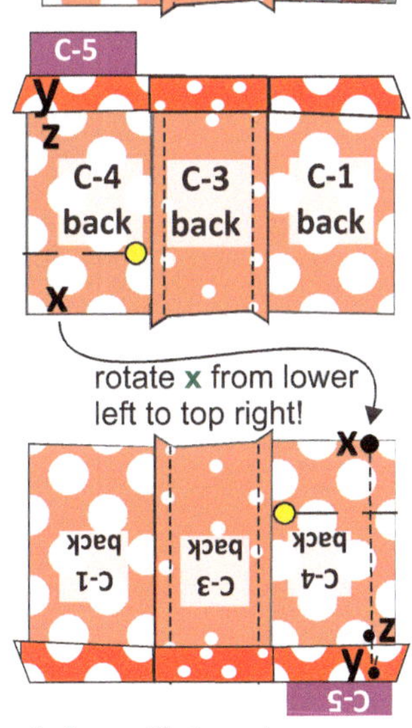

24 Press seam allowance under 4. Press 5's top at an angle, on the green dotted line, diagram **a**. A tiny triangle of C-5 may show above C-4, **b**. Bend it back, press and glue, **c**.

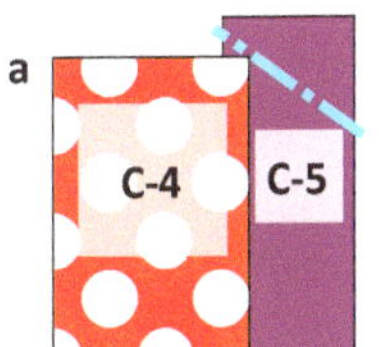

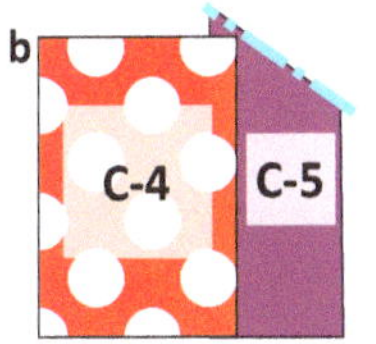

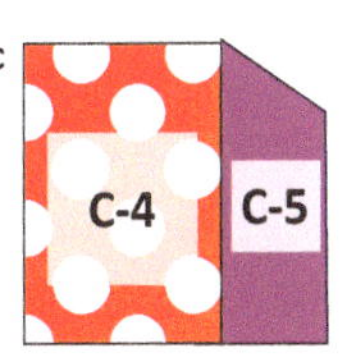

25 Fold the two vertical sides, on C-5 and C-1, inward 1/4" and press in position. Here's the new view from the back.

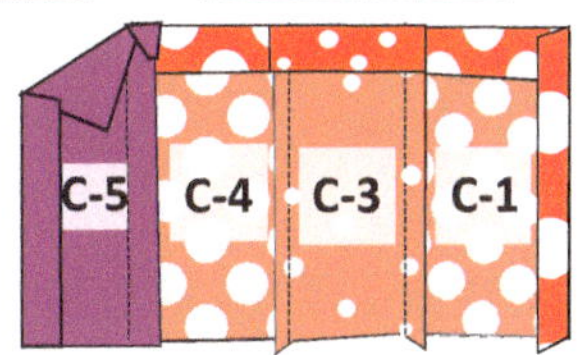

This is the same procedure as for Unit B, but here the pieces are much longer! And if you're using a plaid or other geometric, you'll need to do some thoughtful cutting.

26 Cut the three main pieces so major horizontal lines run across each at the **same** level. Cutting strips next to each other – but not necessarily touching, like the diagram below – helps you get it right. Depending on your cutting strategy, you can create interesting effects.

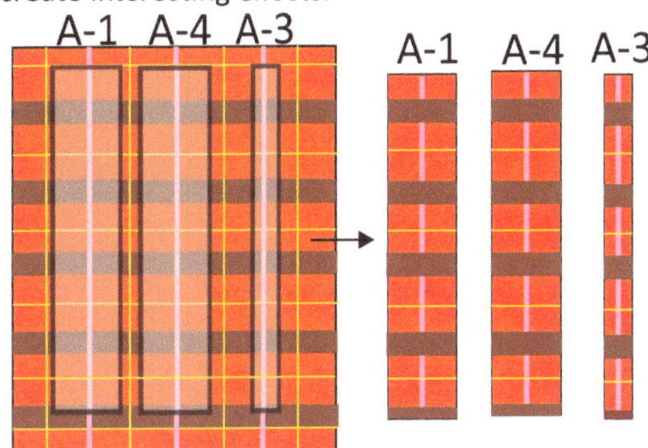

Idea 1: Pieces 1 and 4 are identical. The wide horizontal brown lines flow across each at the same level. Piece 3 is also cut at the same level. All three feature a vertically centered motif (a narrow pink line, down the center). We will eventually MISALIGN piece 3, explained in the box on p. 22.

Idea 2: More exciting: Cut MIRROR IMAGE pieces A-1 and 4. Below, piece 1 has a vertical thick brown bar toward the left; on piece 4, that vertical bar is toward the right. In both, horizontal lines must line up all the way down. (To find a mirror image, you may have to turn your fabric upside down, or even to the back!)

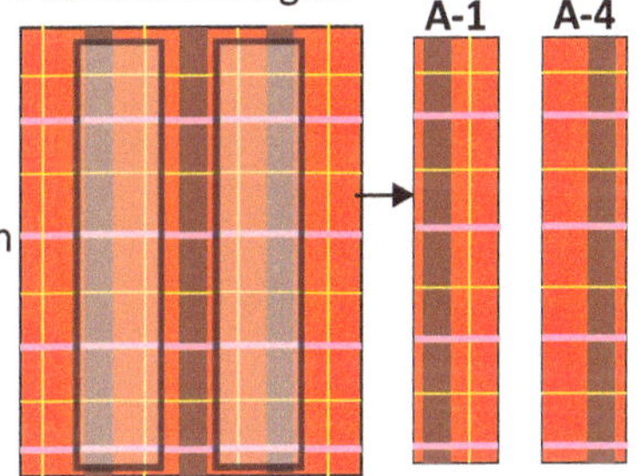

Idea 3: With piece A-3, you don't have to center the same motif as the other pieces. Below, my piece 3 is not quite symmetric; the thicker black vertical line is a bit to the left. But the horizontals still line up with 1 and 4; this will be vital when it's time to mismatch!

27 Press back the top edges of A-1, 3, and 4, 1/4" flat across. Check that the same pattern is now at the top. Here, after pressing, all three have a sliver of a black horizontal line across the top edge.

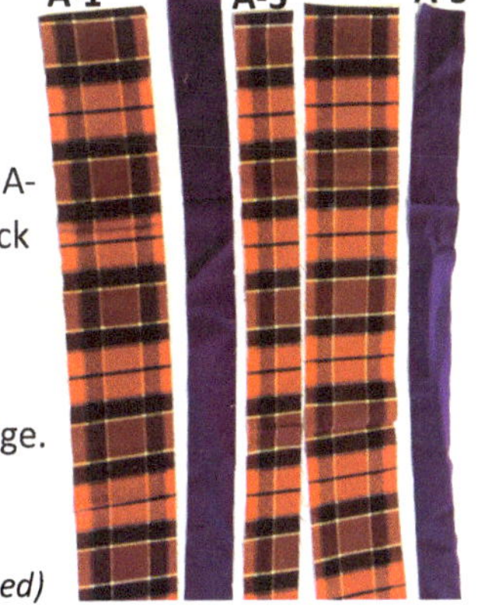

(continued)

28 Flip piece 2, good side down, on 1. The highest raw edge of 2 is 1/4" above the fold on top of 1. Mark two dots on 2: One where you feel the fold underneath on 1 (yellow line); and 1/4" below it (**x**).

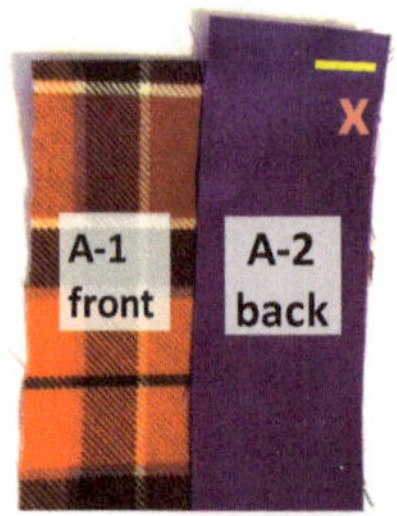

29 Pull up bobbin threads at **x**. **Backstitch** to the yellow line. Stitch straight down, all 21", to the bottom of piece 2 (not shown here.)

30 Unfold and press seam allowance behind 1. The back and front look like this.

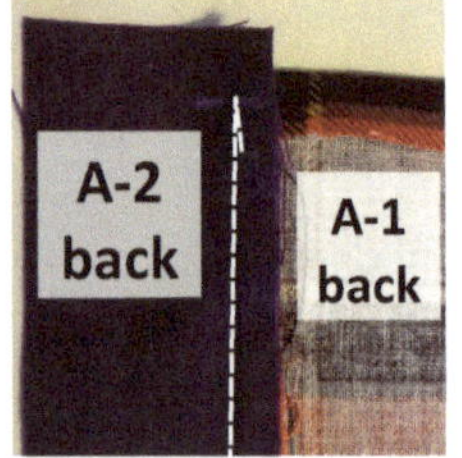

31 Line up A-3 so its top fold is 1/4" lower than the top fold of piece A-1, and 1/2" lower than the top raw edge of A-2. The horizontal stripes on piece A-3 are now OUT of alignment with piece 1, and that's what we want!

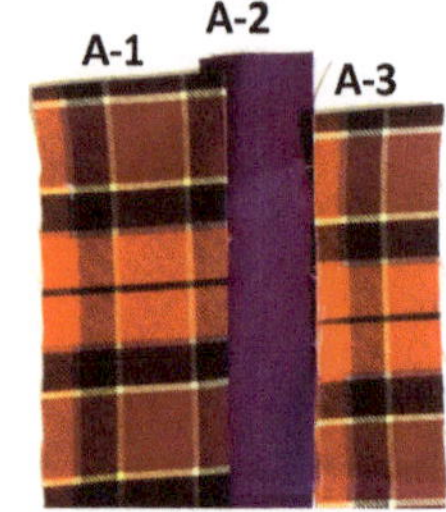

32 Flip A-3 face down onto A-2, matching far right edges. The flap on the top back of A-3 is folded down (with help from a finger).

33 Pull up threads at the black **a**, a bit lower than the flap. Backstitch up and over the flap, to just below the fold, at **b**. Then stitch all the way down to the lower right corner of the A-3 strip (we'll call it **c**).

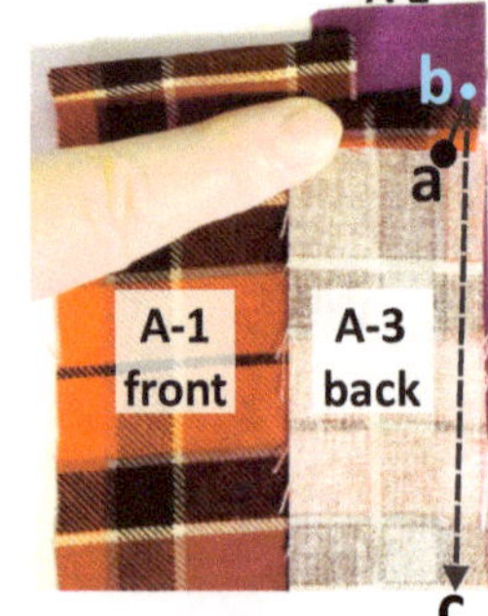

34 Press seam allowance under piece A-2. The front looks like this.

35 Time for A-4. We want its top fold at the same level as A-1. Both will be 1/4" higher than A-3. A-4's horizontal lines must continue those of piece 1 (NOT piece 3's!).

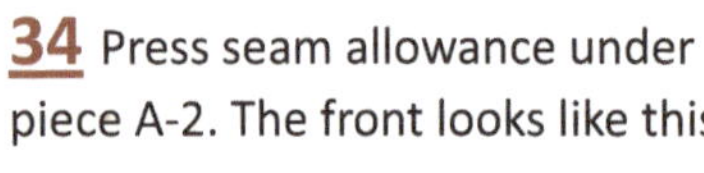

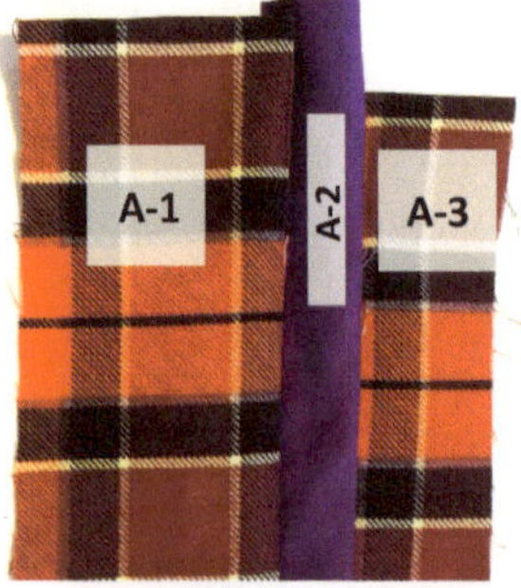

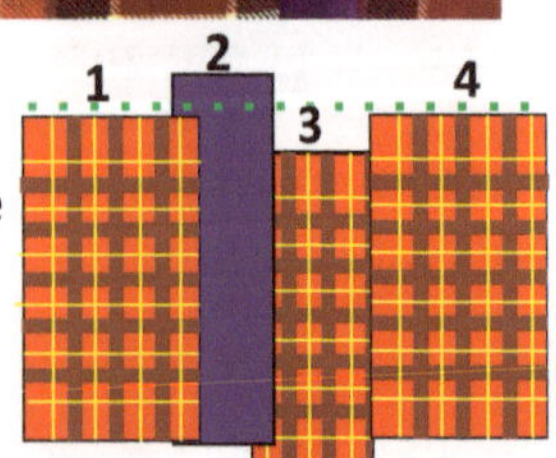

36 Place piece 4 on the table, good side up. Flip the 123 unit face down on it, so the top fold of piece 3 is 1/4" lower than the top fold of 4. Match and pin the left edge.

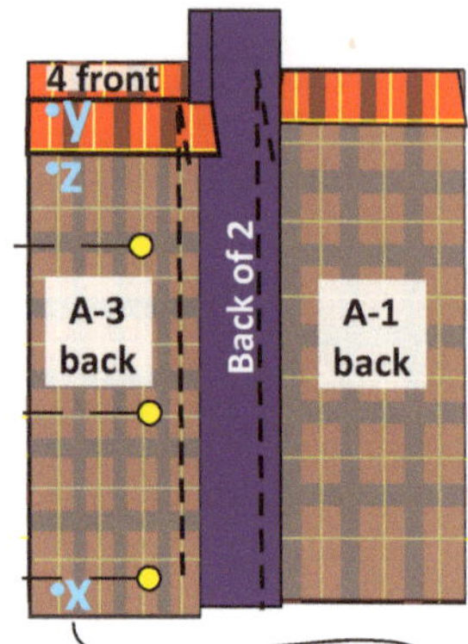

We need to sew the 20 inches between **y** and **x**. What makes this tricky is starting on **bottom** of 3. Such a long seam can distort the alignment at the top. So pin liberally, starting at **y**, the entire length.

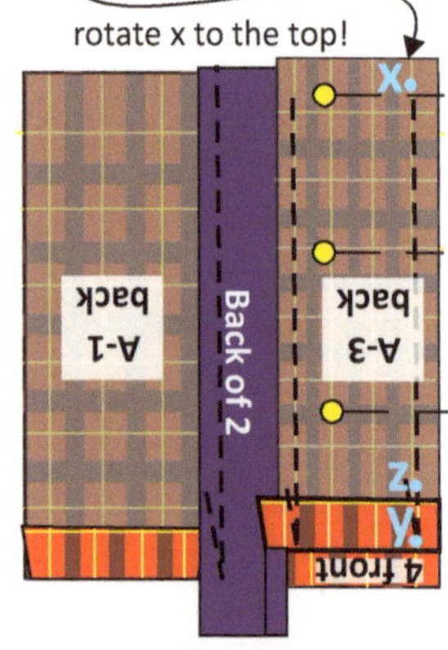

37 Rotate everything to put **x** on the upper right. Bring up threads and start sewing at **x**, where you can feel piece 4 start underneath (no need to backstitch here). Sew to the fold at **y**, sealing the flap shut; backstitch to **z** and cut threads.

38 Press seam allowance toward piece 4. The top front looks like this. The bottom: we don't care. We'll attach a bottom unit straight across there.

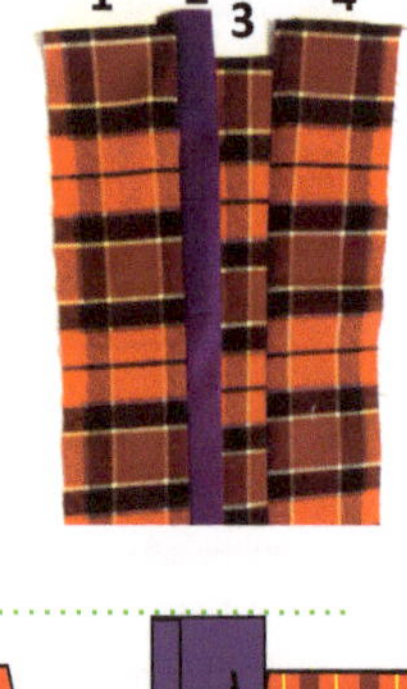

39 Place 5, good side up, on table. Flip 1234 unit on it. Match lower left corners. The top fold of 4 (at the **y**) is 1/4" lower than the top raw edge of 5. Piece 5's top is at the same level as 2's top raw edge. Pin 4 and 5 together.

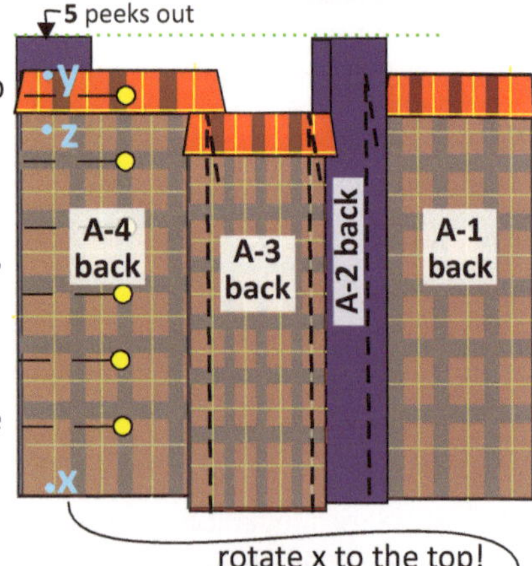

40 Rotate the **x** corner to the upper right, still looking at the back of 1234.

Sew from **x** down to **y**; backstitch to **z** and cut threads. Press seam allowance under piece 4.

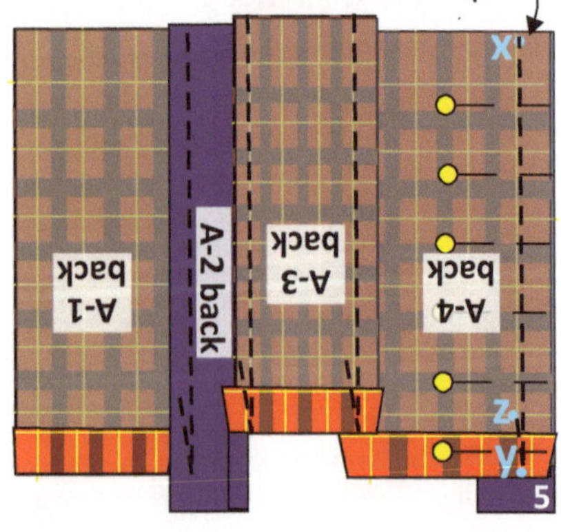

(continued)

41 Fold back tops of the two perspective pieces, A-2 and A-4, on an angle (blue lines). If little corners peep up, fold back, use glue, and press to hide them.

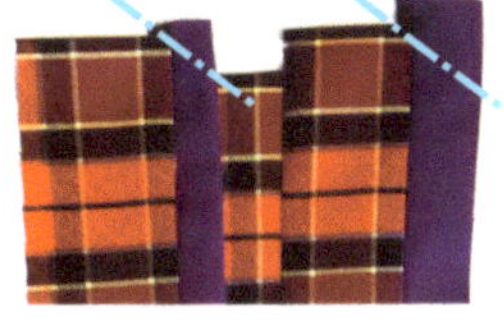

42 The finished top should looks something like this. Press the long vertical raw edges on each side inwards 1/4".

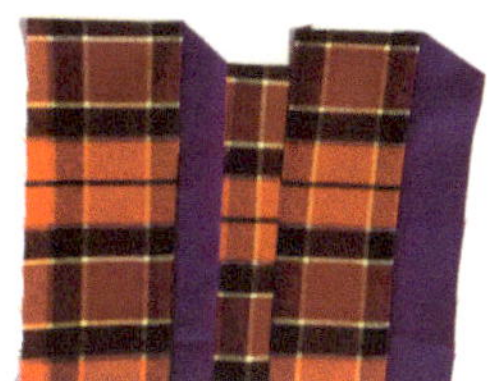

You're done with units A, B, and C. We'll finish piecing the T and D units, and then switch our machine foot, in order to appliqué the components.

The Top and Spire

43 Cut out the three pieces in the top (T) area to sizes on p. 20.

44 Press side edges of each 1/4". Also press in half to make a light crease marking the middle (blue line).

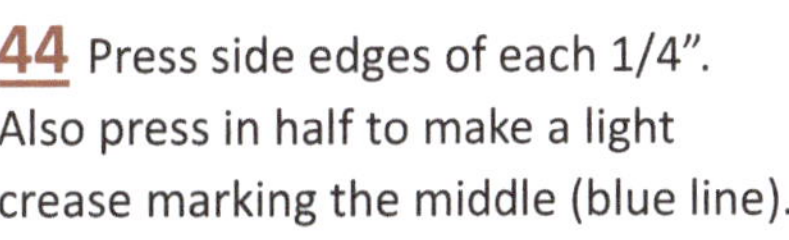

45 Place T-1 on table, good side up. Flip 2 face down on it, matching center creases and top edge. Pin.

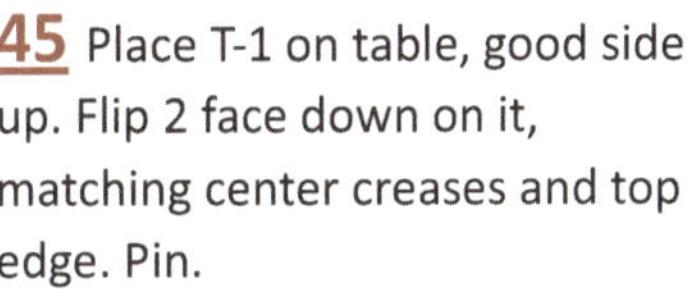

46 Rotate pinned edge to the right side (still looking at the back of T-2). We must secure **both** end flaps with backstitching.

Pull up threads at **a**. Backstitch to **b**. Sew to **c**, the end of the fold. Backstitch to **d**, just beyond the flap, and cut threads.

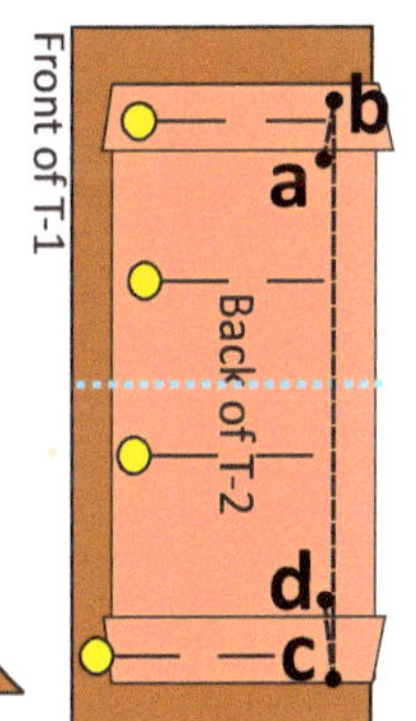

47 Unfold and press seam allowances down to wider level, including extended flaps on top of T-1.

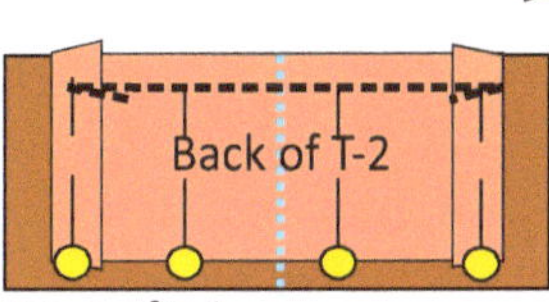

48 Add the next level, T-3, the same way. Flip it, face down, matching centers and raw edges at top. Pin.

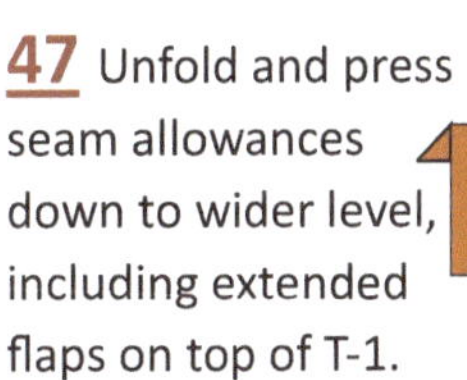

49 Rotate pinned edge to the right (still looking at the back of T-3). Pull up threads at **a**. Backstitch to **b**. Sew down to **c**, just before the fold on T-3. Backstitch to **d**, and cut threads.

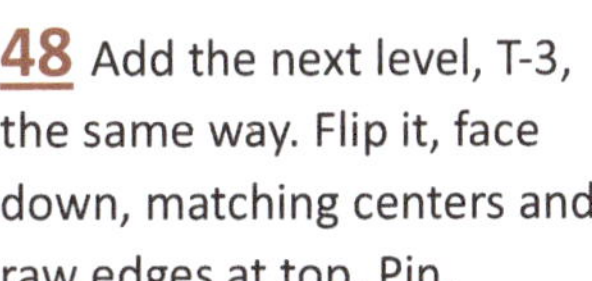
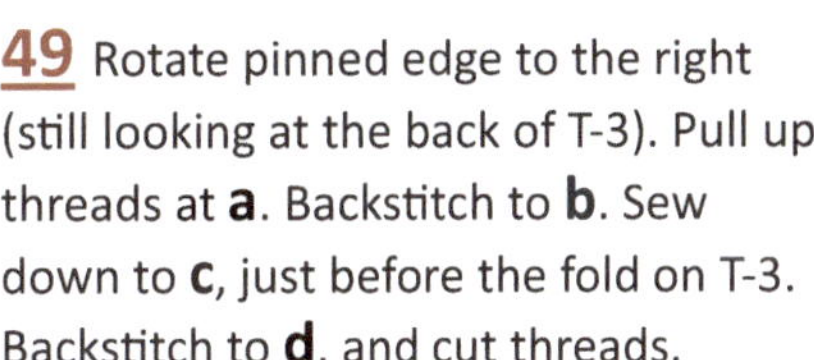

50 Open and press seam allowance down. Here's the back view. Press the top 1/4" of piece 3 down.

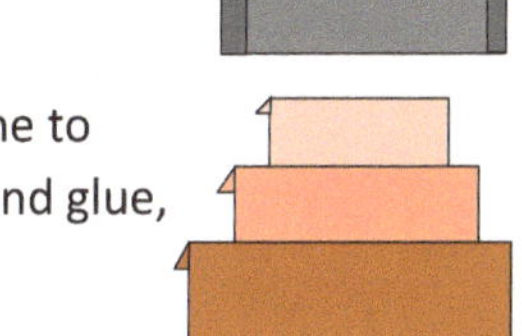

51 Here's the front. This is a good time to wrangle any protruding flaps – press and glue, so they can't be seen from the front.

The Base

52 Cut the four section D pieces in the chart on p. 20. The 1's face front; the 2's are sides in perspective. You can reuse A-2 or B-2 fabrics here.

53 Fold back 1/4" straight across the tops of both D-1 pieces. Do NOT fold anything on the D-2's.

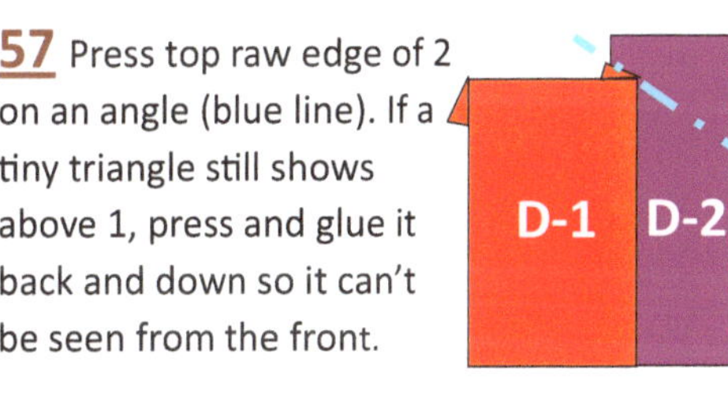

54 Flip a D-1, face down, onto piece D-2, face up, so lower left corners meet at the **x**. Pin left edge.

55 Rotate the **x** to the upper right. Stitch from **x** to **y**, then backstitch to **z**. Cut thread at **z**.

56 Open and press seam allowance **left**, under D-1.

57 Press top raw edge of 2 on an angle (blue line). If a tiny triangle still shows above 1, press and glue it back and down so it can't be seen from the front.

58 Press the two raw side edges 1/4" to the back. Now make another one.

59 Cut straight across the bottom of the A unit. Also, A-1's left edge and A-5's right should be neatly pressed in 1/4" to the back.

60 Place D units along the bottom edge of A. The left D-2's inside seam is about 3/4" from the right seam of A-1. The right D-1's inside seam is 3/4" to the right of A-4's inner seam. Pin, glue, or stitch-baste in position.

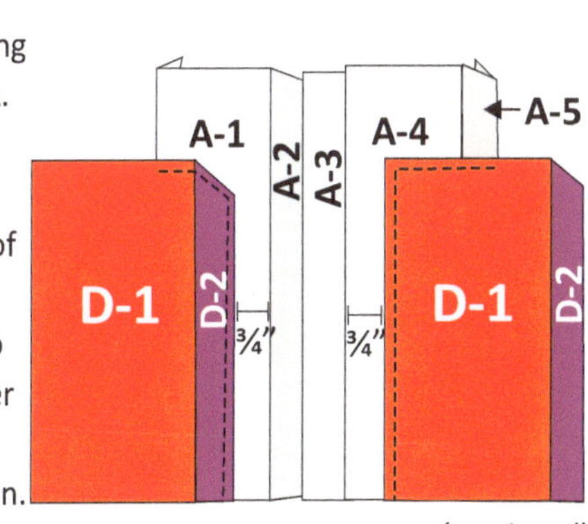

(continued)

Stitch Units Together

61 Install an open-toe foot in your machine. Read pp. 5-6 for appliqué tips. Testing first on a sample is always a good idea. Let's do area D first.

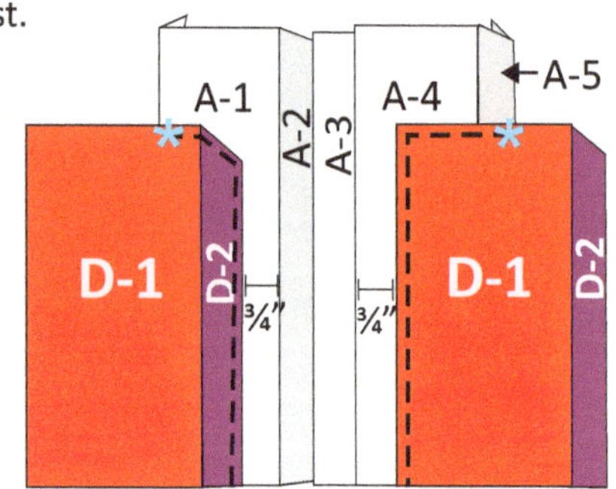

62 Appliqué the areas on the D units along the black dotted lines. A zigzag works well here. Stop and backstitch at the blue asterisks, where the pieces underneath end.

63 Next do the top. Pin or baste unit T behind the top of C. Doing it on a gridded cutting mat helps you place it straight. Use an appliqué stitch, such as a zigzag, where you see the black dotted line in the diagram.

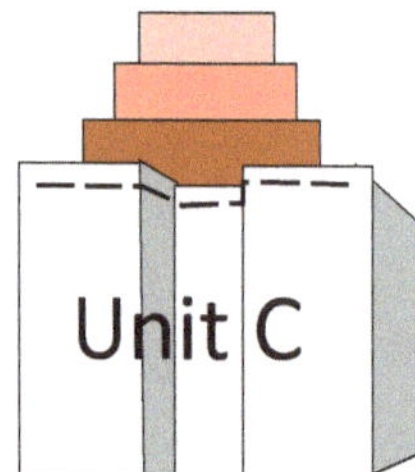

64 To join A, B and C, focus on lining up the strip 3's (marked with red asterisks).

► Place the top edge of B over the bottom edge of C, far up enough that all bottom raw edges of C are covered for at least 1/4". Pin or baste.

► Place unit A's top folded edge over the bottom edge of B. Pin or baste.

► Appliqué stitch the levels together.

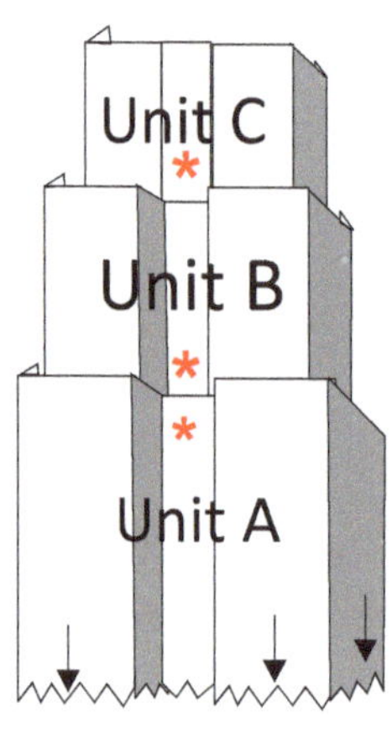

Add the Spire

65 Print out the spire pattern on p. 20. (Do the red box size check).

66 Trace the spire outline onto the paper side of paper-backed fusible web. Cut loosely around the outline.

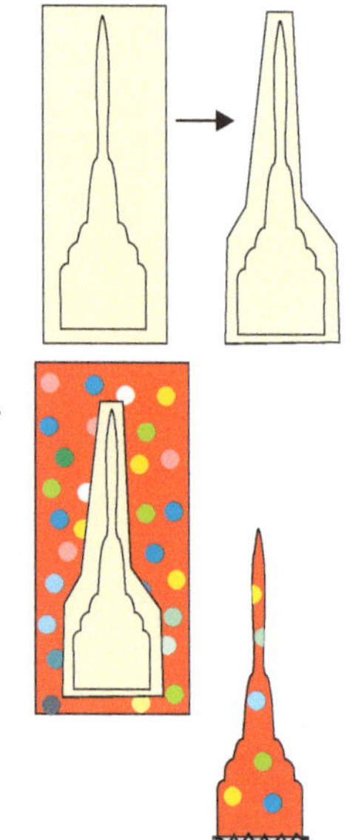

67 Adhere it to the back of the spire fabric. Cut out on the outline. Peel away paper.

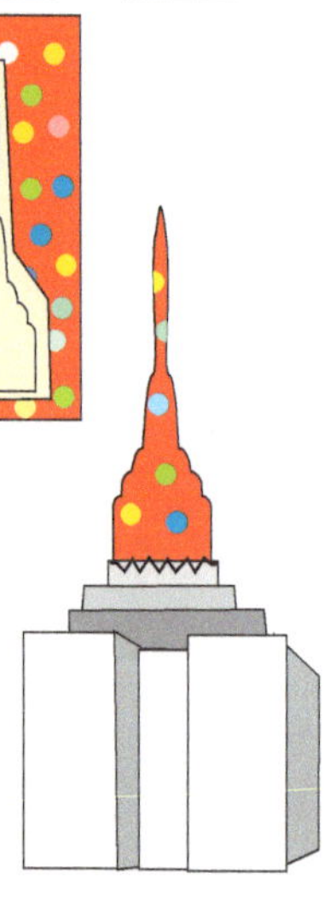

68 Tuck the spire under the top fold of T-3. Pin or baste. Appliqué stitch them together now (or later, when placing the building on the quilt).

Add Base E

69 Cut E to 11.5" x 5".

70 Cut away the extra flaps of A strips that are behind the D pieces (and just inside the appliqué stitches). Leave 1/4" in place.

71 Put E (pink) face up on the table. Center the rest of the building, face down, on top. Be sure the outer flap of D-1 (on its far left), and piece D-2 (on its far right) remain pressed inward 1 /4".

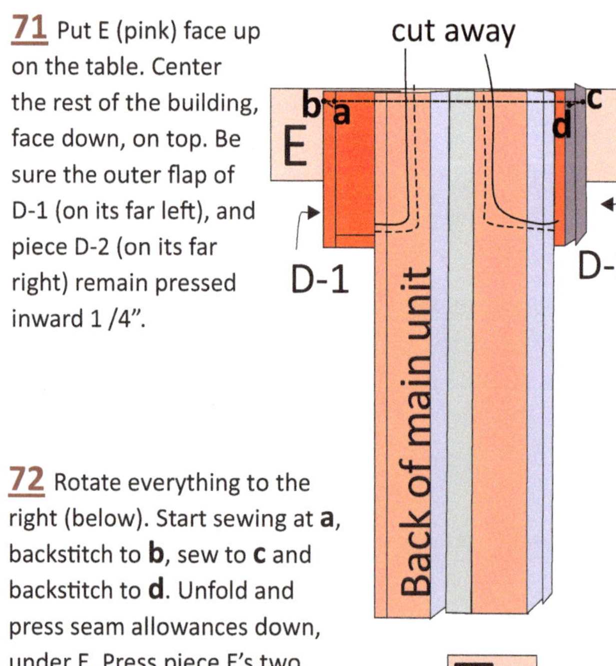

72 Rotate everything to the right (below). Start sewing at **a**, backstitch to **b**, sew to **c** and backstitch to **d**. Unfold and press seam allowances down, under E. Press piece E's two sides 1/4" to the back.

For 'Condensed' quilt (p. 71): No need to press the bottom edge of the building up. You will eventually baste it, matching its bottom raw edge with the bottom raw edge of the background fabric. See next steps on p. 71.

For 'Color Block' quilt (p. 76): Audition backgrounds. In the quilt, mine is dark blue. Cut it to 13.5" x 39.5". Place the building's bottom folded edge 2.5" above the bottom raw edge of the background. This information and next steps are in the quilt directions that start on p. 76. The measurement reference chart is on p. 77.

Quilting ideas: Along with ditch-stitching different sections, I quilted next to the plaid's main lines, vertical and horizontal (about every inch). In the Color Block quilt, I quilted designs into the background that suggest more buildings. See some of them on p. 79.

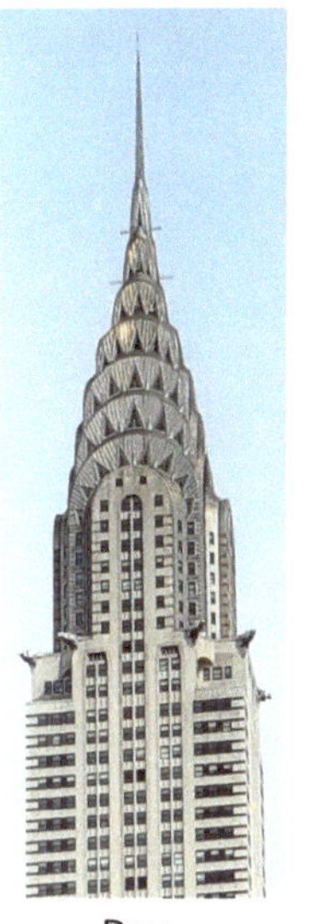

Day

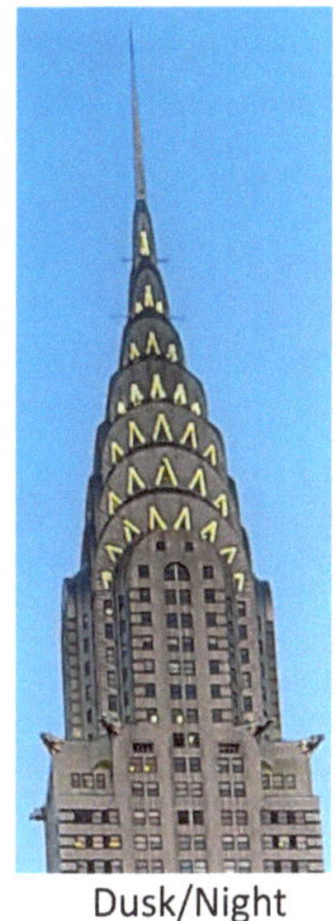

Dusk/Night

The Chrysler Building

It's an Art Deco tribute to the automobile! The edifice boasts stylized steel sculptures representing radiator caps and hood ornaments. Mosaics celebrate hubcaps and fenders. The lobby holds the world's most magnificent elevator doors. Alas, the lobby is now closed to the public, which I learned after entering. The guard promptly escorted me out. But not before I caught a glimpse of the jaw-dropping doors – photos are on the building's website. Soaring above it all is a thrilling steel spire, with its dramatic arches of triangles, dark in daytime, lit up at night.

Of course, what quilters see on top is a "New York Beauty" block. That's no coincidence: Historian Bill Volckening notes that quilt blocks with arches of triangles date to the middle 1800's and had a variety of names like "Crown of Thorns." Then in 1930 – the same year the Chrysler Building opened – Mountain Mist batting renamed the block "New York Beauty."*

Like so many buildings, this one has countless identical windows, which put me off playing with it, until I discovered the joy of plaids!

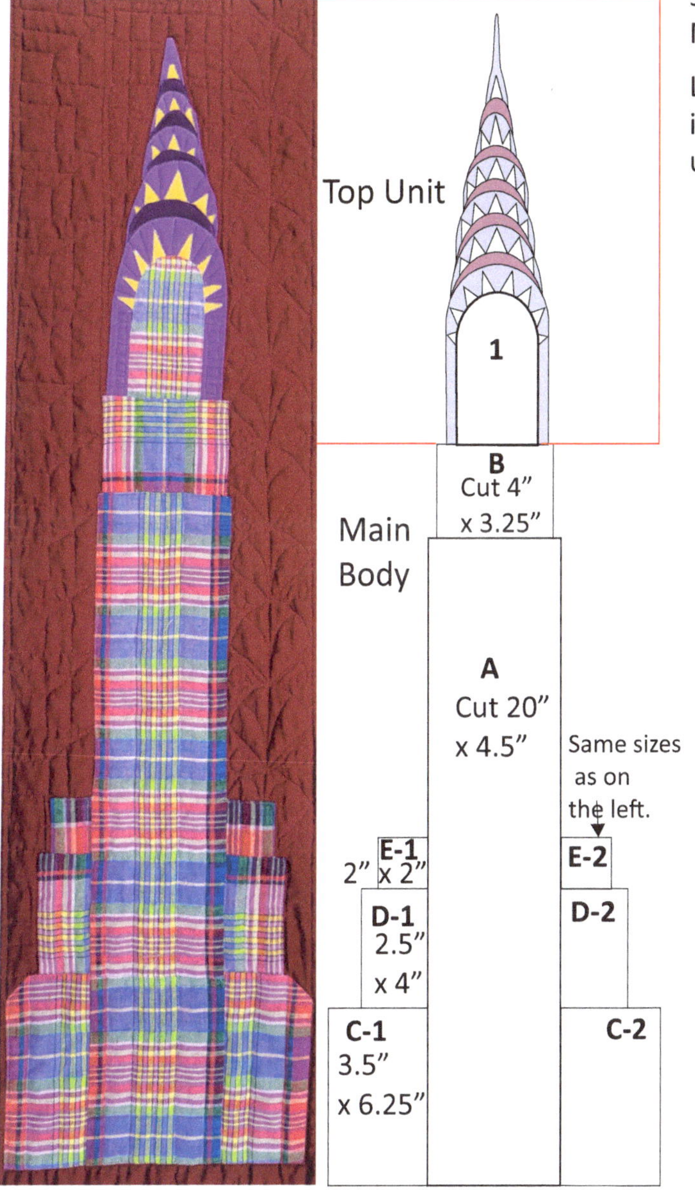

Inspired by the Chrysler Building

Finished size: Approx. 10" x 34"

Fabric

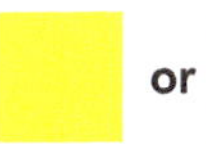

Main body Plaid or geometric print. Fat-quarter, quarter-yard, or half-yard. In the far left photo the plaid is shirting fabric.

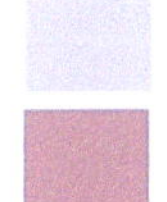

Top triangle windows - For night view, choose very light color. For day, choose very dark. About 8.5" x 10". See p. 30.

Arches behind triangle windows. Two contrasting solids. About 8.5" x 10" of each. See p. 30.

Background, for "Color Block" quilt only, p. 76. Burgundy in the sample quilt. Cut 10.25"x 39.5". A third to a half-yard.

Other supplies:

► Paper backed fusible web, minimum 12" x 13". (Do NOT use web with a back that's sticky when cold.)

► Nonstick "appliqué press sheet" or parchment paper.

► Freezer paper, 8.5" x 11", for shaping piece 1.

► Ironing fluid, like starch or sizing (optional).

(continued)

This is not a licensed product. I am not affiliated or associated with any of the buildings depicted in these quilts.

*Read more about this at http://willywonkyquilts.blogspot.com/2013/02/new-york-beauty-why-that-name.html).

Fussy Cut the Plaid

1 From the main print, select an area for the 20" x 4.5" body. If you want symmetry, the design on the right of center should be close to a mirror image of the design on the left. Here I chose a blue stripe to go down the center.

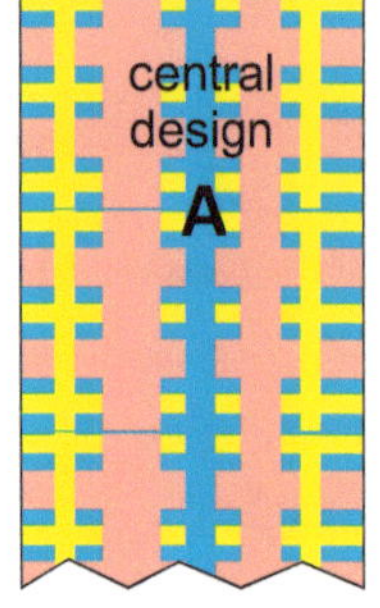

2 For piece B, the 4" x 3.25" rectangle above A, you can find a different area to center if you like – here it's a narrower blue stripe.

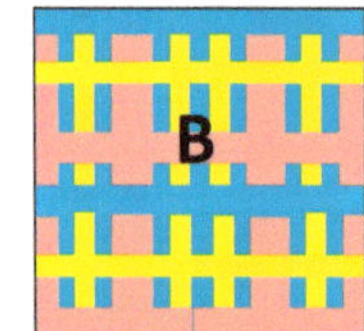

3 Press both vertical edges of piece B 1/4" to the back.

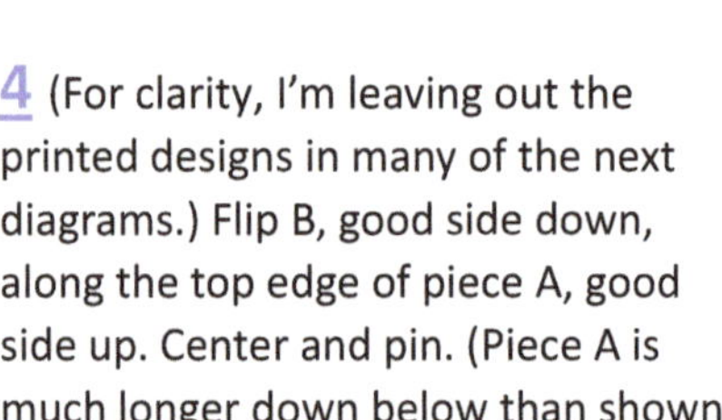

4 (For clarity, I'm leaving out the printed designs in many of the next diagrams.) Flip B, good side down, along the top edge of piece A, good side up. Center and pin. (Piece A is much longer down below than shown! Its sides are not yet turned inward.)

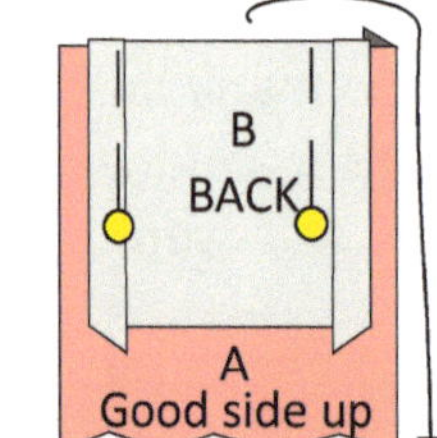

5 Rotate the pinned seam to the right. There are flaps on both edges, so we'll backstitch at the beginning *and* end.

Bring up threads at **a**. Backstitch to the **b**, just below the fold. Sew down to **c**. An awl helps ease the flap shut under the presser foot. Backstitch to **d** and cut threads.

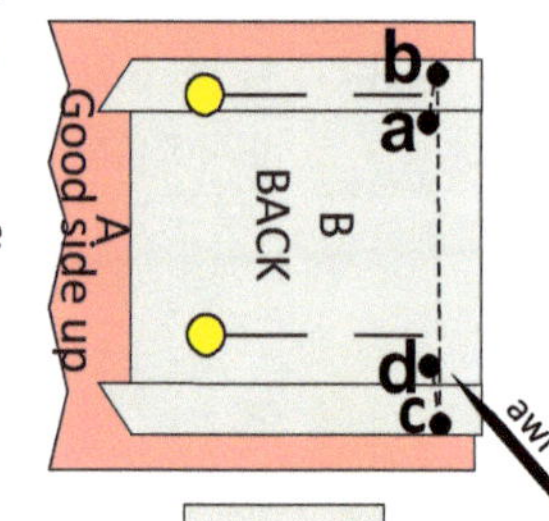

6 Unfold. Press seam allowances down. Also press the extended seam allowance flaps – at the two upper corners of piece A – neatly 1/4" down, with the rest.

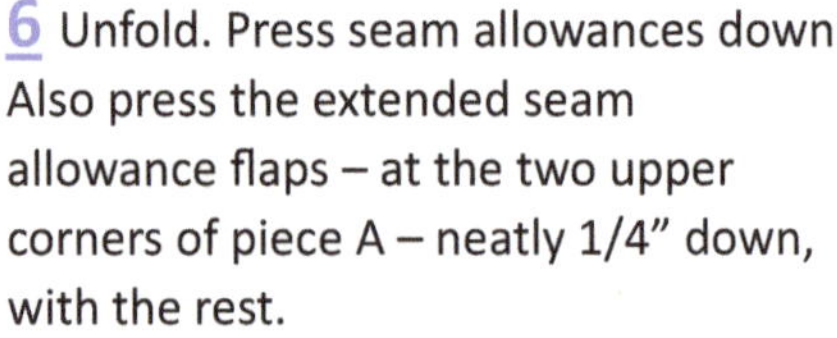

7 Scan your print for C, D, and E levels. You can center motifs, or – more fun – place vertical lines off-center, and mirror them on opposite sides.

For example, if you chose the left area below to serve as piece C-1 – look for its mirror image, like the one on the right.

See how the vertical pink bar on the left of the first sample switches to the right side of the second sample? That's mirror-imaging. It needn't be precise; some minor lines may not be mirrored, but you'll still create the effect.

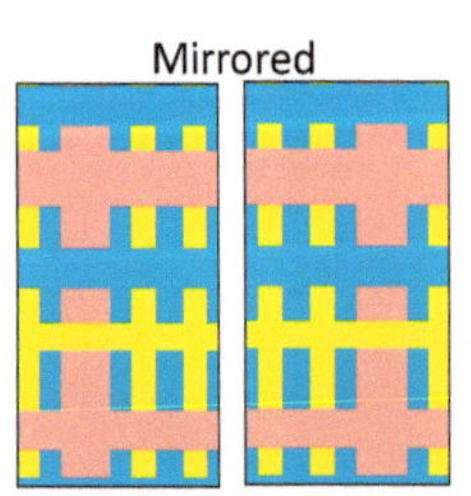

If you're having trouble finding a mirror image, check the plaid's back, upside down, or even turn it sideways.

8 Cut the C-1 pairs, D-1 pairs, and E-1 pairs out to the sizes listed on p. 25.

Join the C, D, and E Pieces

Because the sides are uneven, we must turn some more edges under during piecing. For clarity in these diagrams, I'll show the C-E pieces in different colors.

9 Arrange the main body (AB) and pieces C, D, and E.

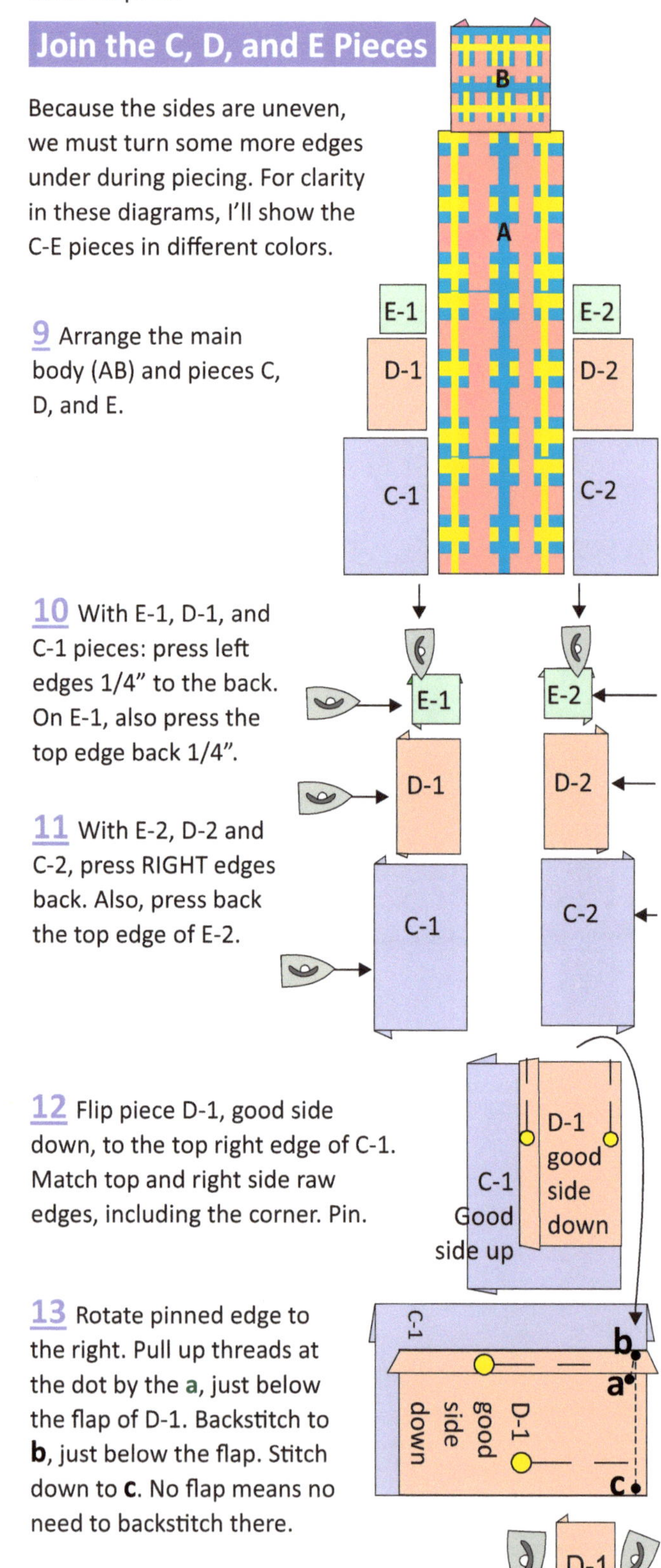

10 With E-1, D-1, and C-1 pieces: press left edges 1/4" to the back. On E-1, also press the top edge back 1/4".

11 With E-2, D-2 and C-2, press RIGHT edges back. Also, press back the top edge of E-2.

12 Flip piece D-1, good side down, to the top right edge of C-1. Match top and right side raw edges, including the corner. Pin.

13 Rotate pinned edge to the right. Pull up threads at the dot by the **a**, just below the flap of D-1. Backstitch to **b**, just below the flap. Stitch down to **c**. No flap means no need to backstitch there.

14 Unfold and press seam allowances down. Also press the extended left edge of C-1 neatly down.

(continued)

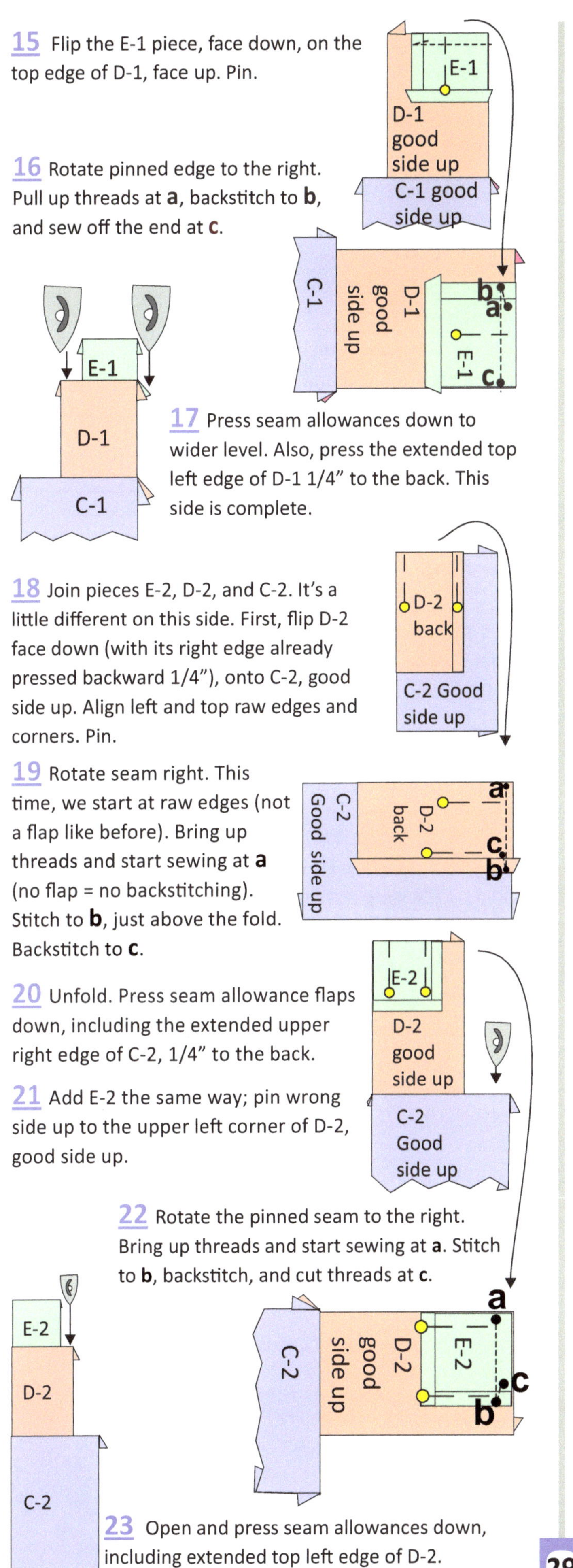

15 Flip the E-1 piece, face down, on the top edge of D-1, face up. Pin.

16 Rotate pinned edge to the right. Pull up threads at **a**, backstitch to **b**, and sew off the end at **c**.

17 Press seam allowances down to wider level. Also, press the extended top left edge of D-1 1/4" to the back. This side is complete.

18 Join pieces E-2, D-2, and C-2. It's a little different on this side. First, flip D-2 face down (with its right edge already pressed backward 1/4"), onto C-2, good side up. Align left and top raw edges and corners. Pin.

19 Rotate seam right. This time, we start at raw edges (not a flap like before). Bring up threads and start sewing at **a** (no flap = no backstitching). Stitch to **b**, just above the fold. Backstitch to **c**.

20 Unfold. Press seam allowance flaps down, including the extended upper right edge of C-2, 1/4" to the back.

21 Add E-2 the same way; pin wrong side up to the upper left corner of D-2, good side up.

22 Rotate the pinned seam to the right. Bring up threads and start sewing at **a**. Stitch to **b**, backstitch, and cut threads at **c**.

23 Open and press seam allowances down, including extended top left edge of D-2.

24 Place CDE-2 unit face down, on lower right edge of main building, which is facing up. Pin. Bring up thread at **a** just below the flap. Backstitch to **b** just below the fold. Stitch down to **c** (no flap means no need to backstitch there).

25 Unfold CDE-2, and press seam allowance left. Also press the entire right edge of A above the new pieces 1/4" to the back.

26 Pin the DE-1 unit to the lower left of the main building, matching bottom left corners.

27 Rotate everything (still looking at the back of CDE-1), to put the pinned seam on the right.

Pull up threads and start sewing at **a**. Sew down to **b**. Backstitch to **c** and cut threads.

28 Unfold and press the new seam allowance right, under the main building. Also press the entire upper left edge of piece A inward 1/4".

The main building is done! In the next page, we'll tackle the top!

(continued)

Most of these pieces are raw-edge appliquéd with fusible web on back. Choose three fabrics, light, medium and dark:

Fabric A For pieces 2A - 6A, the five "shadow" or "echo" arches. Choose a medium shade. In these diagrams, they're violet.

Fabric B Triangle windows. They're secretly attached. Here's 4B, uncovered. For a night version, make B the lightest of the three fabrics. For day, make it the darkest.

Fabric C Directly behind the triangle windows. If B is light, make C the darkest. If B is dark, make C the lightest of the three, as in these

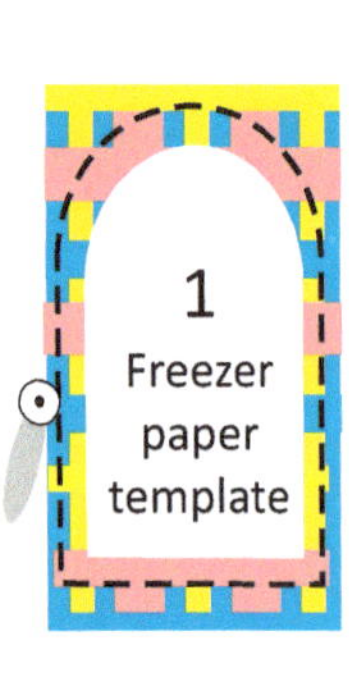

29 Templates are on pp. 33-34. Trace them onto plain paper or freezer paper sheets. (If you are reading a PDF, print those pages on plain paper or freezer paper sheets.) Do the red box size check.

30 Cut piece 1 from the tracing or printout. If it's on freezer paper, cut that out. If it's on regular paper, trace it onto the paper side of freezer paper and cut that out.

31 Find an area for piece 1 on the main fabric. (In my fabric version on p. 27, I centered an area of the plaid that doesn't line up with piece B directly below it.)

32 Press the template to the BACK of the fabric. Cut the fabric a little more than 1/4" bigger than the freezer plate template.

33 Press all, except the bottom edge, inwards and over the arch. Try to distribute the creases evenly. For extra hold, spray a little starch or sizing into a shallow bowl or plastic lid. Paint the seam allowance with it using a craft brush, Q-tip, or finger. Give it a half-minute to spread (while you wash your brush or finger). Press again and smooth out any sharp points that appear.

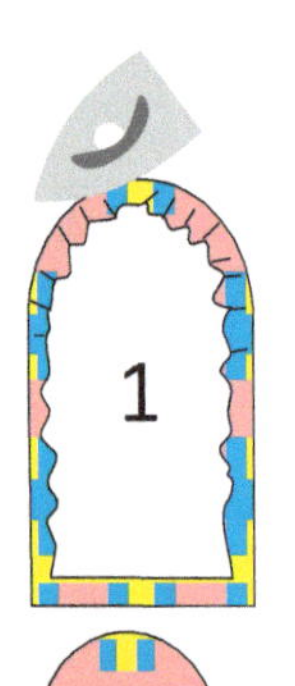
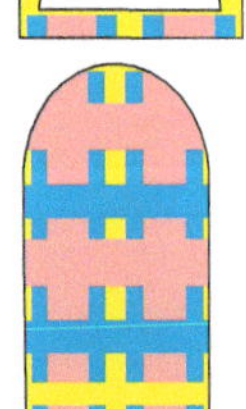

34 Remove template and press again. Only the bottom edge is raw.

35 Lay out enough paper-backed fusible web to fit all the shapes on p. 33 - 34. A 13" square should be plenty. (Use web that doesn't have a sticky back when cold.)

36 In diagrams, fusible web's paper side is yellow. To transfer shapes to fusible, use one of these methods:

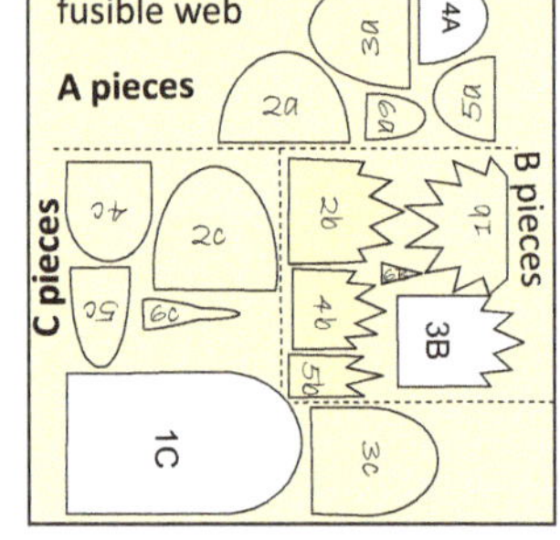

▶ Tape web, paper side up, on top of book pages and trace. Or,

▶ Tape printouts to window or light table; tape web paper side up, on top. Trace. Or,

▶ Glue printout to cardstock. Cut out each shape. Trace around each shape onto fusible's backing paper. Cut just INSIDE the lines.

In all cases, keep letter groups together. Jot number/letter in each shape.

37 Cut apart the paper-backed fusible onto three large pieces, one for each letter group.

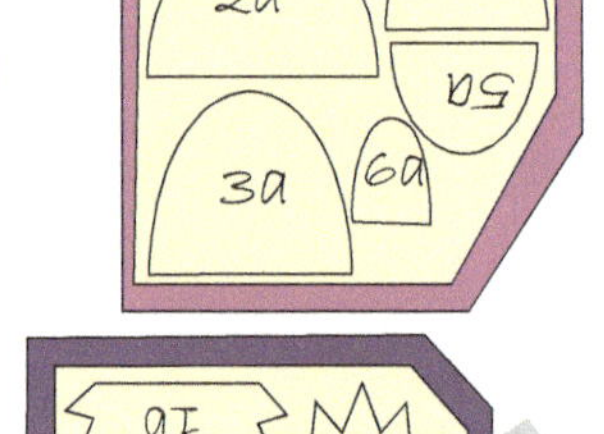

38 Press the **A** group to the back of your **A** fabric. Do the same for the **B**'s, and **C**'s .

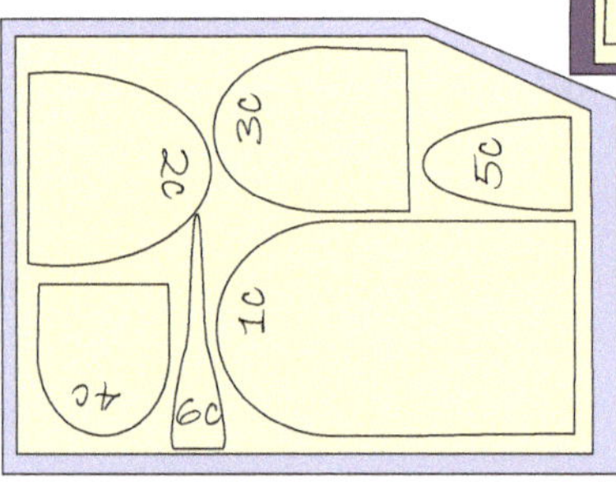

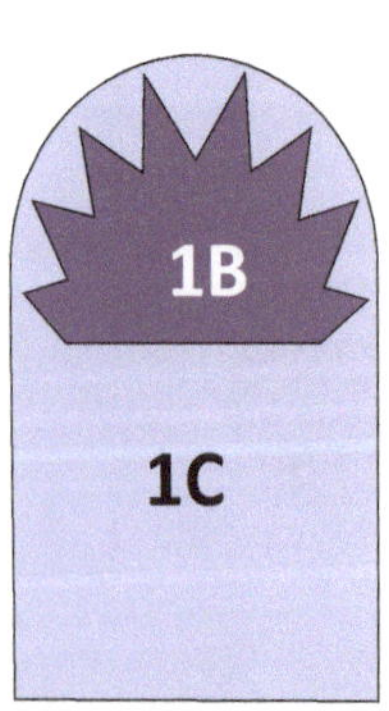

We'll make sandwiches for each number group, and appliqué pieces together. Read the tips on pp. 3-4. Testing a sample first is helpful for choosing thread, stitches, and tension.

39 **Sandwich 1** Cut out piece 1C, but leave paper on back. Cut out 1B and remove paper. Put 1B on C, with triangle points just below C's top edge. The full-size diagram on p. 33 can help with placement.

(continued)

40 Lay parchment paper or a nonstick press sheet on ironing surface. Fuse 1B onto 1C. Peel away 1C's paper after fusing.

41 Use thread that matches B or invisible thread. I use a 1.5 width. Sew the points as shown. You don't have to stitch B's lowest edge.

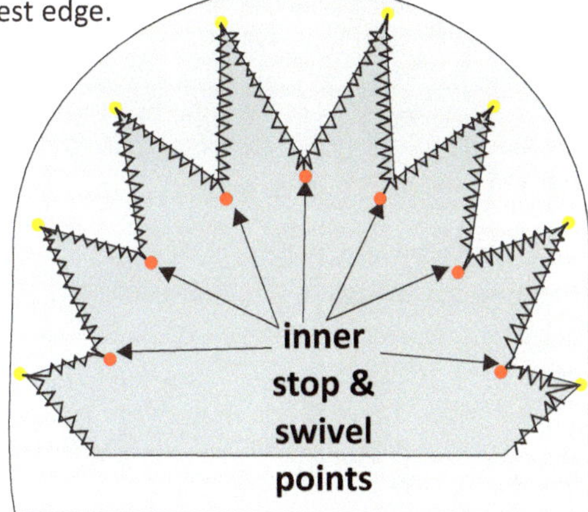

As you approach outer tips, reduce stitch width if needed. At the outer point, stop with the needle down *just* beyond the tip, where the yellow dots are. Swivel and start down the next side. After a couple of stitches you can increase the width to what it was before on each point. Take your time!

42 Place piece 1 on top of 1B and C, hiding triangles' base. Appliqué in place. Read tips on p. 5. Since the edges of 1 are turned under, I like a medium-open zigzag. No need to sew bottom edge.

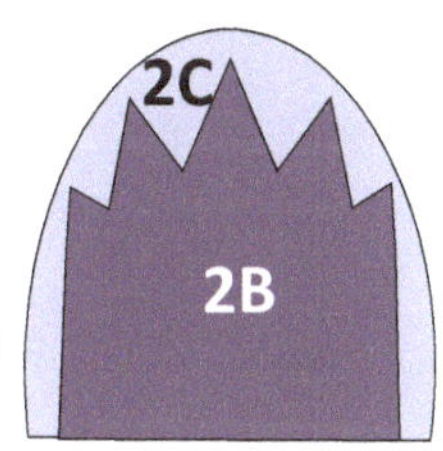

43 **Sandwich 2** Cut out pieces 2A, B, and C. Peel paper from A and B.

Place 2C (with paper) on a press sheet (for extra security). Center 2B on top. Lowest edges *should* match, but don't *have* to – what's important is that 2B's points are a bit below the top arch of 2C, allowing room for stitching.

Place piece 2A on top, to check that it covers the base of the triangles. This is practice, so now remove 2A again.

44 Fuse 2B to 2C. Remove paper behind 2C. Stitch 2B in place. Don't sew across the bottom edge.

45 Fuse 2A on top. We'll sew all the A pieces later, at the same time, to minimize thread-switching (unless you used invisible thread - in which case, you can do all this stitching now). Sandwich 2 is now half-sewn!

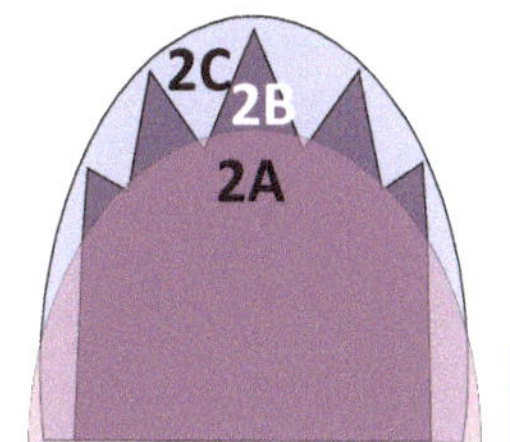

46 **Sandwiches 3, 4 & 5** Do them the same way: place each B on a C, then stitch around the B. Fuse A pieces on top.

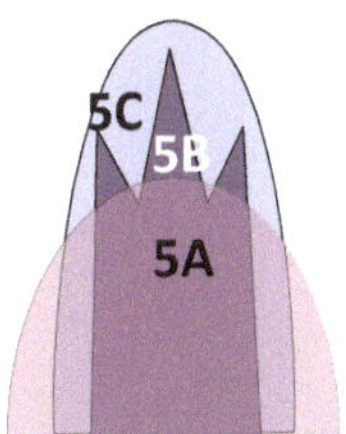

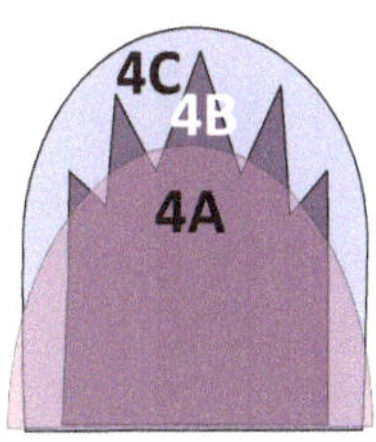

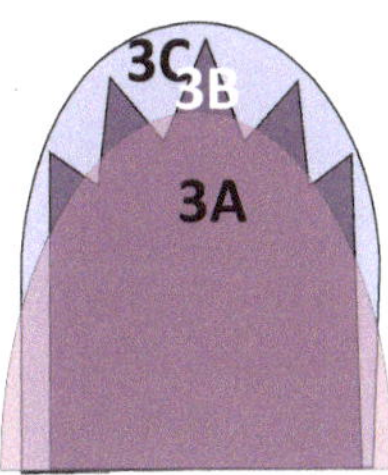

47 **Sandwich 6 including spire** Here, only pieces 6B and 6C's bottom edges match – not 6A's.

Cut out and peel paper from all three pieces. On a press sheet, press 6B to the bottom edge of 6C. This is so small that it's tricky - a wide piece of tear-away stabilizer (or light paper) on back can help you manipulate it. Zigzag up one side of 6B and down the other. Center and press 6A on top so it covers only 1/4"-1/2" of the spire's base.

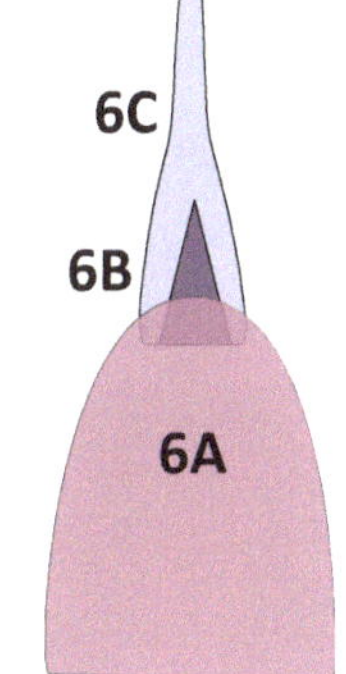

48 Arrange all the components on a press sheet. Again, the full-size diagram on p. 28 is helpful – you can print it out and lay it next to your arrangement. A ruler down the center of your pieces is also helpful in getting them straight.

49 Once pressed, I pin the assemblage on another piece of tear-away stabilizer, or lightweight clean newsprint or tracing paper, slightly bigger than the whole unit. (Don't iron when stabilizer is on back, or your fusible will stick to the stabilizer!)

50 If not using invisible thread, match "A" color first. Stitch along the tops of all the "A" arches. I start with straight stitches, then do a zigzag whose width increases from 1 to 3 at the peak. Stop just above the center, swivel, and sew back down to the other edge, shrinking the zigzag at the end.

51 Change thread to match the C color. Zigzag tops of all C arches. The trick is to avoid stitching into the B pieces! (But no one will notice tiny intrusions).

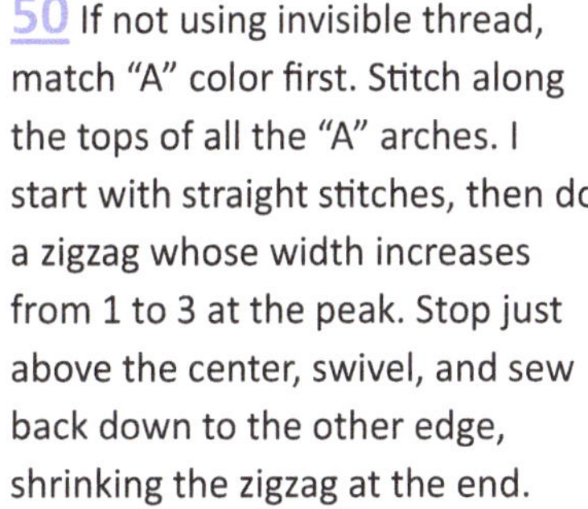

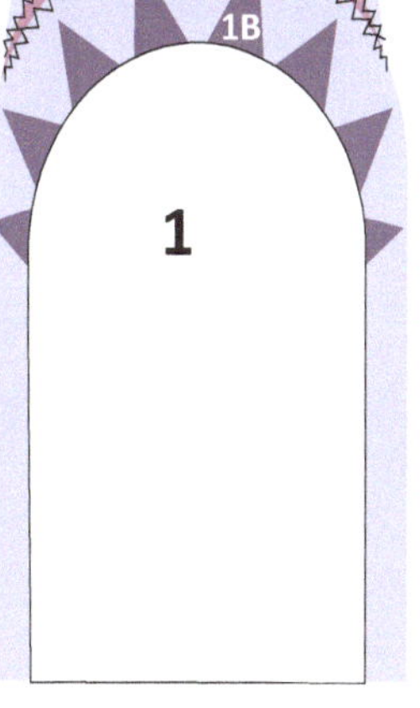

(continued)

It doesn't look good at this stage with so many thread ends and no stitching on the vertical sides. But I promise it will look much better when you appliqué it in place, covering all the remaining raw edges with a tight zigzag that matches fabric C!

52 Place top unit, good side down, centered along the top raw edge of piece B (yellow in the diagram), good side up. Piece B's side edges are pressed 1/4" to the back, but for this seam only, open them. Sew across the back of the top piece, backstitching at both ends (the red dotted line). Fold the side flaps of B closed again.

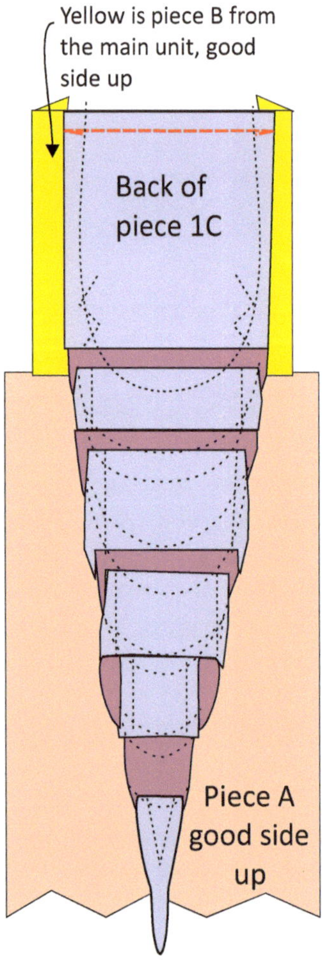

Real life example of what the back looks like! Black zigzags are bobbin thread from stitching B pieces. The white stuff is tear-away stabilizer residue! I don't worry about getting every molecule out.

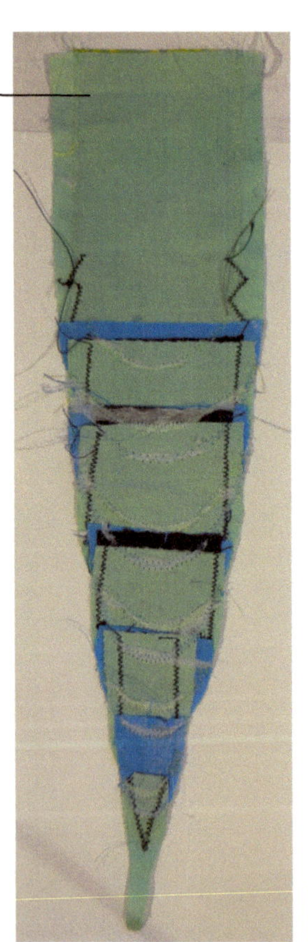

53 Pin or hand-baste the spire behind the building tip. When you're ready to appliqué the building in place, go around the turned edges of the main building with your choice of appliqué stitch (see p. 5). Fuse the top unit in place. Stitch around it using the same thread and stitch that you used inside the top arches. A fairly tight zigzag will cover the raw edges.

For 'Condensed' quilt: No need to press the bottom edge of the building up. See next steps on p. 71.

For 'Color Block' quilt:
Press bottom raw edge of building up 1/4". Audition backgrounds. It's burgundy in my Color Block quilt. Cut background to 10.25"x 39.5". You will place the building's bottom folded edge 3/4" above the bottom raw edge of the background. This information and next steps are in the quilt directions that start on p. 76.

Quilting ideas: I did a lot of straight-line stitching along the major lines of the plaid. On the spire, I outlined the triangle windows and arches, added straight lines between them, and stitched in the ditch around the arches. I followed the path shown here.

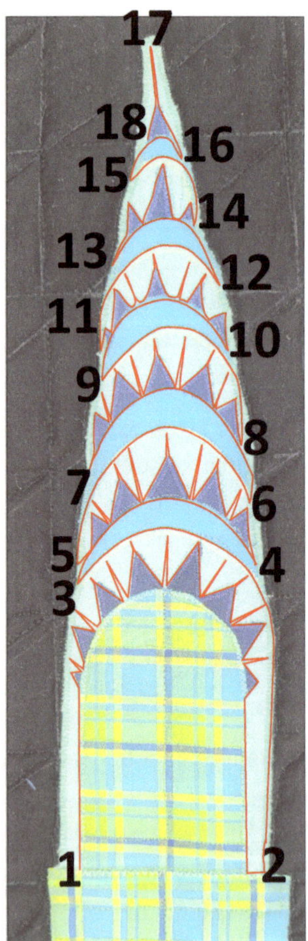

(continued)

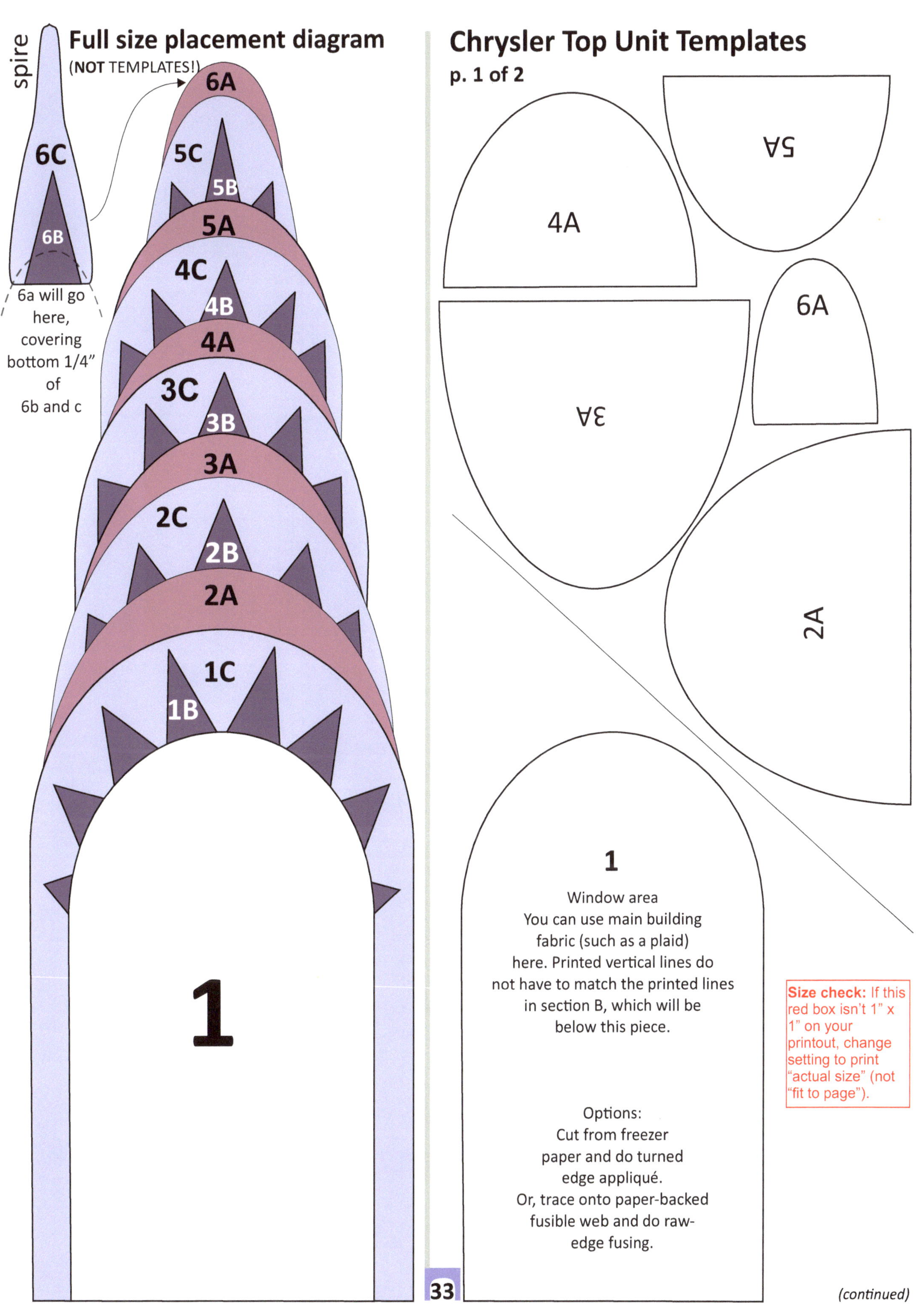
spire
Full size placement diagram
(NOT TEMPLATES!)
6C
6B
6a will go here, covering bottom 1/4" of 6b and c
6A
5C
5B
5A
4C
4B
4A
3C
3B
3A
2C
2B
2A
1C
1B
1
Chrysler Top Unit Templates
p. 1 of 2
4A
5A
6A
3A
2A
1
Window area
You can use main building fabric (such as a plaid) here. Printed vertical lines do not have to match the printed lines in section B, which will be below this piece.
Options:
Cut from freezer paper and do turned edge appliqué. Or, trace onto paper-backed fusible web and do raw-edge fusing.
Size check: If this red box isn't 1" x 1" on your printout, change setting to print "actual size" (not "fit to page").
33
(continued)

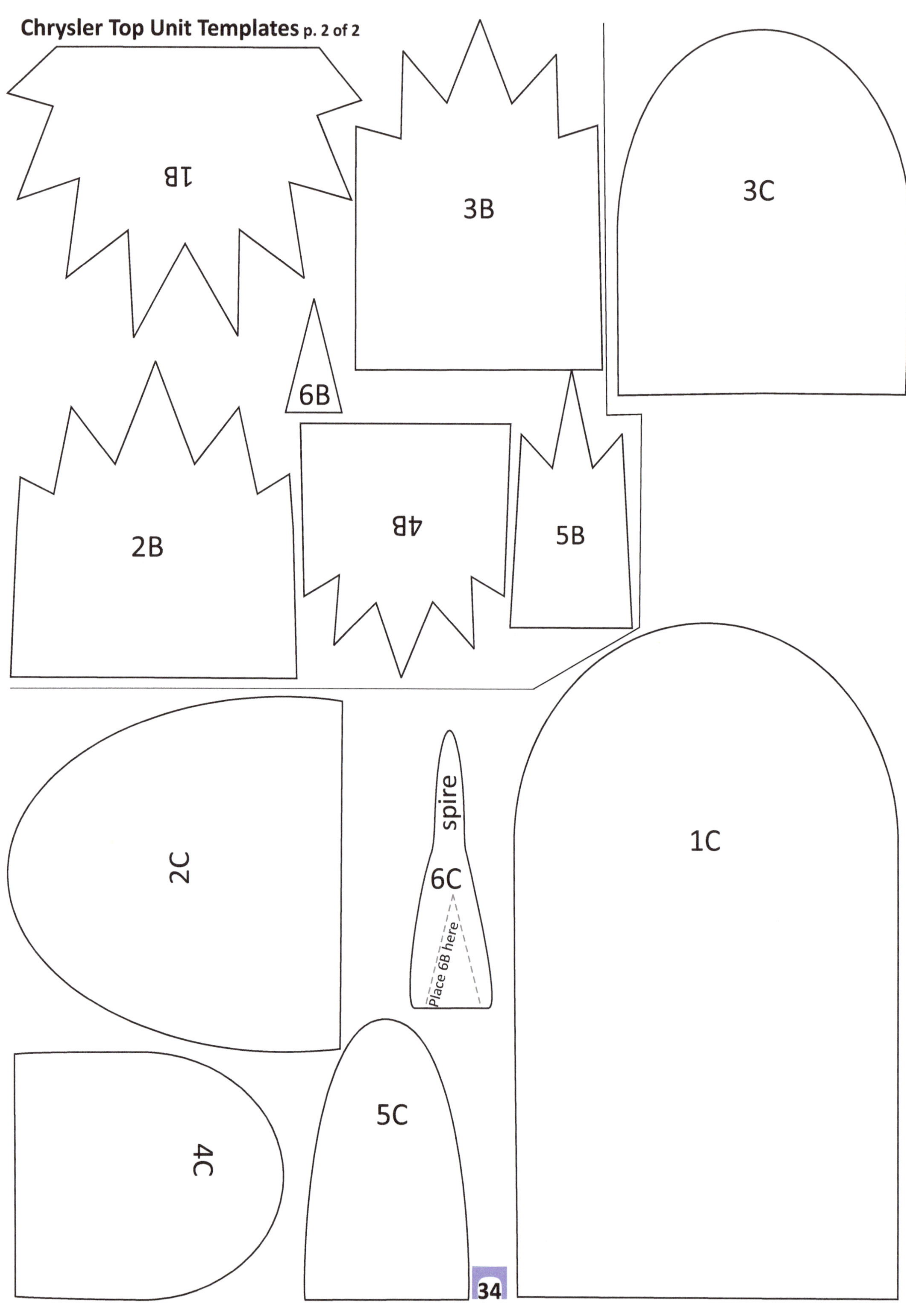

1B
2B
3B
4B
5B
6B
1C
2C
3C
4C
5C
6C
spire
Place 6B here

The Guggenheim Museum

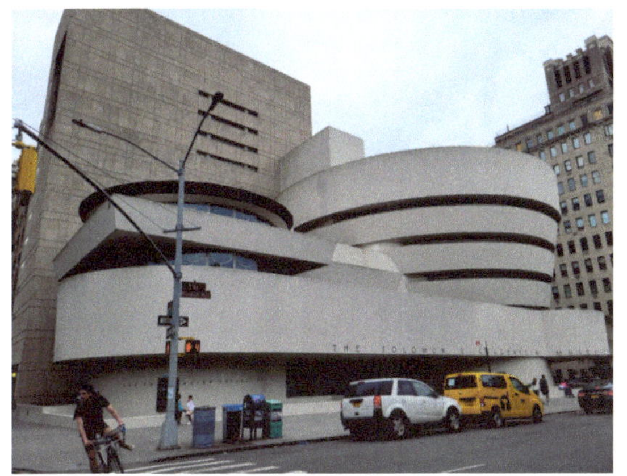

Not many buildings widen as they rise – but this one was designed by America's most famous architect, Frank Lloyd Wright, who, depending which history you read, was inspired by nautilus shells, step pyramids (upside-down), and/or more prosaically, parking garages. Opened in 1959, its round front contains the museum's iconic spiral gallery, which sends patrons climbing in circles for a quarter-mile. It reminds me of the Starship Enterprise – it looks like it flew to New York from an art-loving planet, and parked next to Central Park!

The museum has a less sci-fi annex behind it, built in the 90s. It's the beige box on the upper left of the photo. Dubbed the "Guggenheim Tower," its surface is textured with double-lines forming squares – so that's how I quilted my fantasy version on the left.

We'll use freezer paper (or cardstock), to shape the curved and angled pieces. Most pieces don't need a template – just cut regular rectangles to these sizes.

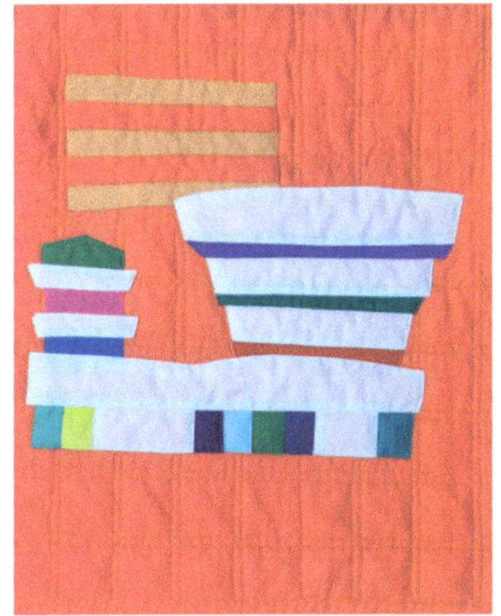

White-and-colors version, above, green version below.

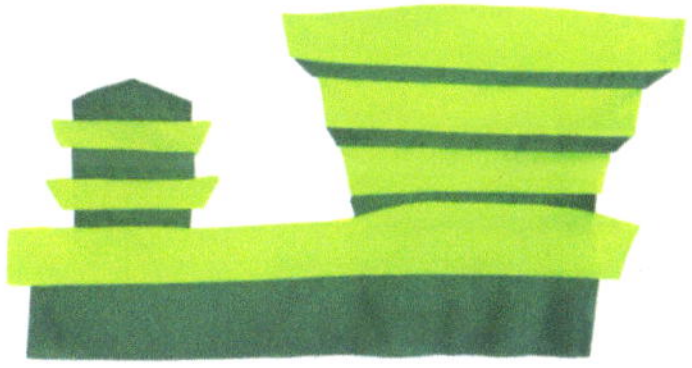

Below, batik version with unique ground-floor curves, by Michele Pusateri

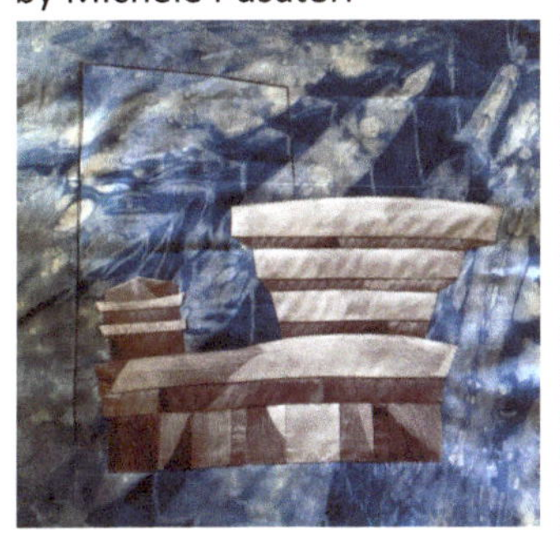

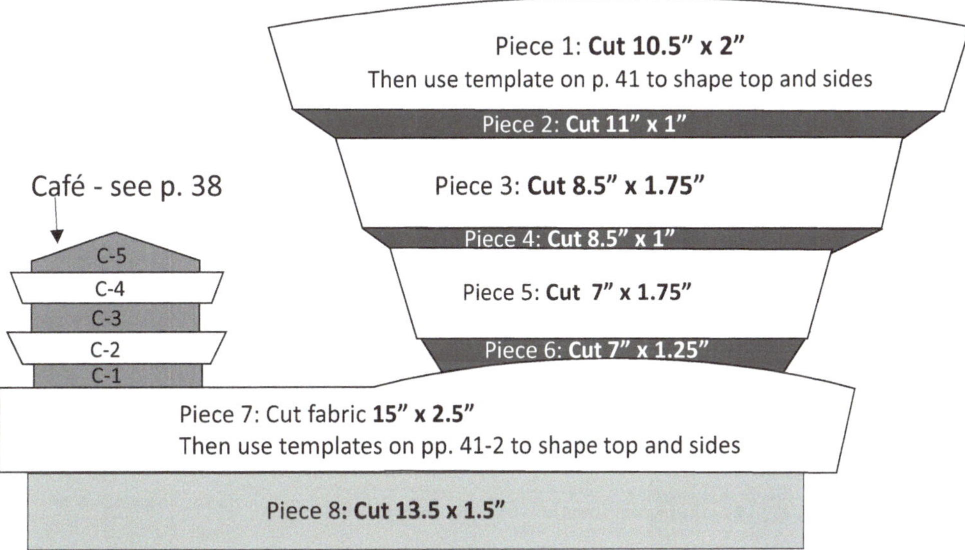

Inspired by the Guggenheim Museum

Finished building: Approx: 15" x 9" for the main building, plus background (in sizes below).

Fabric

Main fabric, the lightest. A quarter-yard or fat-quarter.

Shadow fabric. A quarter-yard or a fat quarter. Assorted scraps for p. 38 rainbow version.

Background for 'Color Block' quilt: 16.25" x 22" plus two 7.5" x 1.5" strips for the back window. Fat-quarter is just enough. Background for 'Condensed' quilt: Cut 18.25" x 15.25", plus same size window strips as in 'Color Block.'

Background window contrasting color. Three strips, each cut to 7.5" x 1.5".

Other supplies

► Freezer paper or cardstock to shape the curved pieces.
► Glue stick (temporary/school glue).
► Spray starch or other pressing fluid is helpful.

(continued)

The Big Spiral

The cone/nautilus on the upper right of the building contains pieces 1-6. Here's how I put them together.

1 Cut out fabrics for pieces 1- 8, to rectangles in the sizes in the diagram on bottom of the previous page, p. 35. No template is needed to cut them.

2 Fold each in half the long way, matching opposite corners. Press a light crease down the center of each (blue dotted line).

3 Use one of the following methods to print or trace pp. 41-42 (or, at a minimum, pieces 1, 7 and all of p. 42) onto:
► Freezer paper 8 1/2" x 11" sheets. Print or write on the non-waxy side (first choice) or
► Printer cardstock, (second choice) or
► Regular copy paper, if that's all you have.
Do the size check and adjust print settings if needed.

4 Cut piece 1 from the printout or tracing. **If it's on regular paper**: trace around the cutout onto the paper side of freezer paper or cardstock and cut that out.

regular paper Piece 1. Cut 10.5" x 2"
Freezer paper or cardstock

5 Place the pattern on the middle back of the piece 1 fabric rectangle. There should be at least 1/4" of fabric on all sides, and maybe a bit more on top. If freezer paper: iron it in place. If cardstock: hold securely in place.

6 Press top edge down over the pattern piece. Option: spray a little starch into a plastic lid and use a craft brush to paint that top edge. Wait a few seconds for the starch to spread. Press well.

7 Press side edges in, around the paper. Do NOT press the bottom edge up.

8 Remove paper. Fold back and press the top corners again, this time with a dab of glue, to keep them from being seen from the front.

9 Prepare pieces 3 and 5. These don't need paper templates, but they do need their sides angled. Mark or estimate 1/4" in from the top corners, 1/2" in from base corners. Fold to the back connecting the marks, and pressing (along red dotted lines).

10 Flip piece 1, good side down, onto piece 2, good side up, matching centers. Pin. The back of piece 1 is on top so you can see the side flaps.

11 Rotate pinned seam to the right. Have an awl (or something similar) handy. Pull up threads about 1/4" below the fold, at the dot by the **a**. Backstitch to the **b** dot (just before the fold). Sew to the **c** dot. (The awl will help you tuck that flap under the presser foot.) Backstitch about 1/4" to **d**. Cut thread.

The backstitching secures the flaps, and hides the thread tails at **a** and **d**, by bringing them further away from the edges.

If you accidentally stitched a bit onto piece 2 at either end, don't worry about it, you probably won't have to take it out!

12 Place piece 3, good side down, on the lower raw edge of piece 2, good side up, matching centers. Piece 3's widest edge is now along the bottom.

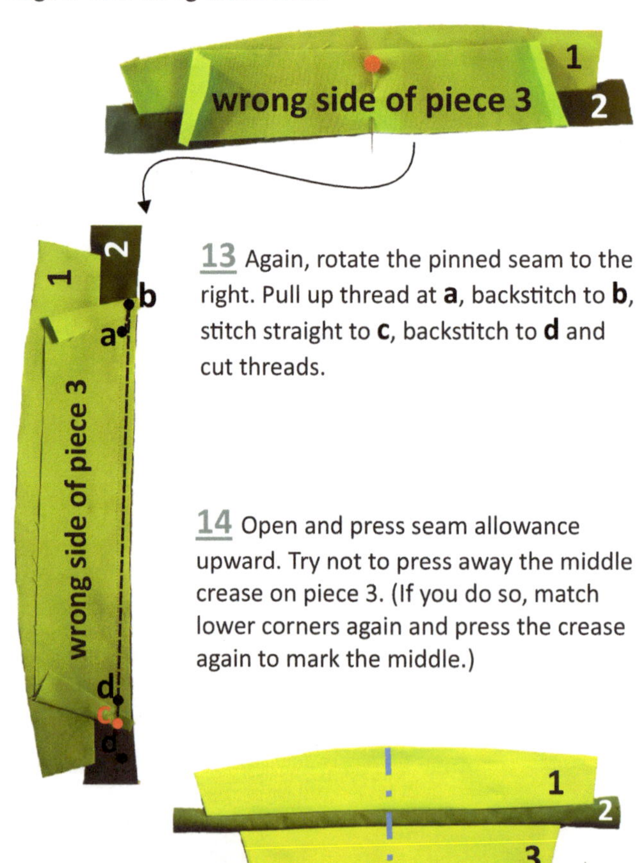

13 Again, rotate the pinned seam to the right. Pull up thread at **a**, backstitch to **b**, stitch straight to **c**, backstitch to **d** and cut threads.

14 Open and press seam allowance upward. Try not to press away the middle crease on piece 3. (If you do so, match lower corners again and press the crease again to mark the middle.)

(continued)

15 Place piece 4 face up on the table. Flip the 123 unit, good side down, onto it. Match center creases, and match the bottom of 3 with the bottom of 4. Pin.

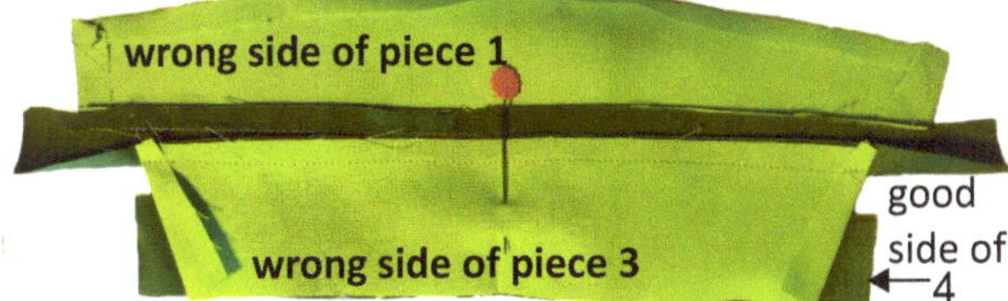

16 Sew before, rotating the pinned seams to the right, and backstitching at the beginning and end.

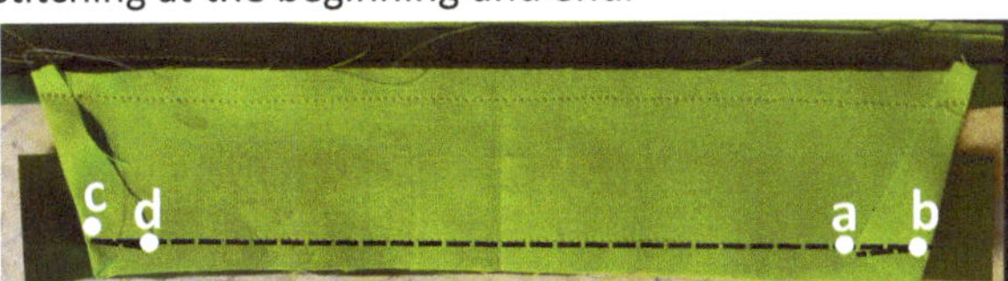

17 Press new seam allowance up.

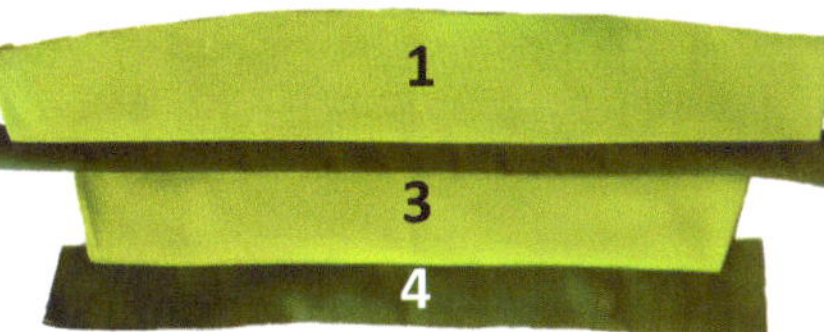

18 Place 5, good side down, to the bottom of 4, good side up, matching centers. Sew as before. Press seam allowance up.

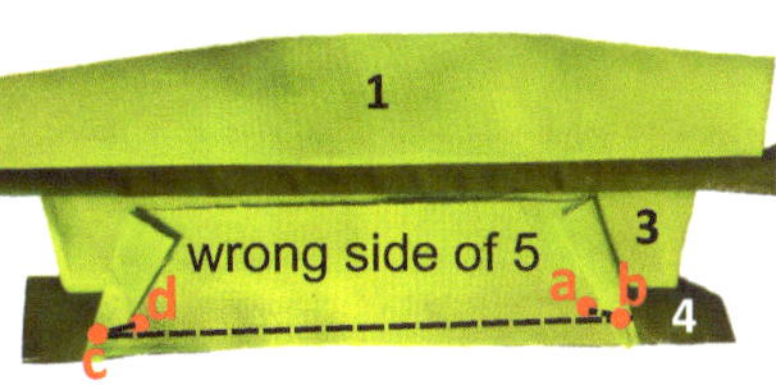

19 Place piece 6, face up, on table. Flip unit 1-5, good side down, along the bottom of 6. Center, pin and sew, backstitching at both ends. Press seam allowance up.

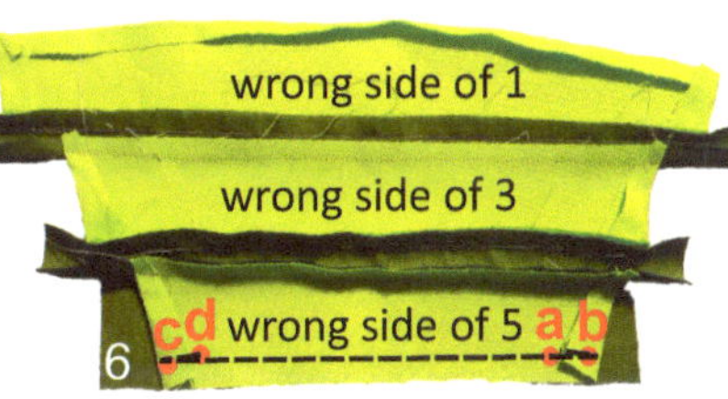

20 You now have a weird unit with light pieces' edges all neatly folded in, and dark pieces' raw edges sticking out.

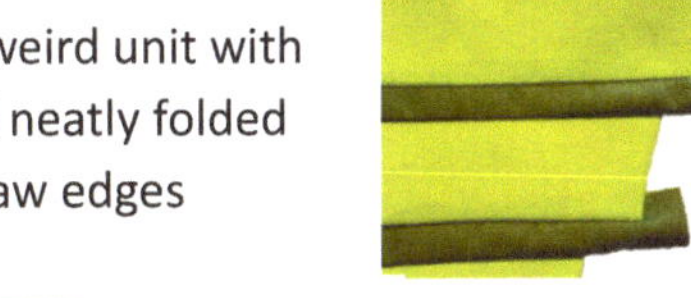

21 Fold and press each dark strips' ends backwards and up at an angle.

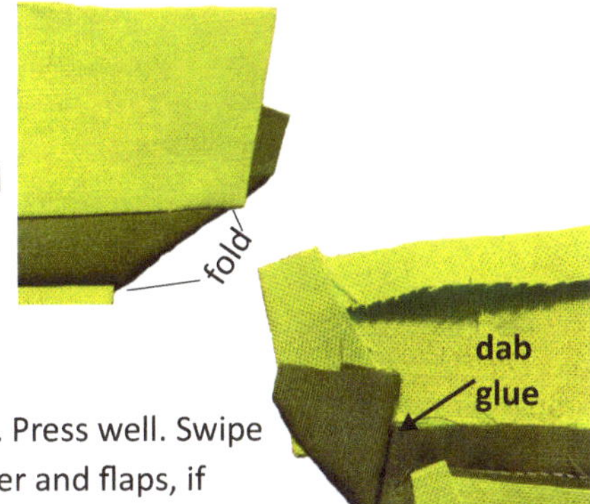

22 Flip to the back. Press well. Swipe glue under the corner and flaps, if needed.

23 Check the front. It's likely that a corner of the dark pieces is still poking out.

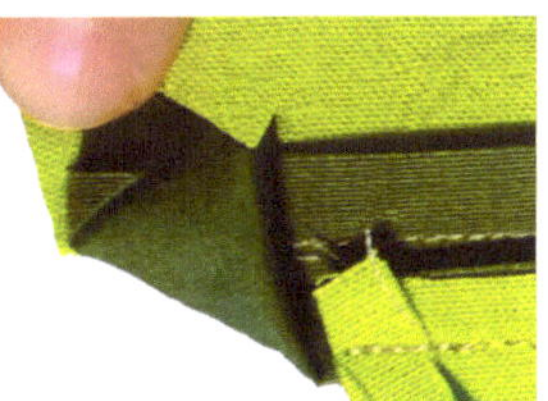

24 Dab glue behind it and fold to the back – on top of the previous fold – so you can no longer see it from the front.

The Lower Body

25 Create the ironing template for piece 7 from the pattern on p. 41 and its extension on p. 42:

► *If you traced or printed templates on freezer paper*: cut out piece 7 and cut the 1.25" x 4" extension from another piece of freezer paper. Iron pieces together with 1/4" overlap. It should look like the diagram below. Skip down to step 27.

► *If you printed onto cardstock* or *copy paper*: do the same as with freezer paper above, but use a glue stick to attach the extension.

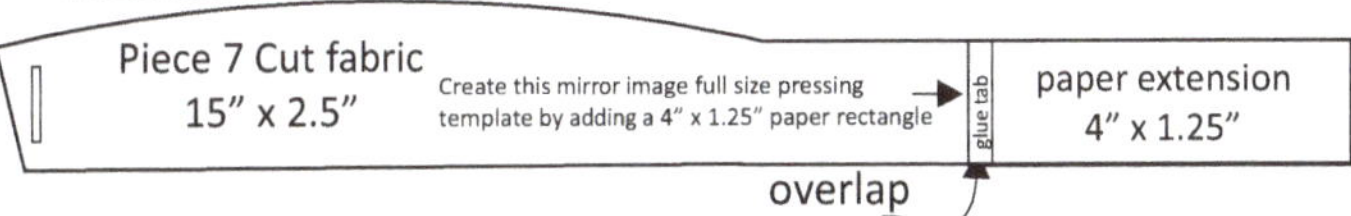

26 For copy paper only: trace the pattern piece onto freezer paper **or** a long piece of cardstock. Cut it out.

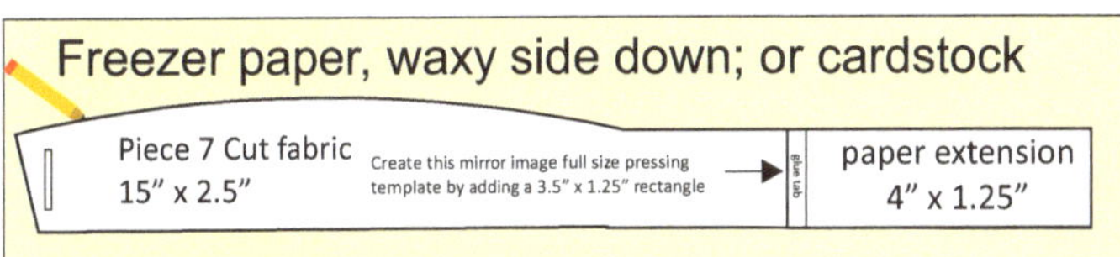

27 Center the paper pattern on the piece 7 fabric strip, and if it's freezer paper, press in position.

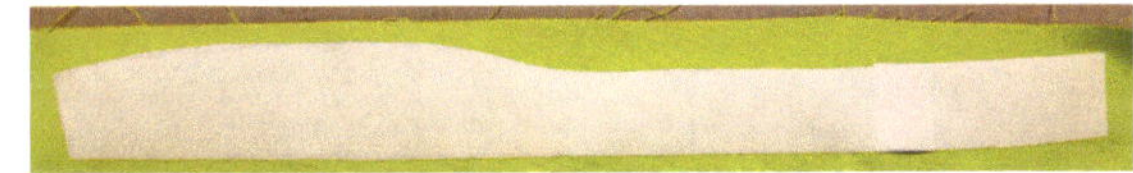

28 Cut the fabric back to 1/4" larger than the paper pattern. With cardstock, make it a generous 1/4" on top. Clip ⅛" into the seam allowance at the concave area.

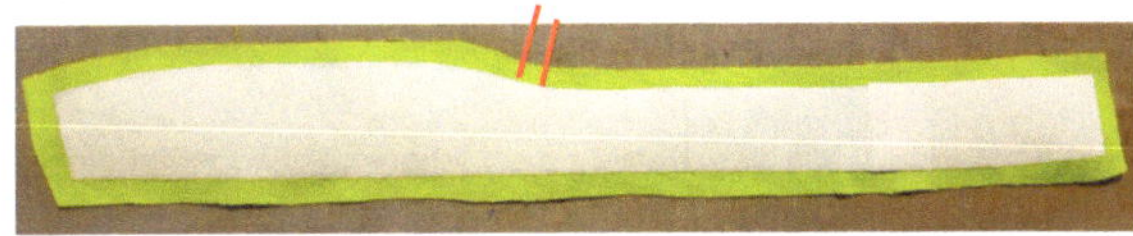

29 Iron the top edge of piece 7 down and over the curve. Fold in the two sides to match the angle of the paper template. Don't fold up the bottom edge.

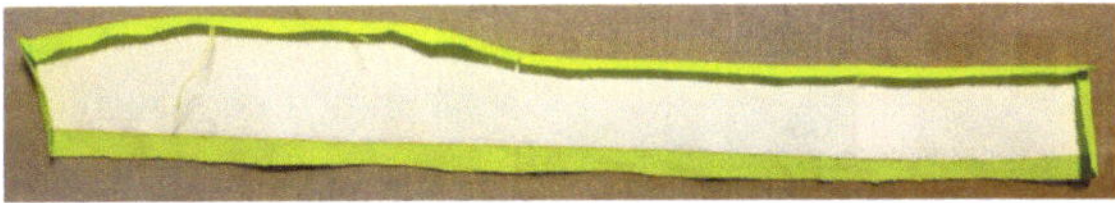

30 Cut piece 8 from dark fabric, 13.5" x 2". It doesn't have any curves, so you don't need an ironing template. But you do have to press and fold its two side edges inward, straight up and down, 1/4" to the back. (If you want a rainbow base, see box on next page.)

(continued)

<u>31</u> Place piece 8, good side down, along the bottom edge of piece 7 (whose good side is up). Pin. Rotate seam to the right and stitch as before, backstitching at both ends.

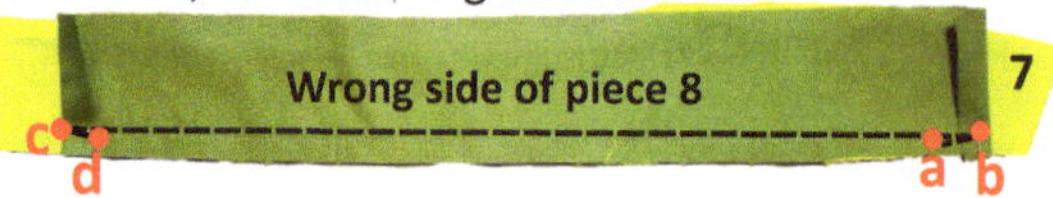

<u>32</u> Press open, and press seam allowance up, to the wider level.

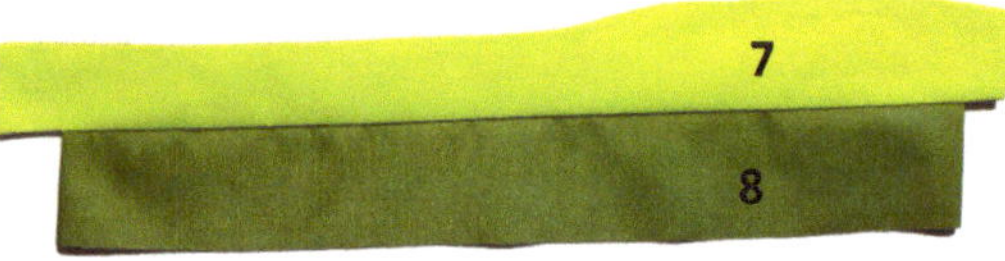

<u>33</u> Place the 7 + 8 unit over the bottom of the spiral piece, covering most of piece 6 and checking that at least ¼" of piece 6's bottom edge is covered.

If you can do this on a grid, like a cutting mat, it will help you align the sections straight across. Pin or stitch-baste in position.

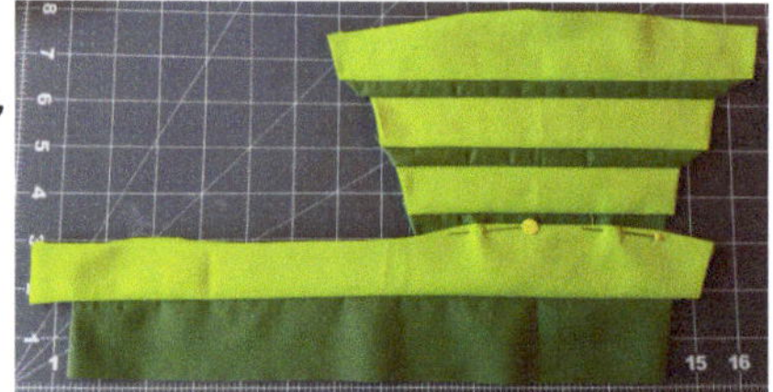

<u>34</u> Sew 7 to 6 with hand or machine appliqué. Machine stitch options include straight, zigzag, blanket, or blind hem. See pp. 5-6 for more information.

The photo below shows my finished line of blanket stitch appliqué, using matching thread.

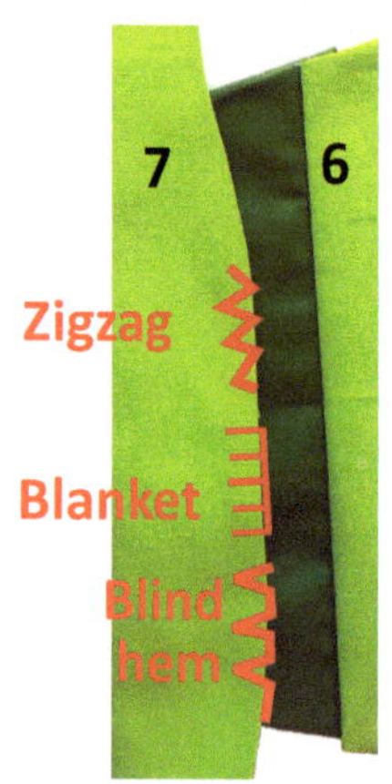

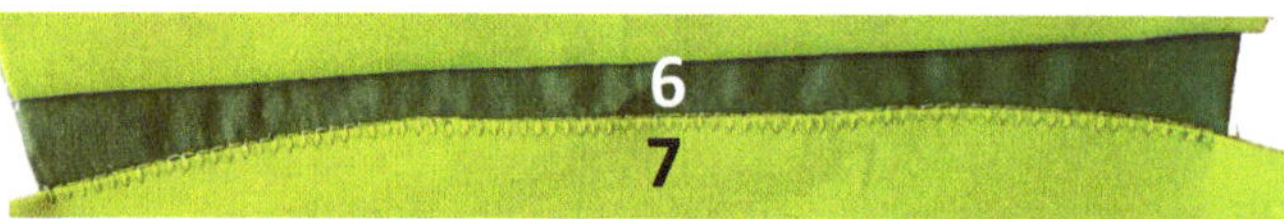

With any machine stitch, start and end with a few straight back stitches or zigzags in place.

Rainbow Base

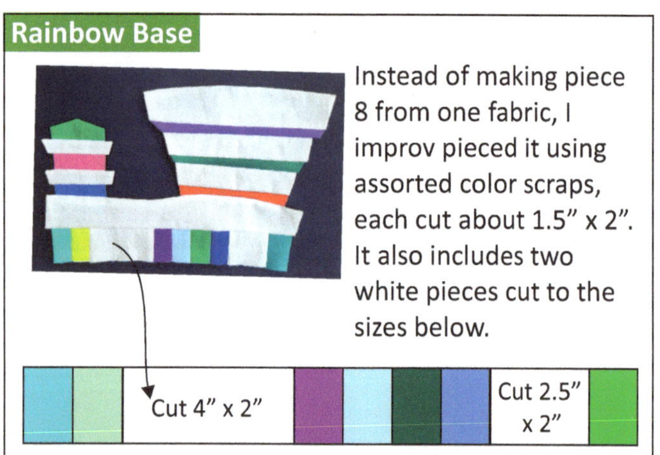

Instead of making piece 8 from one fabric, I improv pieced it using assorted color scraps, each cut about 1.5" x 2". It also includes two white pieces cut to the sizes below.

The Other End – Have a Snack!

Every museum visit should include a trip to the café! The full size templates are on p. 42.

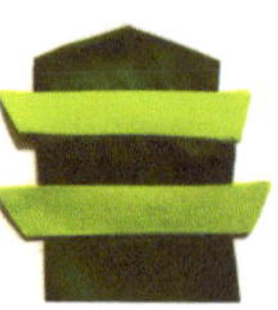

Tail cutting diagram (not full size)

Piece C-5 (Dark)
cut fabric 1.5" x 3.25"
or read steps 37-9 below

Piece C-4 (light)
cut fabric 1.25" x 4.5

Piece C-3 (dark)
cut 1.25" x 3.25"
or read steps 35 - 7 below

Piece C-2 (light)
cut fabric 1.25" x 4.5"

Piece C-1 (dark)
cut fabric 1.25" x 3.25"
or read steps 35 - 7 below

<u>35</u> To speed-cut the dark pieces above: Cut a 3.25" x 4" rectangle from fabric. Press its side edges in to the back, 1/4".

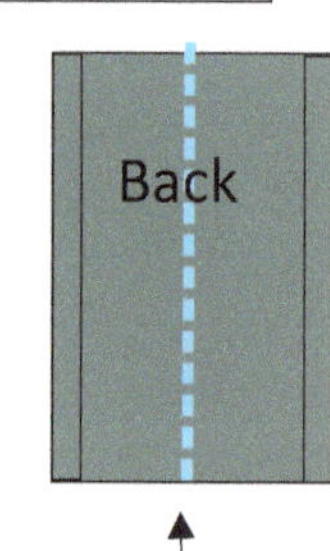

<u>36</u> Bring side folds together to lightly press a vertical crease down the center (blue line.)

<u>37</u> Make two cuts 1.25" apart. The top two will become pieces C-1 and C-3. The remaining piece is 1.5" high. It will be piece C-5.

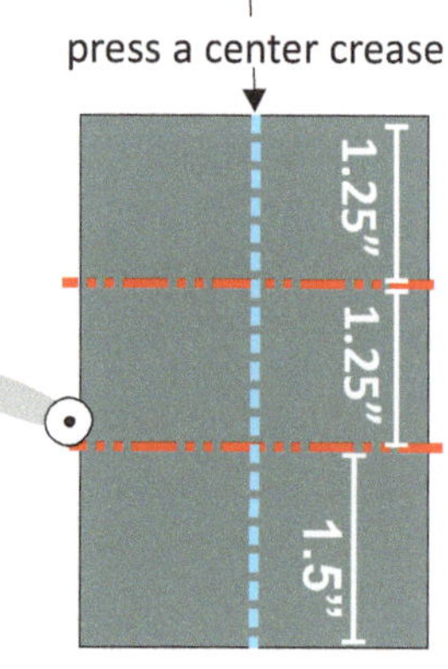

<u>38</u> Cut pieces 2 and 4 from light-colored fabric, both to rectangles 1.25" x 4.5".

<u>39</u> If you haven't already, trace or print out p. 42, for the full size tail templates.

► If you printed on freezer paper or cardstock: Cut out pieces 2, 4, and 5. Go to step 40.

(continued)

► If you printed or traced on copy paper: Cut out piece 5, and either 2 or 4 (they're identical). Trace 5 once and 2 or 4 twice, on the paper side of freezer paper or on cardstock. Cut out the three pieces.

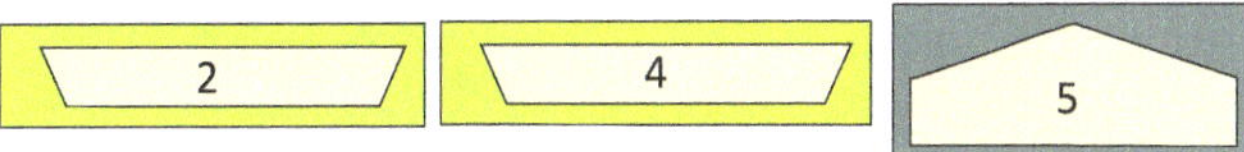

40 Center pieces 2, 4, and 5 on their fabric rectangle. If freezer paper, press in position. If cardstock, place in position on top of fabric.

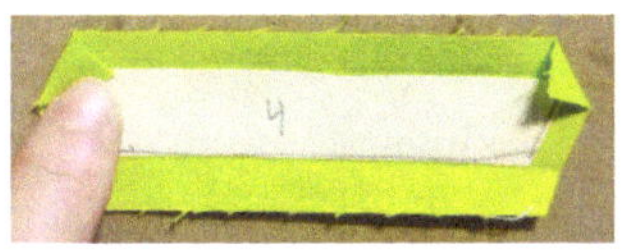

41 On pieces 2 and 4, trim the fabric's sides about 1/4" from the sides of the freezer paper or cardstock templates, at an angle.

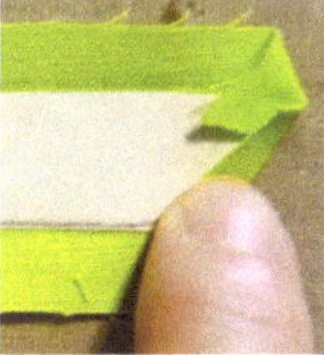

42 For pieces 2 and 4, bring each upper corner in and down as far as possible, without folding the paper underneath.

You should feel those paper or cardstock corners behind the fabric triangles you fold inward. Press.

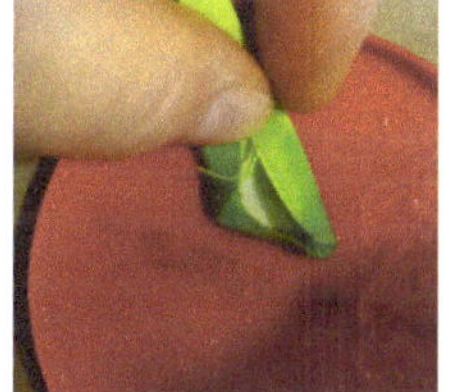

43 Fold and press each side inward, tight against the paper's side edges. A bit of glue helps, or...

44 ...Or, spray pressing fluid into the back of a flat lid. Dip a corner into the shallow puddle. Give it a few seconds to spread. Then press everything folded in place again.

45 Press top and bottom seam inward, but you don't need to starch or glue these.

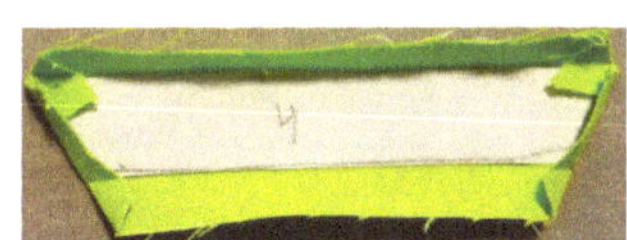

46 Remove freezer paper or cardstock template. Bring two short sides together and lightly press in half, matching side folds, to establish the center. Press a light crease.

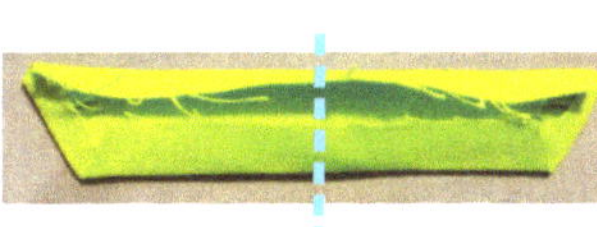

47 Center piece 5 template between the side folds of the fabric. There should be 1/4" of fabric below the template.

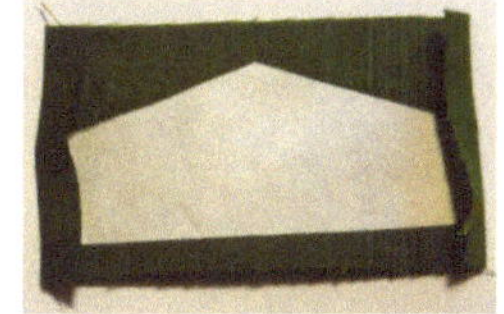

48 Cut the top edge of the fabric 1/4" above the slanted top edge of the paper template.

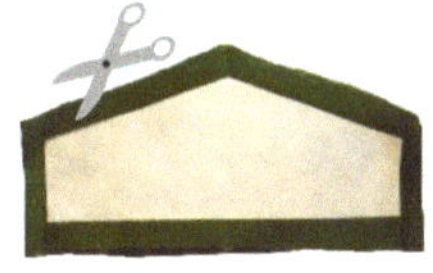

49 Press top edges down and re-press side edges in. Use pressing fluid or a little glue to hold them (try to not glue the template).

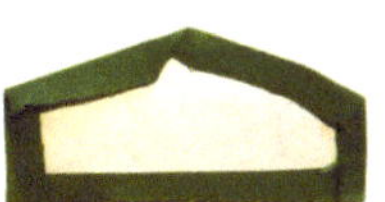

50 Remove template. Check that vertical crease still shows.

51 Sew it all together! We'll mostly sew from the back of the dark/narrower pieces, so we can see and stitch their side flaps inward. With each new piece match center creases.

52 Place piece #1 face down, onto the bottom edge of piece 2 facing up. Wider edge of piece 2 is along the top. Match and pin center creases. Rotate seam to the right, with a/b on top.

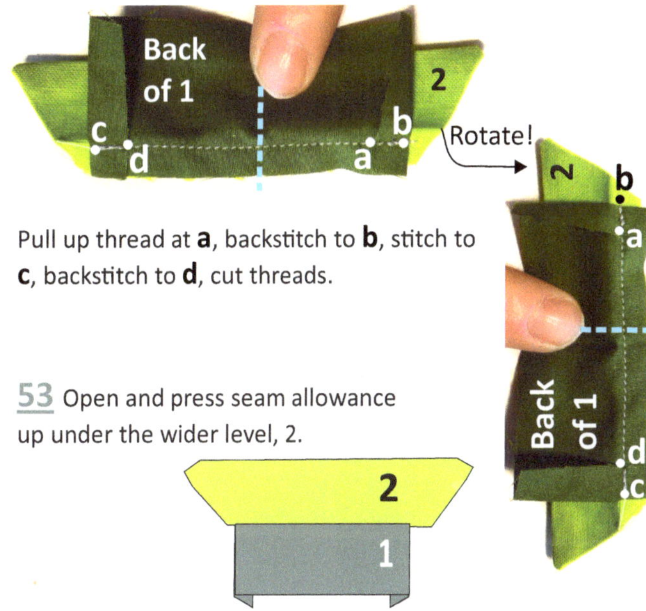

Pull up thread at **a**, backstitch to **b**, stitch to **c**, backstitch to **d**, cut threads.

53 Open and press seam allowance up under the wider level, 2.

54 Flip piece 3, good side down, on top of unit 1 and 2, good side up. Match center creases. The top raw edge of piece 2 should stick up, as in the photo. We're matching that raw edge with what will become the bottom edge of piece 3. Rotate right, and sew as before, sealing top and bottom folds with backstitches.

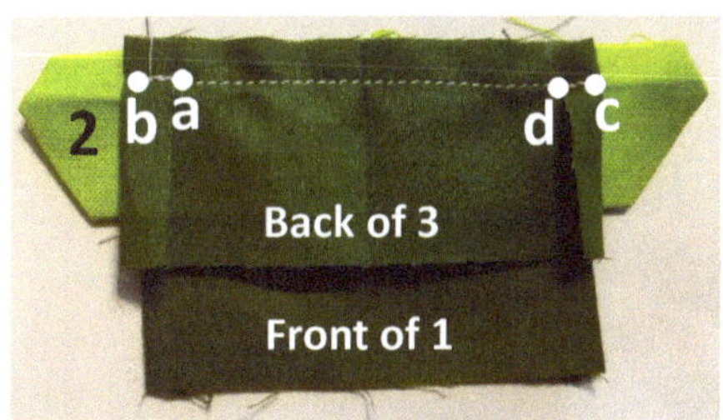

55 Opened, it looks like this. Press new seam allowance down under the wider piece 2.

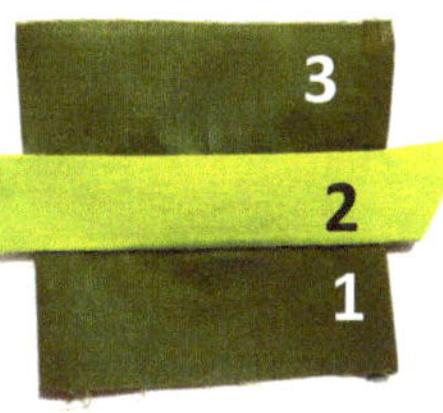

(continued)

56 Place unit 4 on table, good side up, shorter edge along the top. Flip the 123 unit, face down, on top of 4. Match centers and top edges. Pin.

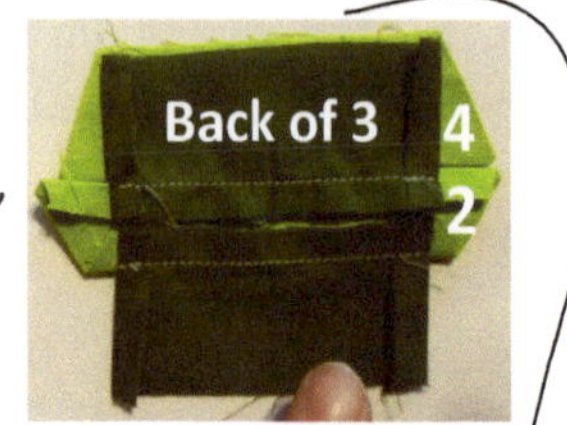

57 Rotate pinned edge to the right. Sew as before, backstitching at both ends.

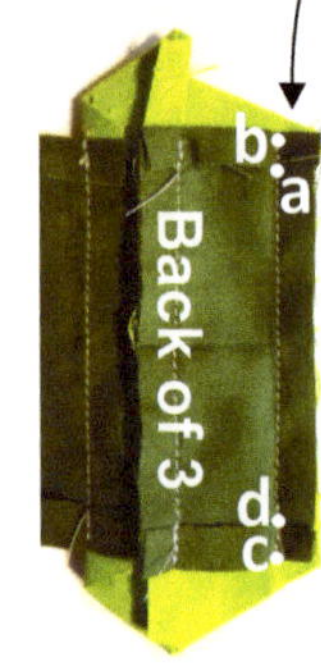

58 Flip piece 4 open, and press the seam allowances upward, under the bottom of piece 4.

59 Place the lower raw edge of piece 5, good side down, on top of unit 1234. Match centers and top raw edges. Sew as before, backstitching at both ends. Press seam allowance down under the wider level, behind piece 4.

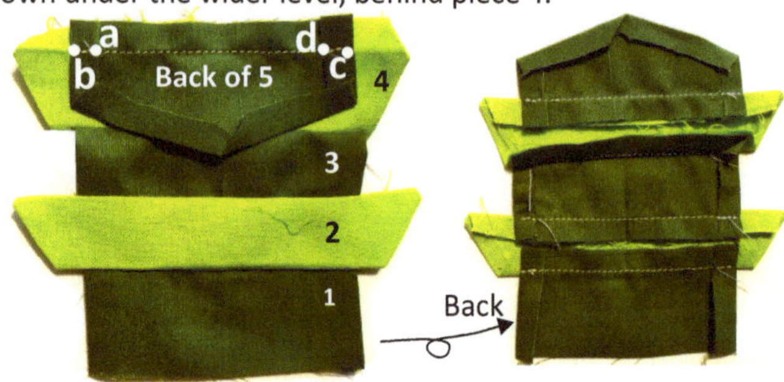

60 Tuck the unit's bottom raw edge 3/8"- 1/2" under the upper left end of the museum's body. Appliqué it to the main building as you did with the right section.

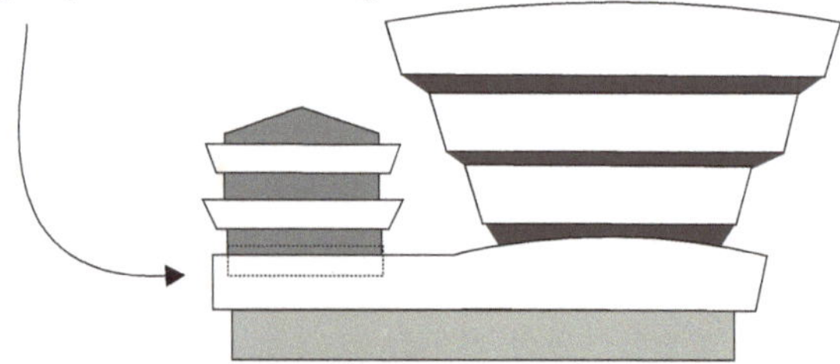

Create the Background

61 Audition backgrounds. I chose orange for my white building and plaid for my green one. *For 'Condensed' quilt: cut background to 18.25" x 15. 25". For Color Block quilt: cut background to 16.25" x 22".*

62 Windows: cut 5 strips, two from the background color, and three lighter. All are cut 8" x 1.25".

63 Stitch together in the order shown. The top and bottom strips should not be the background color.

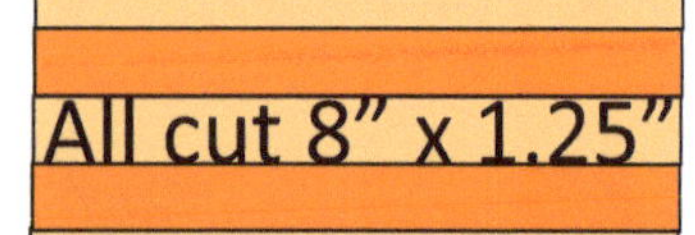

64 Press all four raw edges of the window to the back 1/4".

65 Place it on the background and figure out where you want it in relation to the main building. The photo above right shows how I overlapped pieces for the 'Color Block' quilt. But for my 'Condensed' quilt, below right, I used a busy plaid background, and decided it didn't even need a window!

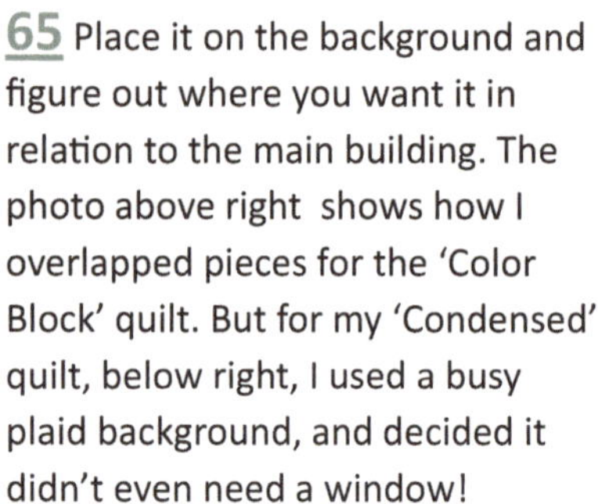
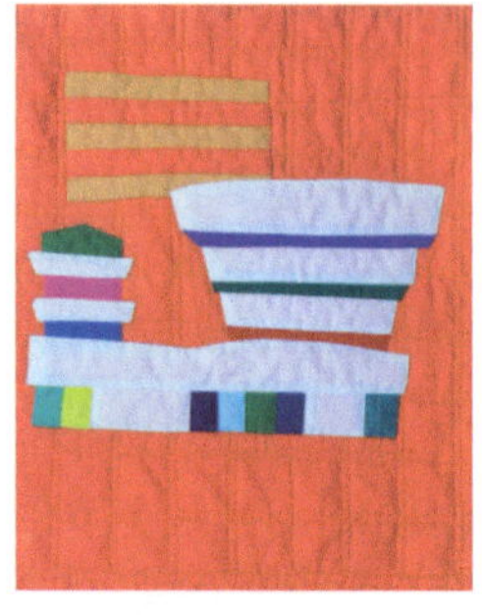
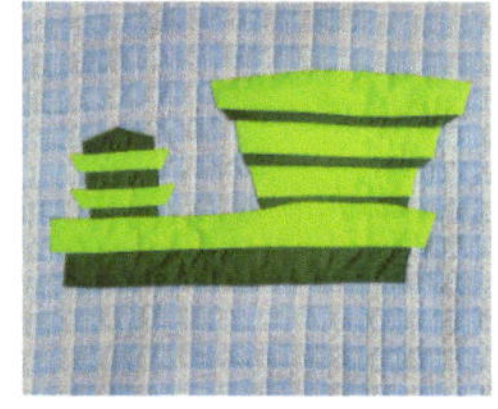

66 Appliqué the window to the background first. I used invisible thread and a zigzag stitch. (Appliqué tips are on pp. 5-6.)

67 Appliqué the main building in place.

For 'Condensed' (p. 71), or 'Color Block' (p. 76): The main building is already appliquéd to a rectangular background, so all you have to do is sew it in place when the quilt directions indicate!

Quilting Ideas: I did my ditch-stitching (the white dotted lines in the diagram below), just inside the edges of all the dark-color (shadow) areas, to push them back, popping the lighter areas forward.

For my 'Color Box' quilt's orange background, I quilted double lines that cross at 90 degree angles, forming squares. I marked 2" intervals in both directions, and drew lines 1/4" apart.

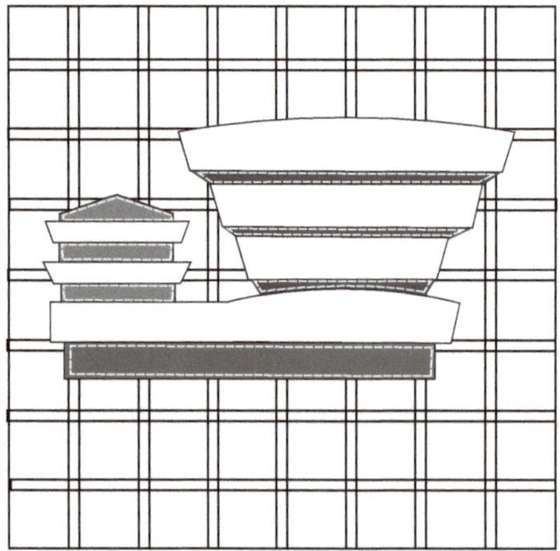

For the background on the 'Condensed' quilt, I simply quilted along major lines of the plaid, which alternates 3/4" with 1" lines.

(continued)

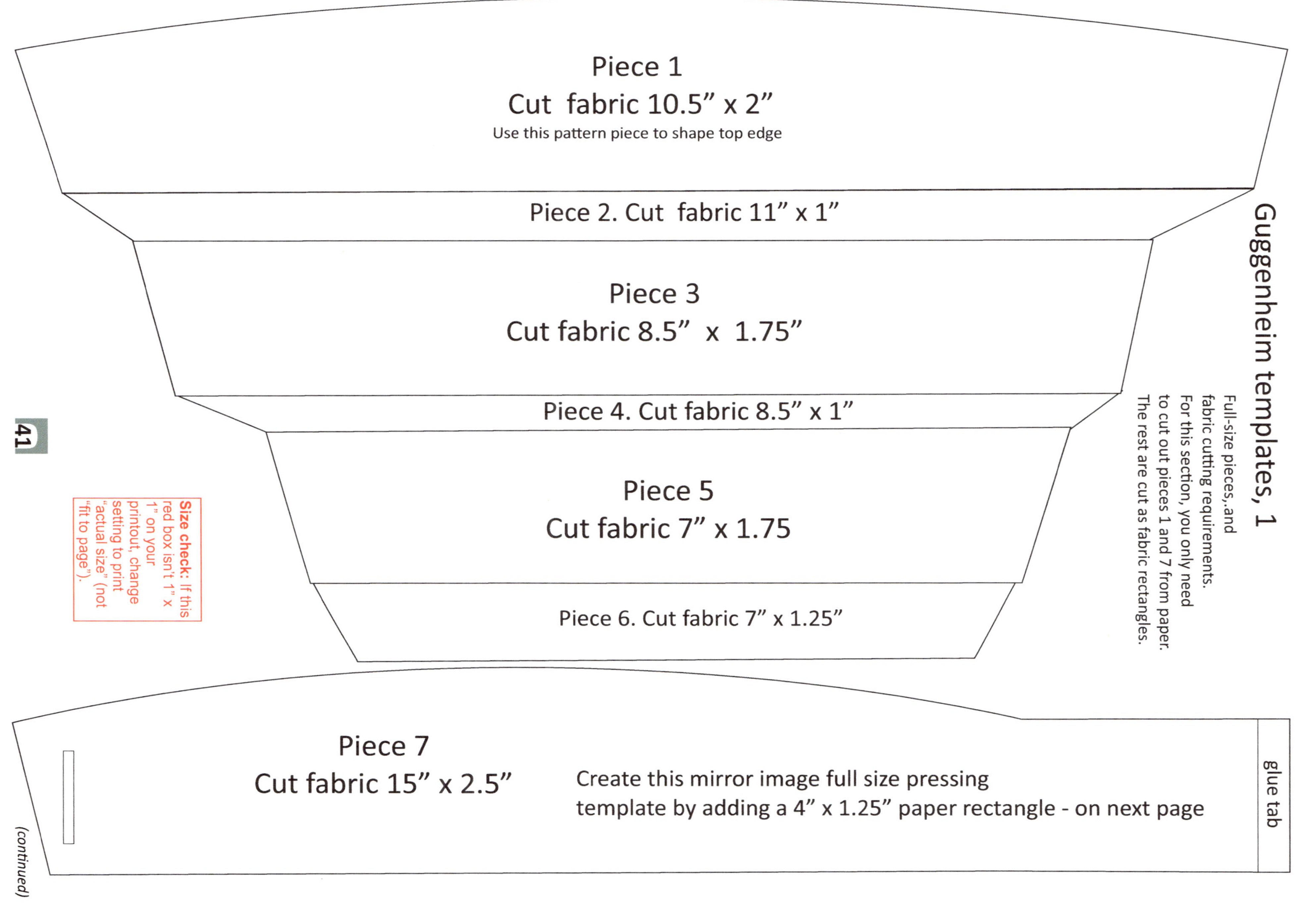

Piece 1
Cut fabric 10.5" x 2"
Use this pattern piece to shape top edge

Piece 2. Cut fabric 11" x 1"

Piece 3
Cut fabric 8.5" x 1.75"

Piece 4. Cut fabric 8.5" x 1"

Piece 5
Cut fabric 7" x 1.75

Piece 6. Cut fabric 7" x 1.25"

Piece 7
Cut fabric 15" x 2.5"

Create this mirror image full size pressing
template by adding a 4" x 1.25" paper rectangle - on next page

Guggenheim templates, 1
Full-size pieces,.and
fabric cutting requirements.
For this section, you only need
to cut out pieces 1 and 7 from paper.
The rest are cut as fabric rectangles.

glue tab

Size check: If this red box isn't 1" x 1" on your printout, change setting to print "actual size" (not "fit to page").

41

(continued)

Guggenheim templates, 2

Tail full size templates:

Piece 5 (Dark)
Cut fabric 1.5" x 3.25"

Piece 4 (light)
Cut fabric 1.25" x 4.5

Piece 3 (dark)
Cut 1.25" x 3.25"

Piece 2 (light)
Cut fabric 1.25" x 4.5"

Piece 1 (dark)
Cut fabric 1.25" x 3.25"

glue tab

You don't need to cut out this paper pattern for a rectangle, but if you do want a full size mirror image template for any reason, add a 4" x 1" piece to its far right end. Template for that piece is here:

Piece 8 Cut fabric 13.5" x 1.5

Main body
Piece 8 extension
4" x 1"

overlap glue tab

Main body -
Piece 7 extension
4.25" x 1.25"

overlap glue tab

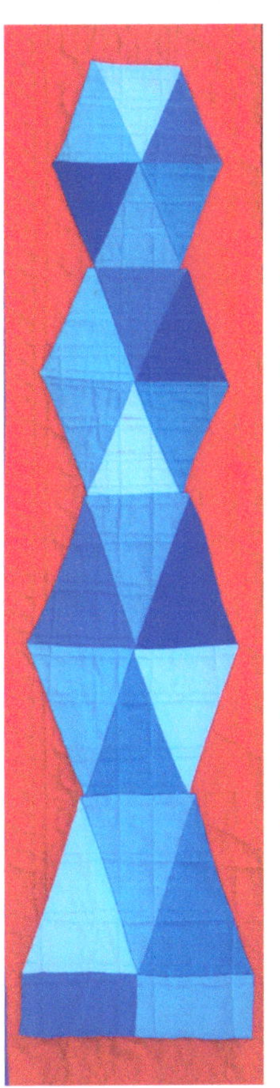

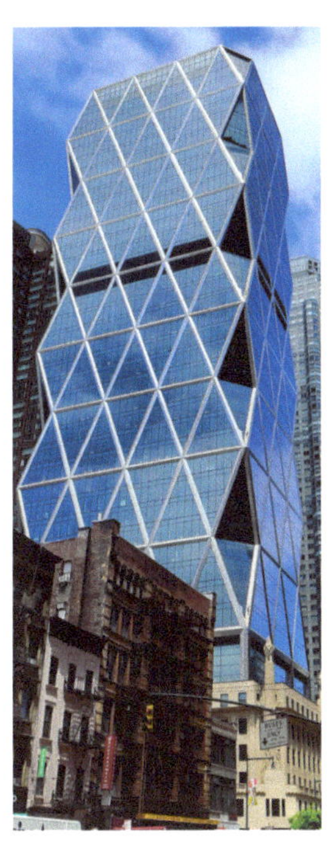

The Hearst Tower

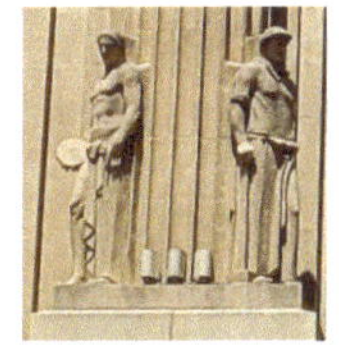

On the ground floor – and for six stories up – it's a lovely 1920s sandstone office building, designed by architect Joseph Urban for William Randolph Hearst. Scantily-clad classical figures gaze benevolently from the second floor. (Hearst was a statuary fan, as anyone who's visited his California castle or seen the movie 'Citizen Caine', knows.)

But throw your head WAY back, and – whoa! There's a tower of glass and steel isosceles triangles! When you step into the front door, four seconds before the guard throws you out, you see that the old building is just a shell, hiding a stupendous modern lobby! It's well worth exploring at its website (https://www.hearst.com/real-estate/hearst-tower).

The sight of this unique triangle stack makes me so happy and has inspired so many different ideas. This one is the most fun, and you can do it following my templates or working improvisationally.

Layout

Fourth Floor
3.5" x 4" triangles

Third Floor
3.75" x 4.5" triangles

Second Floor
4" x 5.5" triangles

First Floor
4.25" x 6.5" triangles

Base 2.5" x 4.5" rectangles

Inspired by the Hearst

Finished size: Approx. 7" x 30"

Fabric

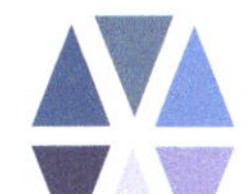

Building: 6 variations of one color family. 8.5" x 11" of each. Or, if working with scraps, see box below. Full-size templates are on p. 48.

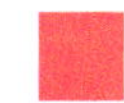

Background for "Color Block" quilt only, p. 76. Mine is deep red/magenta. Cut 8.25" x 39.5". A quarter-yard (not a fat-quarter) or a third-yard or half-yard.

Scrapping the Tower

If you want to use scraps rather than yardage, you can make old-fashioned cardstock templates. Instead of doing steps 1-6 on the next page, do this:

► Print out or trace the template page, p. 48 (Do the red box size check). Glue the page to cardstock as shown on the right. Cut out each piece on its black outlines.

► Bring templates to scrap stash, to check that pieces are big enough. Then use the templates to cut at least 6 different fabrics of each size.

► Have fun throwing in oddballs, prints, a bright reflective window – and maybe even a rose bud? (See:"Citizen Caine".)

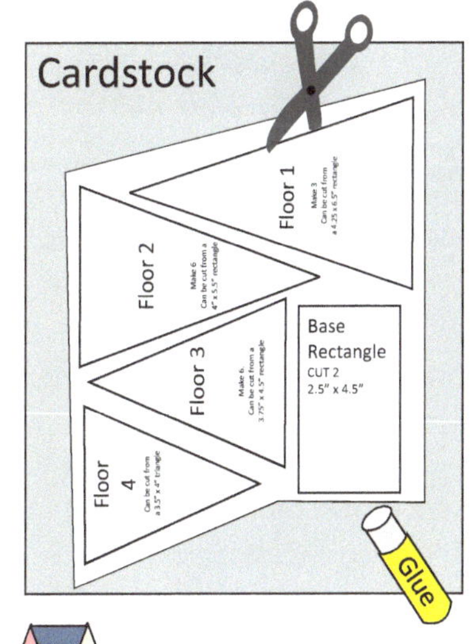

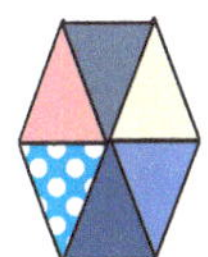

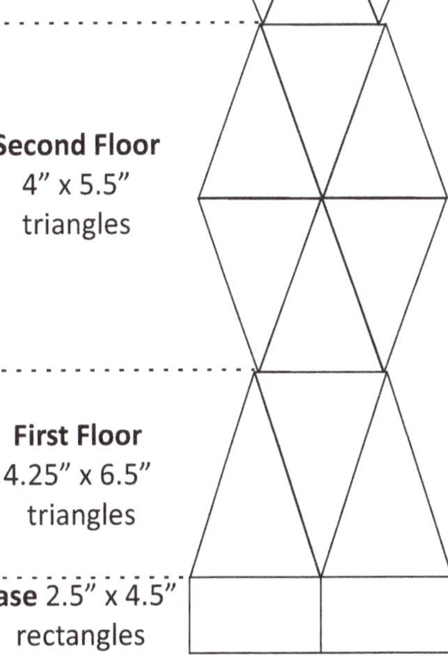

(continued)

 This is not a licensed product. I am not affiliated or associated with any of the buildings depicted in these quilts.

*If you're starting with scraps, read the box on bottom of the previous page and then **skip** steps 1-6 below. If starting with "yardage" - pieces 8.5" x 11" or larger - speed things up with the first 6 steps below:*

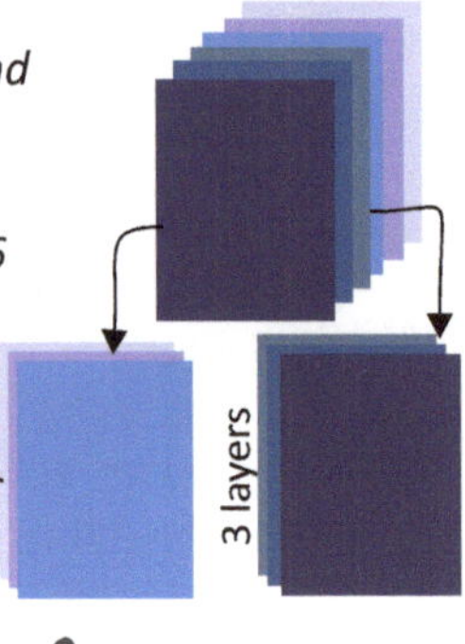

1 Cut an 8.5" x 11" rectangle from each of the 6 different fabrics.

2 Stack them in two groups of 3, matching edges.

3 Trace or print out p. 48. With a printout, do the red size check. Cut tracing or printout *outside* the triangle grouping (green dotted line here), and also outside the base rectangle.

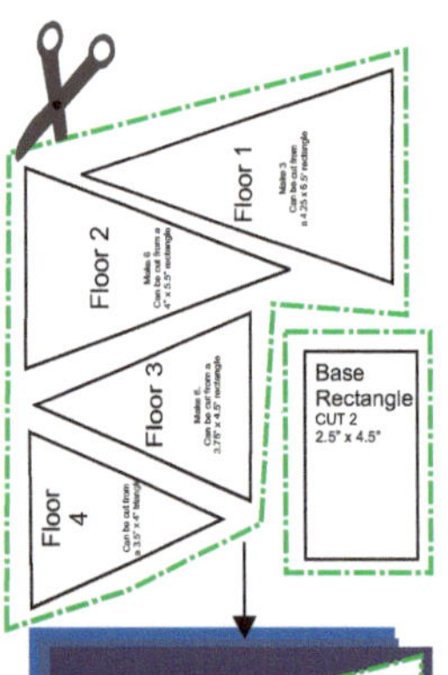

4 Choose either fabric stack to start. Don't pin the base rectangle pattern to this stack, just the triangles. Pin center of each, through all layers.

5 Cut out triangles on their black lines, through paper and fabric layers. (Use rotary cutter or scissors.) Sort into four piles by size (all 1's together, all 2's, etc.).

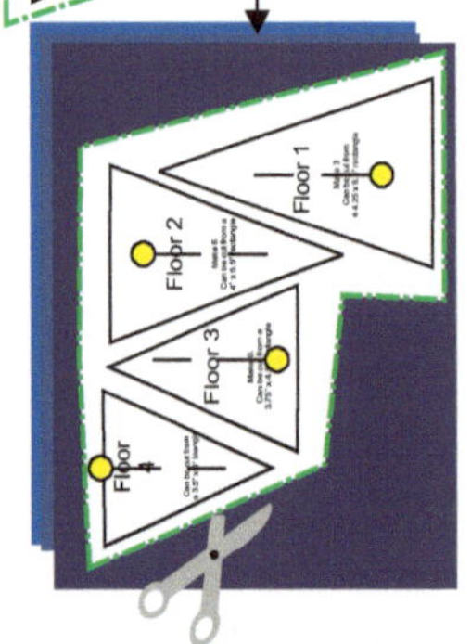

6 Unpin the paper templates. Floor 1 needs only 3 pieces, so set that template aside – you won't use it again. Pin remaining templates to the second 3-layer stack. Also pin the base rectangle pattern there. Cut pieces through all three layers (The paper is already cut.) You will wind up with one extra rectangle (sorry).

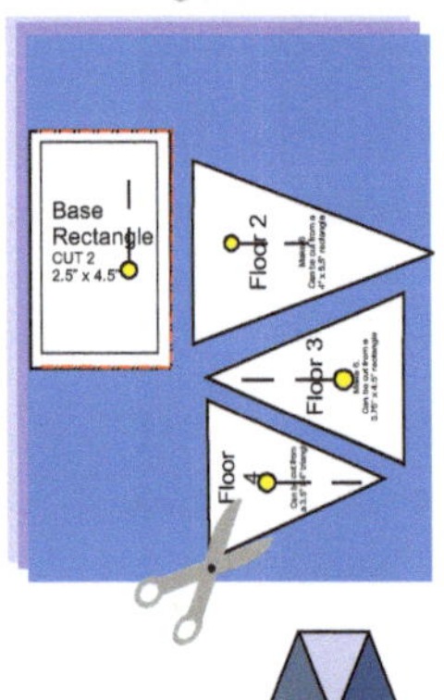

7 You should have 21 triangles (plus three rectangles). Arrange by size into floors. Each floor has six triangles, except the first floor, which has 3 triangles and 2 rectangles.

Avoid putting the same fabrics next to each other; avoid making each hexagon's layout the same; and avoid putting a triangle into the wrong size group!

If you find you want more variety, use templates to cut different pieces.

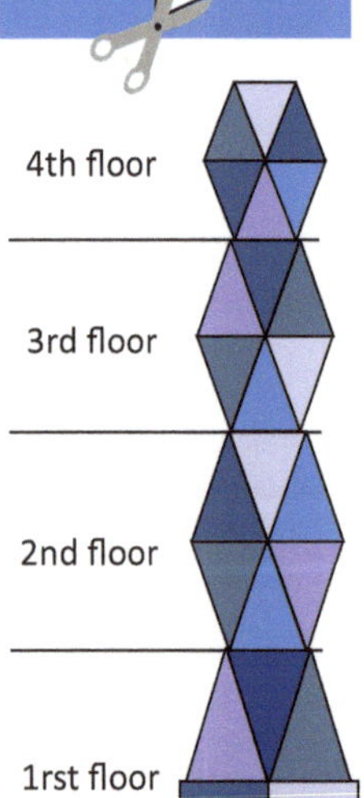

Floors 2-4 have two horizontal rows of triangles that form a hexagon. I sew each row outward from the central triangle (1 or 4). Here's how.

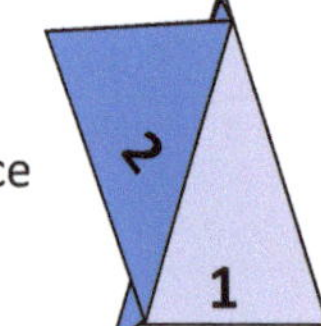

8 On any bottom row (except floor 1): Flip piece 2, face down, onto piece 1, face up, aligning left raw edges. A tiny triangle of piece 1 peeps out on top. The bottom of piece 2 extends a bit beyond piece 1. Both areas are circled.

9 Pin perpendicular to the seam (above right). Sew with the usual 1/4" seam allowance. (starting at the base of piece 2).

10 Unfold piece 2 and press seam allowance left, under piece 2.

11 Press left edge of piece 3 to the back 1/4" (pink dotted line).

12 Hold 3 on top of the 1 + 2 unit, and figure out where it goes to create a straight edge across the top; and an intersection about 1/4" below the top center.

13 Holding 3 in position, pin it face down on top of 1 + 2. Test placement one more time by pinning through the seam allowances, PARALLEL to the seam as shown, and opening to check.

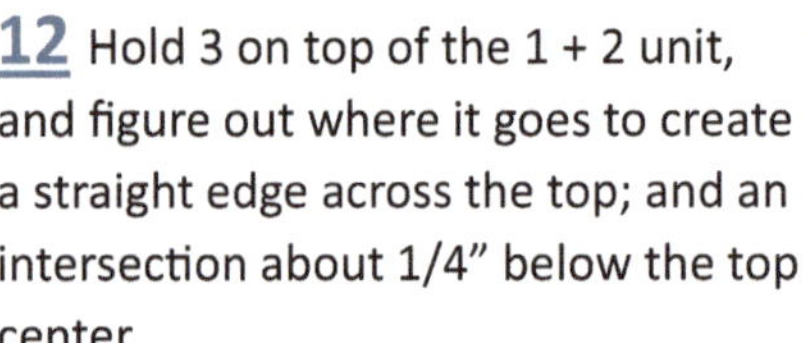

14 Here's the test opening – good enough! (I am here to have fun!)

15 Pin perpendicular to the seam. Sew down the crease, sliding away the pin before you get there.

16 Press piece 3 open and press the seam allowance outward, underneath piece 3.

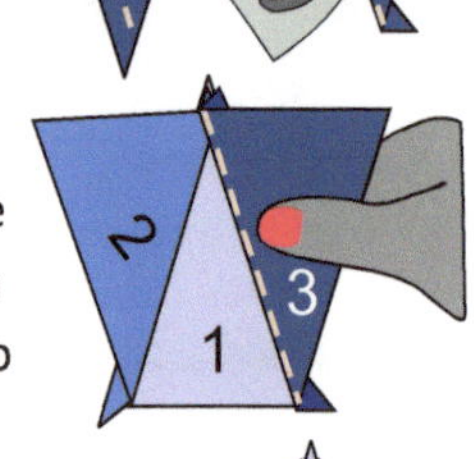
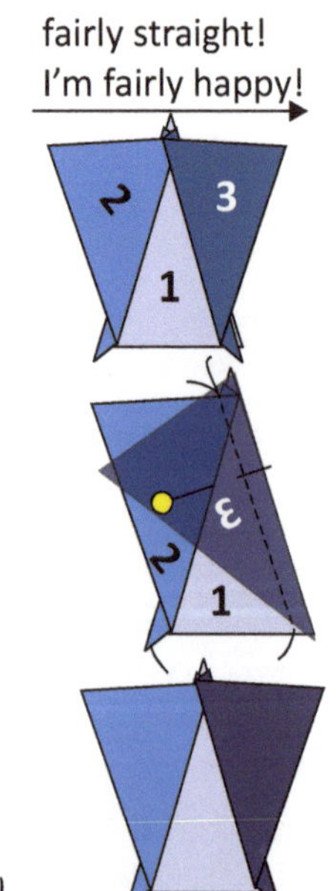

(continued)

17 Trim the top straight, cutting off as little as you can get away with! This row is now finished. Next is the row that will go directly on top of it.

18 Here are the top row pieces. Place piece 5, face down, along the left edge of 4, face up. The tip of 5 will protrude a bit on top, past piece 4. The bottom corner of 4 will protrude on bottom, beyond 5. Both areas are circled.

19 Pin perpendicular to seam. Sew down the pinned edge. (Start sewing from bottom of piece 5.)

20 Press pair open, pressing seam allowance left, under piece 5.

21 Do the advance pressing trick with 6. Press its left raw edge (when looked at from the front), 1/4" to the back (pink dotted line is the fold).

22 Hold piece 6 on the 4+5 unit, to determine where it goes to create a straightish line across the bottom; and an intersection of pieces 4, 5, and 6 about 1/4" above the bottom center. Pin the seam allowance and test open to make sure.

23 When you like the position, turn the pin perpendicular to the seam, and sew down the crease, sliding pin away before you get there.

24 Press piece 6 open and press the seam allowance under it.

25 Trim the bottom edge straight, cutting off as little as possible to make it straight.

26 You now have the two halves needed for this floor:

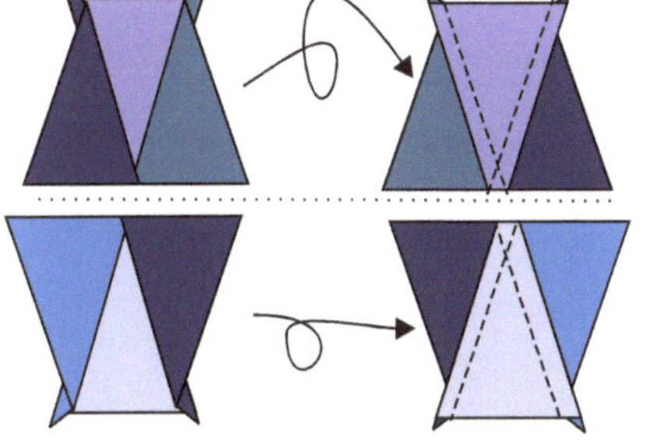

Front view   Back view

27 Flip the top half face down onto the bottom half, face up.

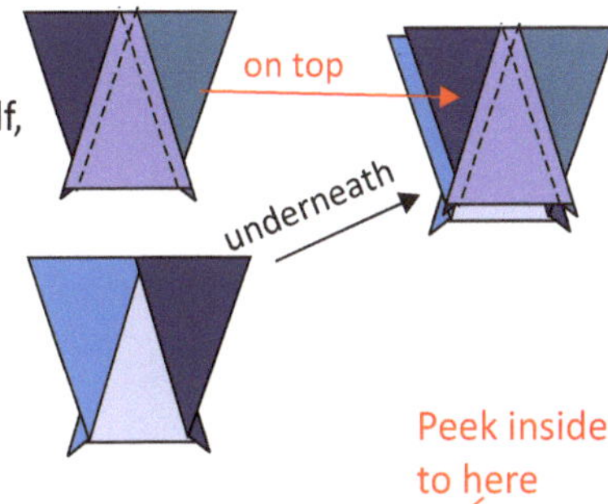

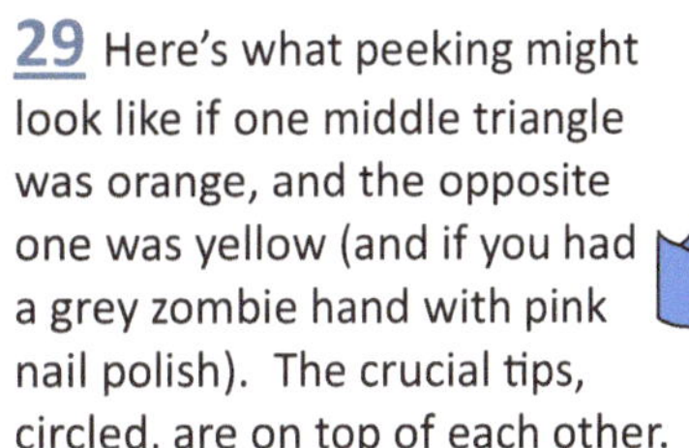
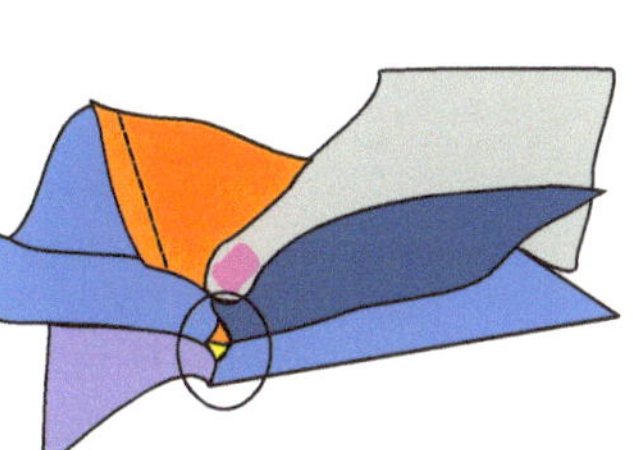

28 Peek between layers at the top to check that the tips of the two middle triangles are directly on top of each other.

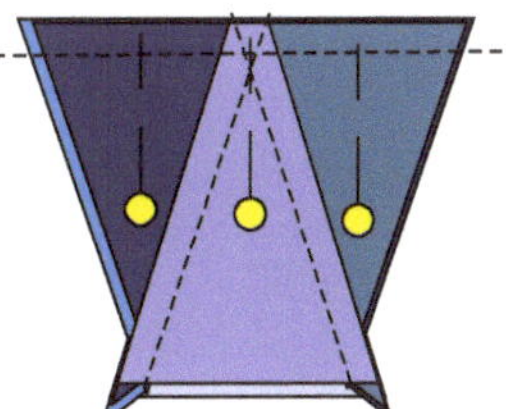

29 Here's what peeking might look like if one middle triangle was orange, and the opposite one was yellow (and if you had a grey zombie hand with pink nail polish). The crucial tips, circled, are on top of each other.

30 Pin perpendicular to the seam. Sew across to join halves with the usual 1/4" seam allowance. There's no need for backstitching.

31 Open halves and press the central seam allowance open, as in diagram **a**.

32 Press all but the top and bottom horizontal edges 1/4" to the back – the four edges that the arrows point to in diagram **b**. A little glue helps. We'll show the process now:

In **diagram c**, only the lower right edge is pressed in.

In **d**, we've pressed the upper right edge too.

Finally, press in the two left edges. When done, it looks something like **e**.

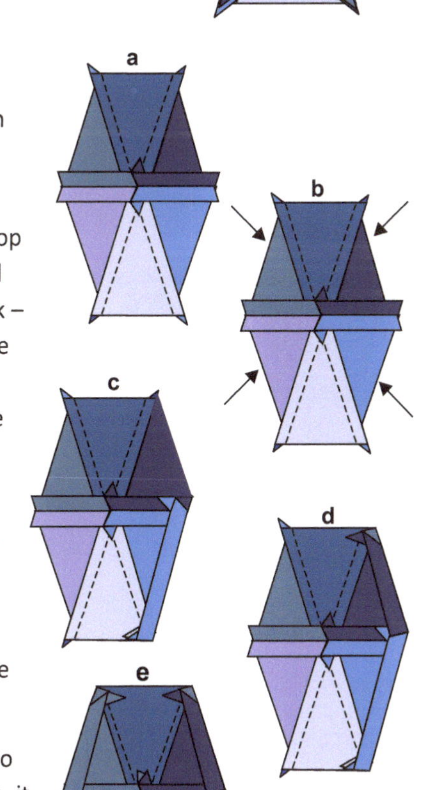

(continued)

33 Repeat steps 8-32 to make floors 2, 3, and 4. The first floor (right) has just a top row. Stitch its triangles together and press in the two side edges, but do NOT glue them at their base – we'll open them again soon.

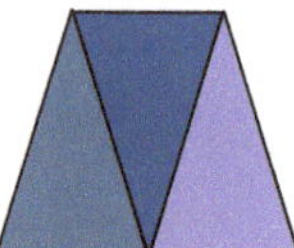

First floor

Assemble the Tower

34 Flip the 4th floor hexagon, face down, on the 3rd floor, face up. The 4th is slightly smaller, so center it, with equal amounts of the 3rd floor sticking out on both sides. Pin.

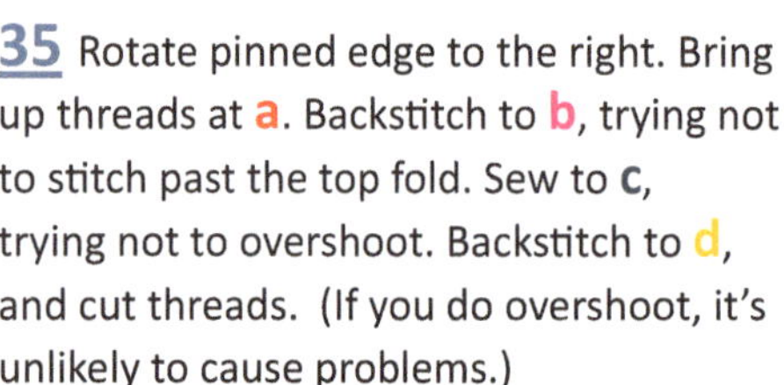

35 Rotate pinned edge to the right. Bring up threads at **a**. Backstitch to **b**, trying not to stitch past the top fold. Sew to **c**, trying not to overshoot. Backstitch to **d**, and cut threads. (If you do overshoot, it's unlikely to cause problems.)

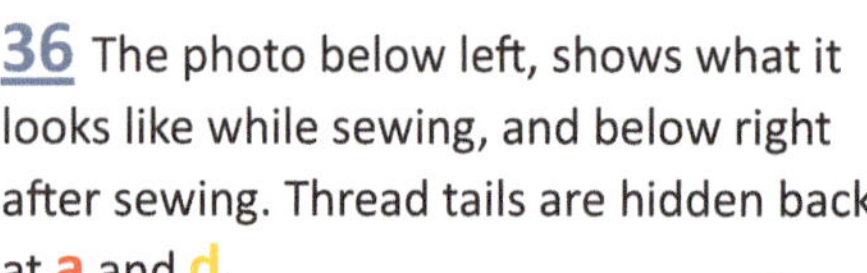

36 The photo below left, shows what it looks like while sewing, and below right after sewing. Thread tails are hidden back at **a** and **d**.

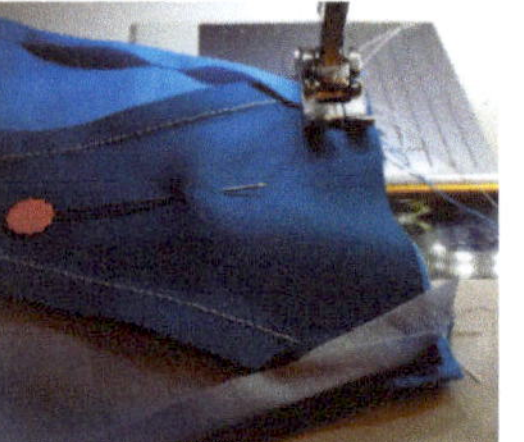
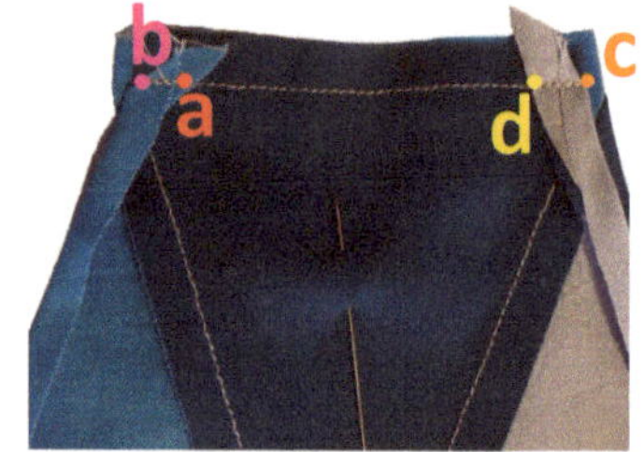

37 Press seam allowances down (below, left). It hides flaps better than pressing them open, plus I like that, from the front, it makes each succeeding level appear a little more set back (below, right.)

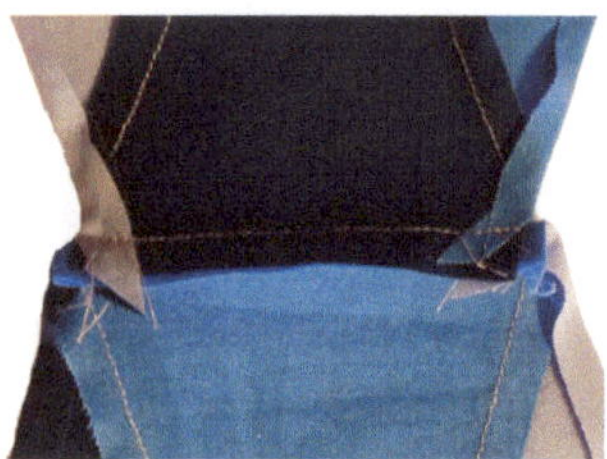
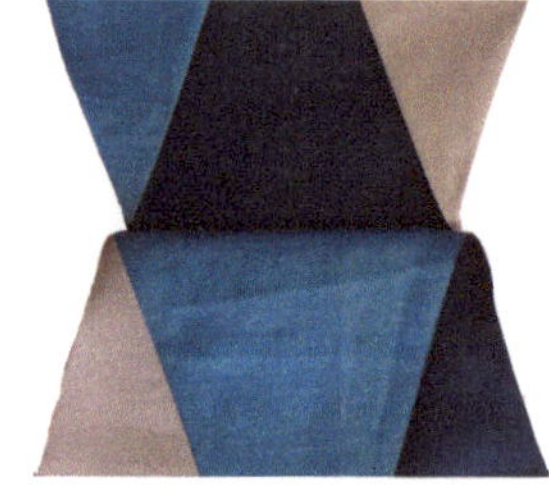

38 Repeat this procedure to add the second floor, and the top of the first floor.

39 First floor: You've pressed the two sides inward 1/4", but now we're going to open the two bottom corners. The pink line is the crease you pressed into the triangles earlier. We only need to open the bottom, not the top.

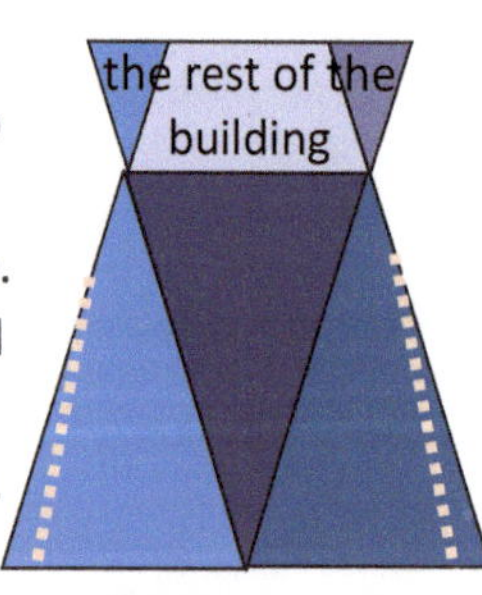

40 Sew the bottom rectangles together side by side. Press seam allowance either way.

41 Turn the half-hexagon, good side down, onto the rectangle pair, good side up. Match the widest edge of the joined triangles with the rectangles' bottom edge. Center. Triangles' side flaps are open at the bottom. Pin.

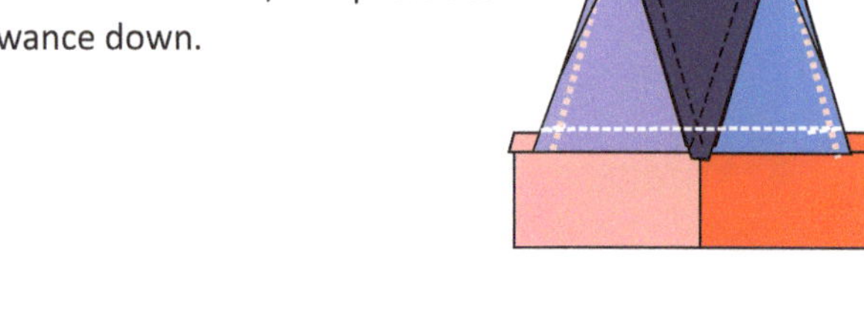

42 Rotate pinned edge right. This time, we will NOT sew the flaps shut. But do start and end with back stitches to create a secure join.

Bring up threads at **a**. Backstitch to **b**, just before the triangle ends. Sew to **c**, just before the triangle ends. Backstitch to **d**, and cut threads there.

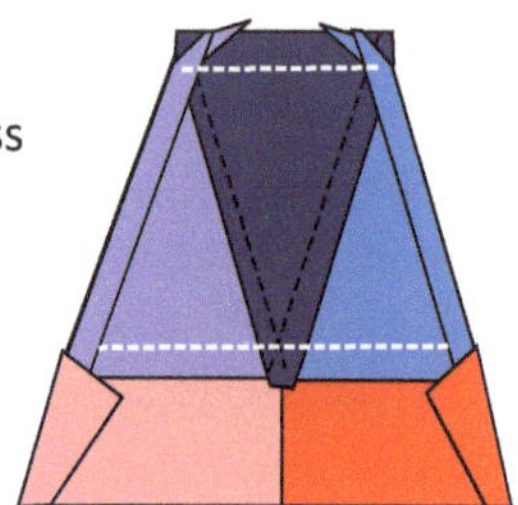

43 Unfold the base, and press seam allowance down.

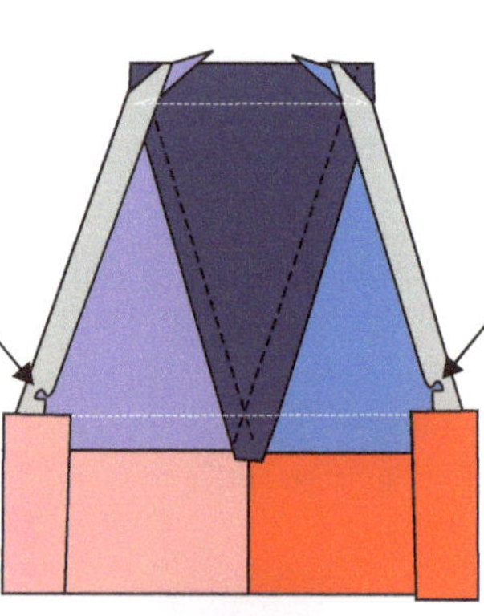

44 Re-press the side creases on both side triangles. When you press them inward, with the base attached, it will look like this.

45 Just a little more pressing is needed to make the base sides straight up and down.

From the back, readjust base flaps so they are vertical instead of angled. You want the side flaps on the triangles – grey in this diagram – to change direction at the base. Do this by pressing a tiny crease in the seam allowance flaps - the little dark loops where the arrows point. Iron firmly!

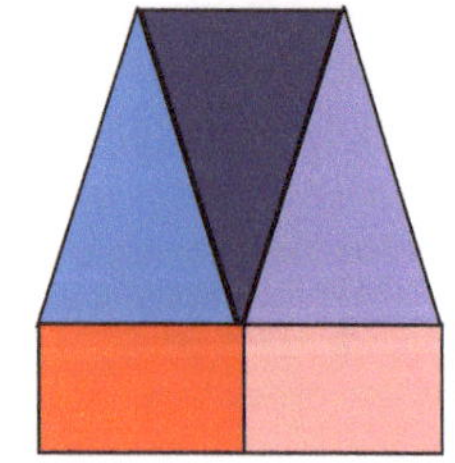

46 Check from the front that the fold transitions neatly from a diagonal to dropping down straight.

47 Press the building's top edge down 1/4" (not shown).

(continued)

For 'Condensed' quilt: No need to press the bottom edge of the building up. See next steps on p. 71.

For 'Color Block' quilt:
Press bottom raw edge of building up 1/4". Audition backgrounds. In the sample quilt, it's magenta. Cut background to 8.25" x 39.5" from a quarter-yard (not a fat-quarter). This information and next steps are in the quilt directions that start on p. 76; the measurement reference chart is on p. 76.

Quilting Ideas
On the Hearst Tower, each of its triangular faces is made up of many rectangular windows. That inspired my quilting, subdividing each triangle into thirds vertically (red lines) and half horizontally (blue lines). The horizontal quilting lines are doubled.

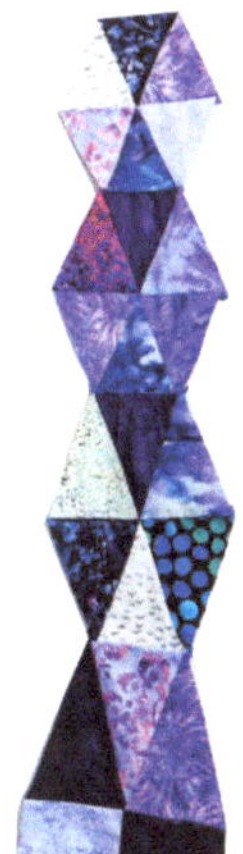

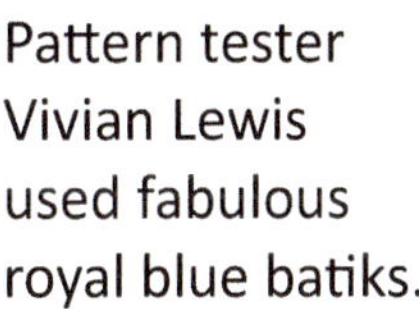

Pattern tester Gail Solomon used a variety of purple batiks for her version.

Pattern tester Vivian Lewis used fabulous royal blue batiks.

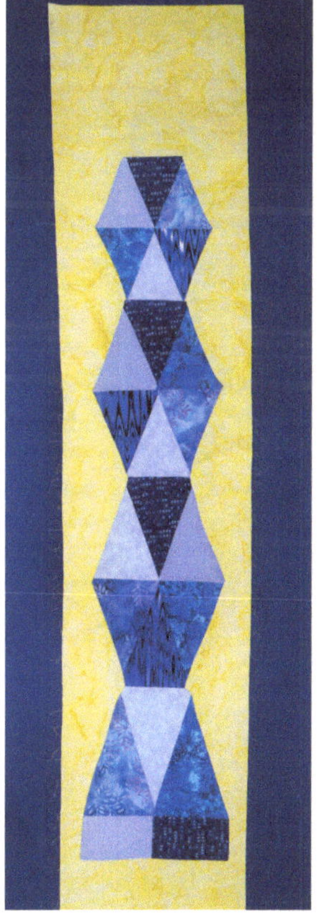

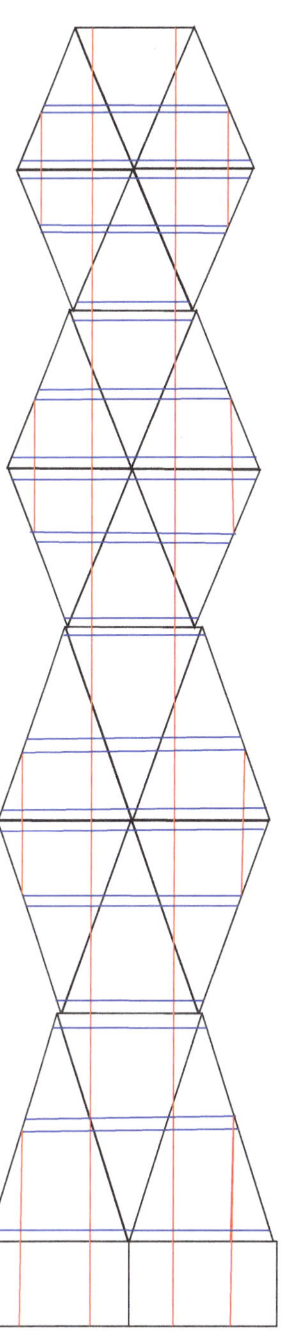

(continued)

Hearst Templates

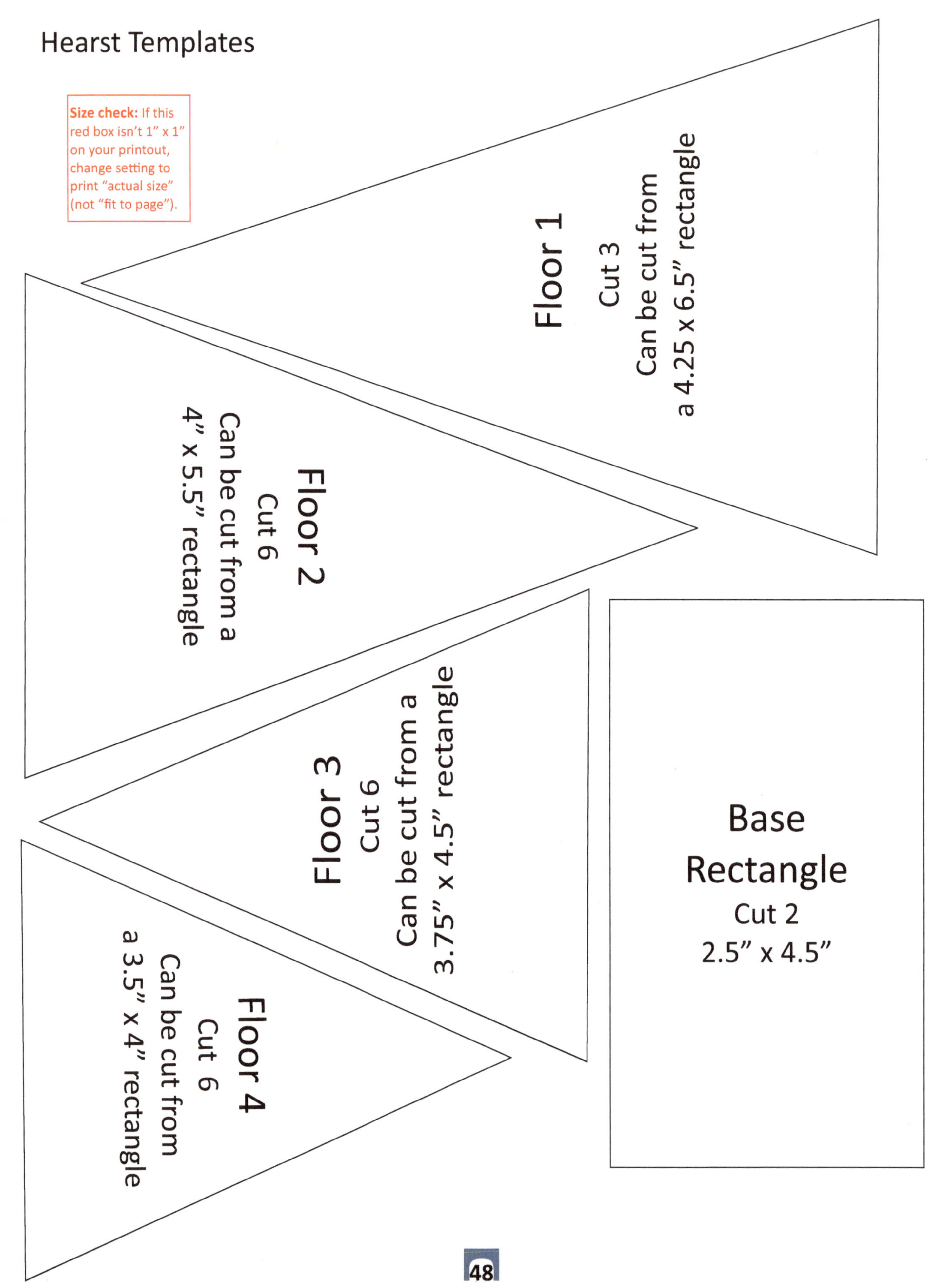

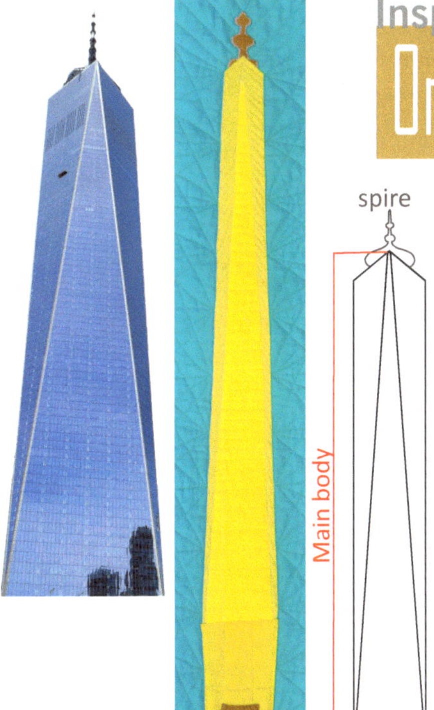

One World Trade Center aka Freedom Tower

Guarding the hallowed grounds of the lost Twin Towers, this prism-like building opened in 2014. It's the tallest building in New York and the US; and the 6th tallest in the world, at 1776 feet (honoring the Declaration of Independence). It will be the tallest on your quilt.

Its geometry is fascinating. The main body has 8 vast triangular surfaces – depending on where you stand, you can see a central triangle pointing up or down. The building is square at the bottom; a regular octagon halfway up (the middle of each triangle forms a side); then square again at the top – but the top square is rotated 45 degrees from the base! 45 also happens to be the number of miles you can see from the building's observation deck!

Because we are dealing with long pattern pieces here, have spray starch (or other ironing fluid) handy, to help you make sharp, straight folds.

Inspired by One World Trade

Finished size: Approx. 36.75" x 4"

Fabric

Main body, front (Back is medium grey in these diagrams): 4.5" x 31.5", or one quarter-yard (NOT a fat-quarter).

Central triangle, front (Back is light grey in diagrams): 4.5" x 31," or one quarter-yard (NOT a fat-quarter).

Pedestal: 4.5" x 4.5", and Spire, 3.5" x 4"

Door: 3.25"x 2.25"

Background rectangle, for Color Block quilt. 7.75" x 39.5". A quarter-yard (NOT a fat-quarter).

Other Supplies

► 3.5" x 4" piece of paper-backed fusible web for the spire.

► A temporary fabric marker whose marks are not set by ironing (see step 11).

► Yardstick

► Spray starch, sizing, or pressing fluid

► Fray-checking fluid

► Invisible monofilament thread, or thread matching the central triangle

This is not a licensed product. I am not affiliated or associated with any of the buildings depicted in these quilts.

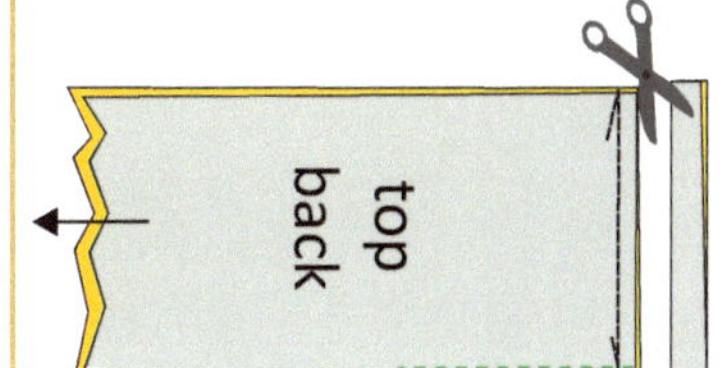

Make the Main Body

1 Cut main body fabric to 4.5" x 31.5".

2 Bring two top corners together, good sides meeting, so you're looking at the back. Finger-press the center fold for the top 1" or so (the green dotted line). Pin top edge.

3 Rotate pinned edge to the right, and sew down the top, 1/4" from the top edge, as on the left, starting and ending with backstitches. I sew towards the fold.

4 Trim about 1/8" off the top (left). Reach into the little pouch you've formed (right), and then....

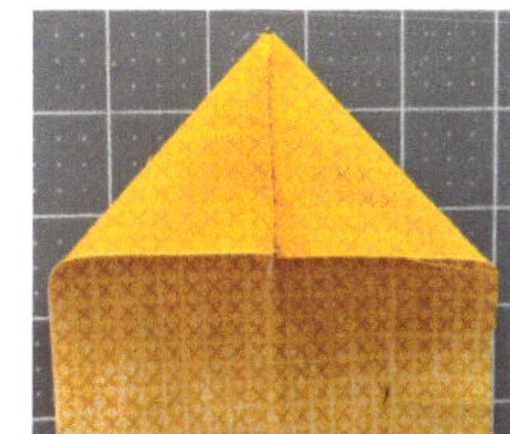

5 Turn the tip right side out. Push out the tip using a chopstick, or something with a smooth point, so you don't poke through.

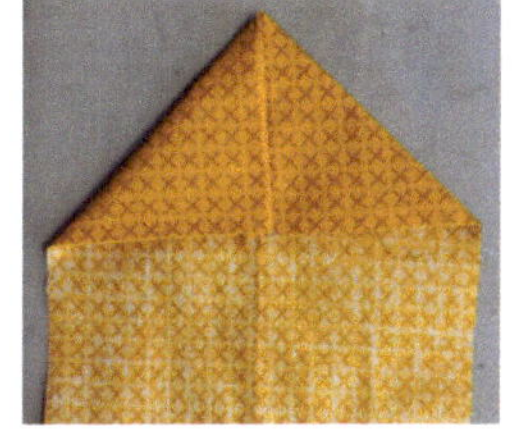

6 Arrange the tips' sides symmetrically. Press well. Then spray the entire back with starch and press the whole piece. The back now has a nice, flat self-lining behind the tip.

(continued)

7 Press both long sides inward 1/4". At the top, you'll be pressing small side folds on top of the triangle folds created in step 5.

Don't glue these two side creases in position yet, especially at the base. We're going to temporarily open them again, in order to attach the pedestal.

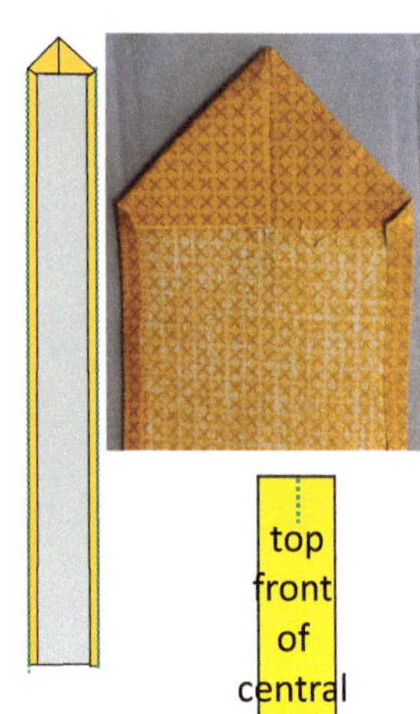

Make the Central Triangle

8 Cut central triangle fabric to 4.5" x 31" (a half-inch shorter, and same width, as you cut the main building). Spray with ironing fluid and press well.

9 Press in half and crease the center top for an inch or so (the green dotted line in the diagram).

10 Press the top edge of the strip 1/4" down to the back.

11 Mark 1/8" from the center top in both directions. These are the two red lines on top. Use a marker whose marks are not set by ironing. **Avoid using the purple air-erase, or the blue water-erase pens for this and the next few steps, because ironing can make those lines permanent.**

12 On bottom, mark two more lines 1/4" in from each lower corner.

13 Use a yardstick and your non-heat set marker to draw two lines on back:

The first line goes from the hashmark on top right (on the fold), down to the mark that is 1/4" in from the right bottom corner.

Press as hard as you dare. But if you can't press hard (for example, you're using a mechanical pencil), mark lightly, then go over the line with a "hera" marker or the edge of a credit card. Denting the lines will help you fold them accurately!

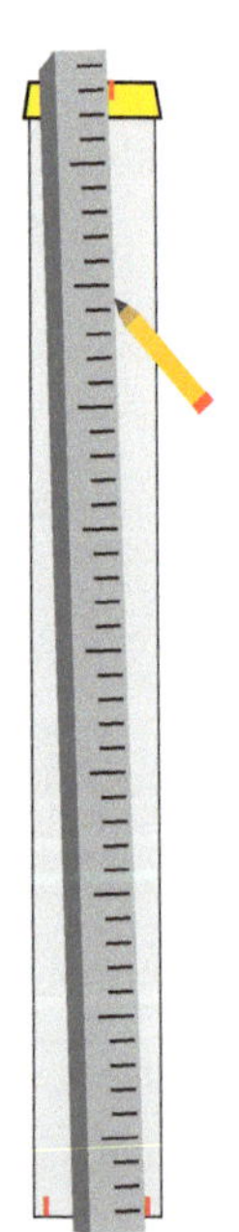

14 Do the opposite side, connecting the hashmark on the top left to the one on the lower left, the same way. Result is in the middle.

15 Use rotary cutter and ruler to cut away all the fabric that's more than 1/4" from these side folds. Make these cuts as smooth as you can.

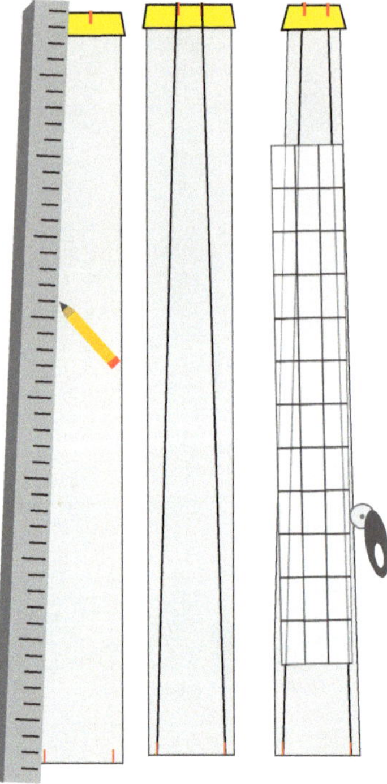
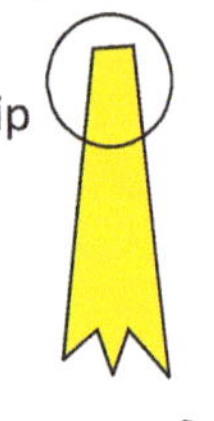

16 Practice fold: The tip is already pressed down. Now try pressing one side down (on one of the long lines), on top of it. Then press the opposite edge inward on the other line.

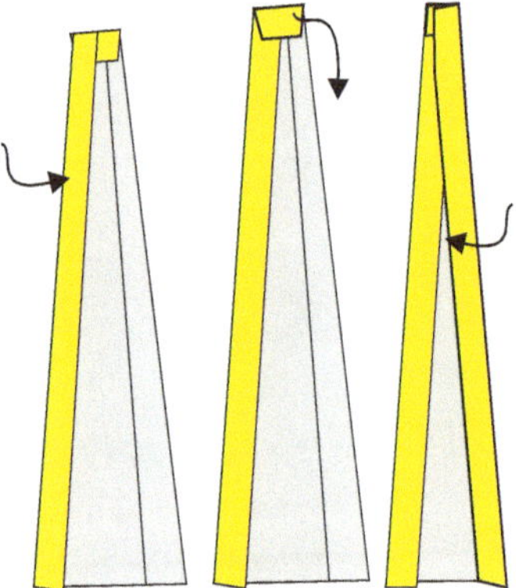

When you look at it from the front, the tip looks like this. There are probably some flaps or threads sticking out. Let's clean those up.

17 Test a scrap of the same fabric with a couple of drops of fray-stopping fluid. Give it at least 15 minutes to dry. Once you know it dries invisibly, proceed. Unfold the tip and drip fray-stopping fluid on the top half-inch or so. Let dry.

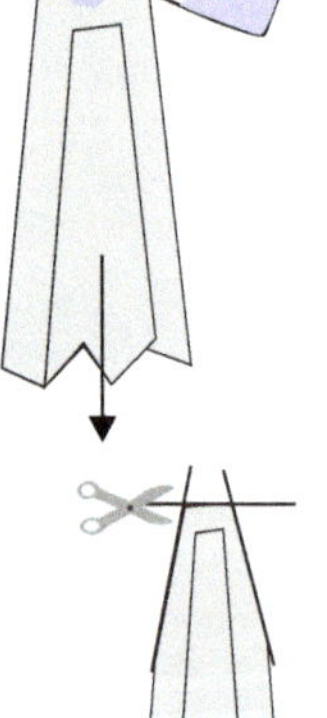

18 Trim around the tip area to just under 1/4". Do this for the top 2" or so.

19 Rearrange and re-press flaps into the position that best hides edges. Experiment with folding the top flap down first, second, or third – see which order works best! When you figure it out, use a glue stick to hold edges back. Press well.

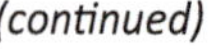

(continued)

20 On the lower part of the main building, open the side flaps for about 6". The green dotted lines show where the fold lines are opened.

Center the large triangle on the main building, matching bottom raw edges. At the top end, you want the triangle's tip at least 1/2" below the main building's tip. (This leaves room for stitches, and allows for the fact that this appliqué may stretch upward as you sew it in place.) Use lots of small pins; or hand baste; or glue-stick the large triangle securely in place.

21 Appliqué the triangle. I've tried hand- and machine-appliqué for this piece (on different versions), and it's remarkable how alike they look. Machine appliqué suggestions are on pp. 5-6. A tension and stabilizer test before you stitch the real thing is a good idea.

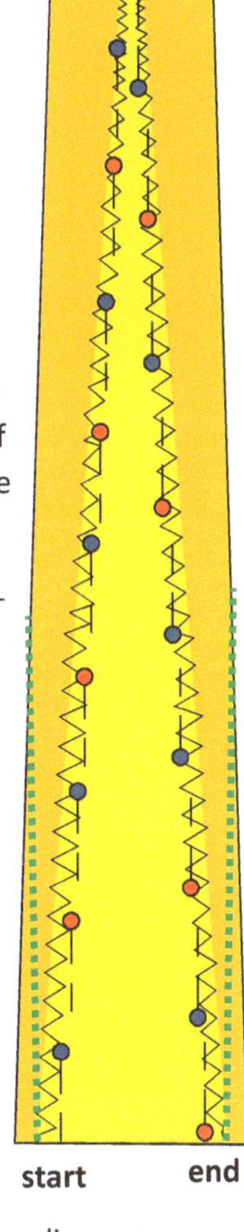

start   end

Start sewing at a base side (lower left in the diagram above). Do a few back-and-forth straight stitches, then go around. With a zigzag, each stitch starts JUST outside the appliqué, then takes a deep bite into it. At the top, if your machine stitch is a zigzag, stop with the needle outside the appliqué, and swivel several times - there's a blue dot on each of the likely swivel points in the diagram below (but more or fewer is fine).

End on the lower right of the building with a few more tiny back and forth stitches.

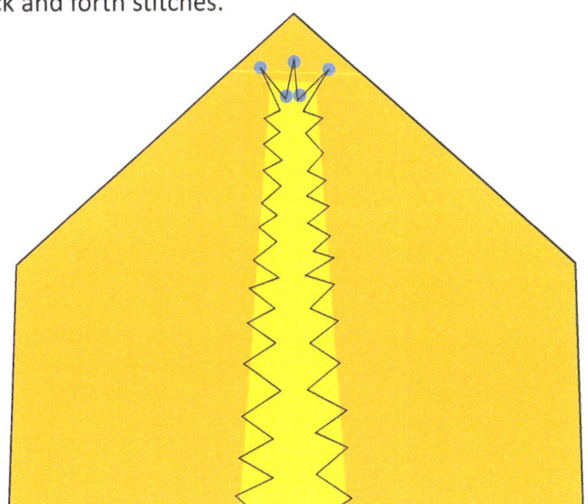

22 Cut the pedestal to 4 1/2" x 4 1/2".

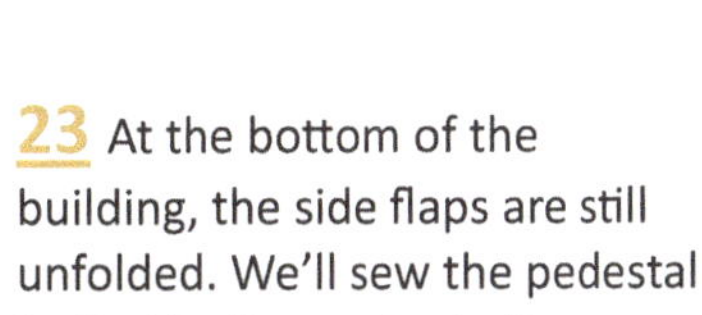

23 At the bottom of the building, the side flaps are still unfolded. We'll sew the pedestal to that bottom edge in the traditional way.

Lay the pedestal, good side down, onto the bottom edge of the main building, with its good side up. Three raw edges now meet along the bottom edge: the building's main body (good side up); the triangle on top of it (sewn in place, good side up), and the pedestal (good side down). Sew across with a 1/4" seam allowance. I backstitch at both ends here, just for security.

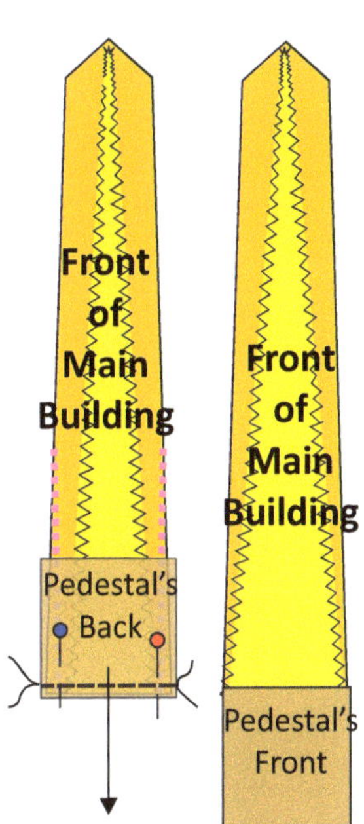

24 Unfold the pedestal. Your building has just grown by 4"! Press the seam allowances downward. Refold the 1/4" creases on the lower sides of the main building. Fold the pedestal's sides 1/4" in, pressing as smooth a transition as you can between the seam allowances on the main body and those on the pedestal.

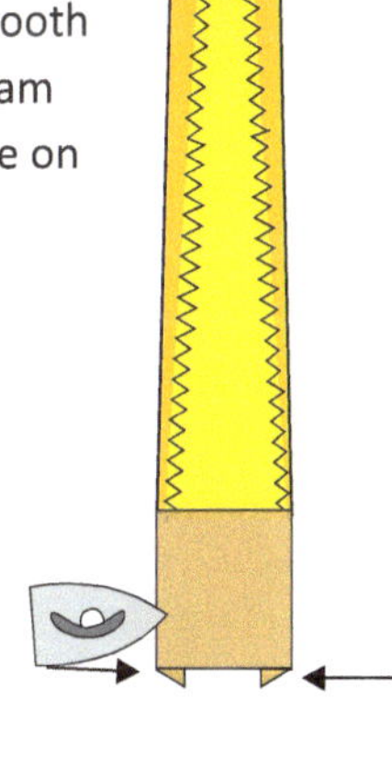

25 For a door, cut a rectangle to 3.25" x 2.25". Press the sides in 1/4" and apply a little glue in the corners to hold them. Press top edge down, and use a little more glue in the corners to hold it. Don't press the bottom edge up. Appliqué the doorway to the bottom middle of the pedestal, matching lowest raw edges.

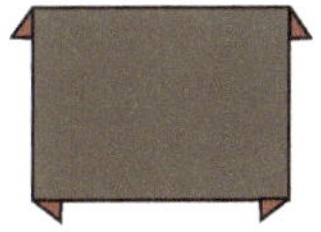

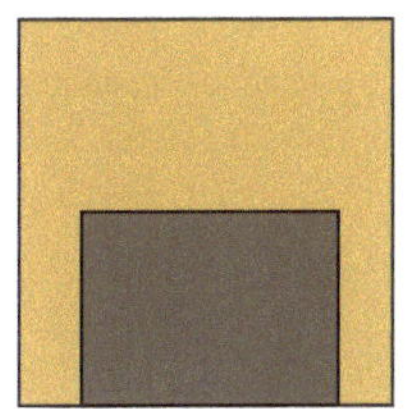

(continued)

26 Print this page for spire pattern. **Check size on your printout: spire height should be 3.5".** (If not, set printer to "print actual size.")

27 Trace the spire's outline on the paper side of paper-backed fusible web.

28 Cut paper-backed web out loosely, beyond the outline.

29 Press cutout to the back of spire fabric.

30 Cut spire and paper following the outline. Peel away paper.

31 Baste the spire behind the building tip. I suggest doing some hand basting to hold them together short-term. When you're ready to appliqué the building in place, go around the turned edges of the main building with whatever appliqué stitch you like. Then fuse the spire down, and do a tight zigzag around the spire area that shows – from lower left, up and around, to the lower right, to cover its sides and top. Appliqué tips are on pp. 5-6

For 'Condensed' quilt: No need to press the bottom edge of the building up. See next steps on p. 71.

For 'Color Block' quilt: Press bottom raw edge of building up 1/4". Audition backgrounds. In the sample quilt, it's teal, cut to 7.75" x 39.5". (This requires a quarter-yard or half-yard, NOT a fat-quarter.) You will place the building's bottom folded edge about 2.5" above the bottom raw edge of the background. This information and next steps are in the quilt directions that start on p. 76.

More quilting ideas. I quilted in the ditch just outside the central triangle and door. Horizontal lines are stitched across the central triangle, becoming diagonal on the two sides, for a bit of perspective. I stitched a grid over the base. I did a little echo quilting inside the doorway. The background is quilted with emanating lines.

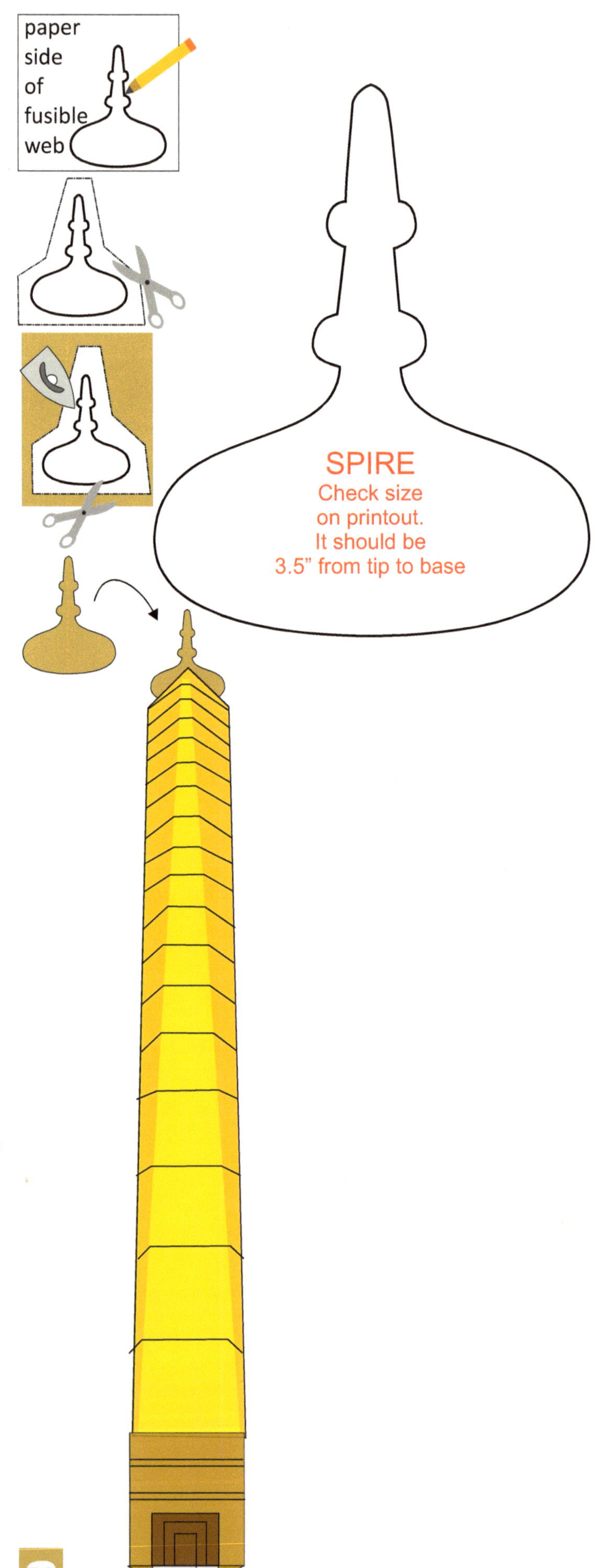

Metropolitan Opera House

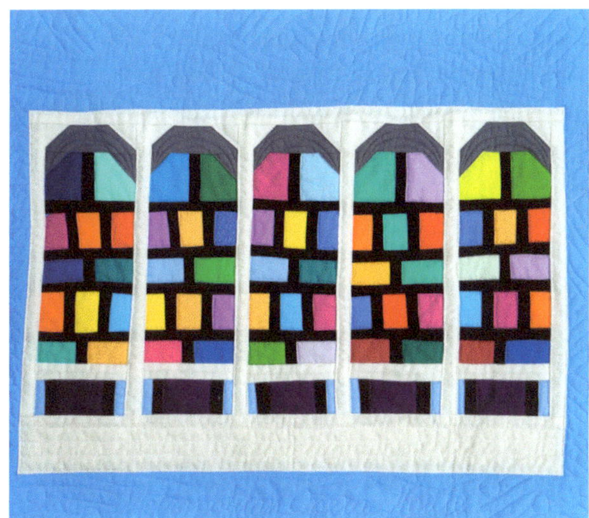

The windows fronting Lincoln Center's Metropolitan Opera House (aka "the Met") are clear. But lit up, they remind me of stained glass, because of the dark lines of leading, and colors shining through from a splendid lobby adorned with two huge Chagall murals, seasonal banners, explosive chandeliers, and well-dressed opera lovers. It's a temple to the arts!

This version is a scrapbuster – it winnowed my solid and black scraps significantly. It's long and low, perfect to front your skyscrapers. Or, use this approach to make a more traditional worship house. These windows are similar in shape to those at Temple Emanu-el on 5th Avenue, and the Riverside Church in Morningside Heights.

Read through the chapter before cutting. The diagram on the next page is for reference; the directions will take you through the cutting step-by-step, with speed-sewing and organization tips. I found it helpful to lay it out on a design surface that can easily be rotated 90 degrees, such as posterboard.

(continued)

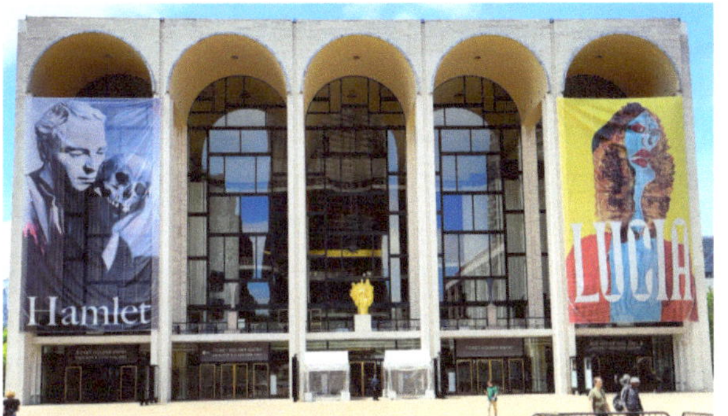

Daytime, with banners

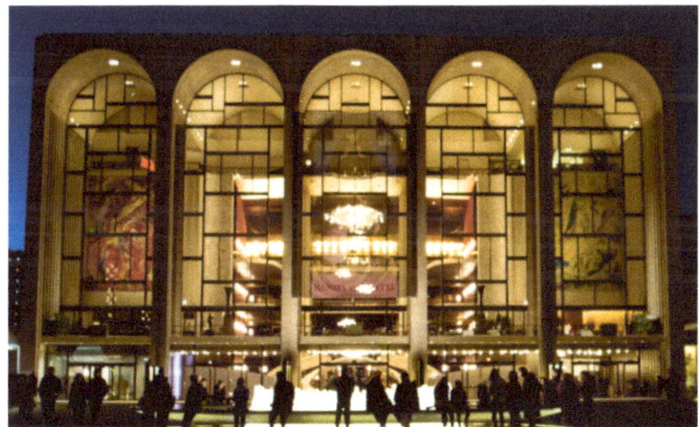

Night   via Pixabay

This is not a licensed product. I am not affiliated or associated with any buildings depicted in these quilts.

Inspired by the Met

Finished size: Approx. 23.5" x 16"

Fabrics

Window colors. The more you include, the easier it will be to mix them up. At least 16 different fabrics. Small pieces, at least 1.5" x 2" or larger, will give you what you need.

Building color. Use the real building's color, white, or go fanciful. Start with 1/3 yard.

Grey. For the top shadowed arches. A quarter-yard or fat-quarter.

Black or dark navy. Window leading. Scraps, or a fat-quarter or regular quarter-yard (or more). Will be cut into 1" strips.

Doorway. One piece, 10" x 2.5". See p. 56 for strip piecing directions. Use any dark color. I used purple.

Background rectangle for Color Block quilt, p. 76. Blue in that quilt. Cut 25.25" x 22". A half-yard.

1 All the black (or navy) strips are 1" wide, and lengths vary – adding up to about 220" total. It needn't be continuous! You can cut ten 1" strips off the long (22") edge of a fat-quarter; or four strips from 44" wide yardage. I keep these "master leading strips" handy to subcut as I do the next four steps and beyond.

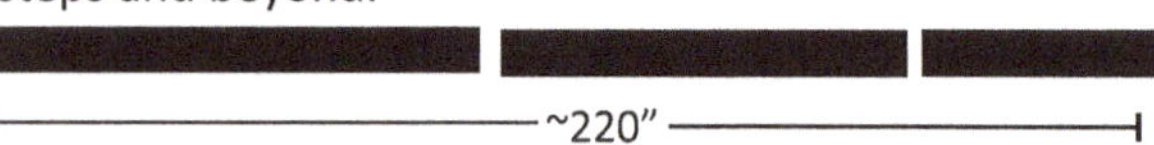

~220"

2 **Cut Row A pieces**. Each of the five sections has two Row A's. To fill them, cut 30 colorful rectangles to 1.5" x 2". Use at least 7 different fabrics – cut 4-5 pieces of each. (A few extra are good!). Different shades of the same color are fine, like the peach and orange pieces below. They must contrast in some way, value and/or color.

– For all the vertical black strips in all Row A's: Cut 20 pieces off your master leading strip, each 1" x 2". Keep all Row **A** pieces together.

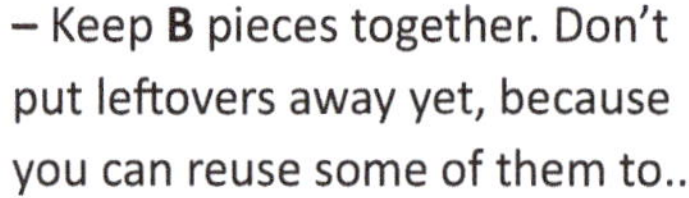

3 **Cut Row B pieces**. There are two Row B's in each of the five sections. Cut 20 colorful rectangles to 2.25" x 1.5". Use at least 6 fabrics (3-4 of each). Try not to reuse fabrics from A rows.

– Cut 10 Row B black strips, each 1" x 1.5"

– Keep **B** pieces together. Don't put leftovers away yet, because you can reuse some of them to...

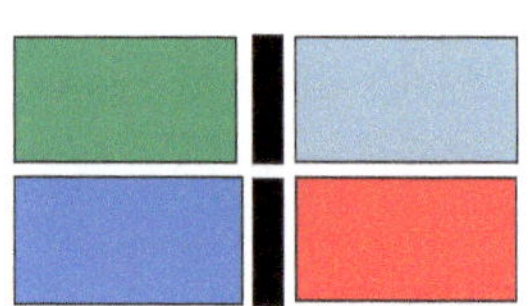

4 **Cut Row C pieces.** This is the highest colorful row in each section. There are two **C** pieces per row. Cut 10 colorful rectangles to 2.25" x 2.5". It's okay to repeat Row **B** fabrics here, but not Row **A**, because A is directly below this row (and we're avoiding repeating a fabric above itself.)

– Cut five black strips 1" x 2.5".

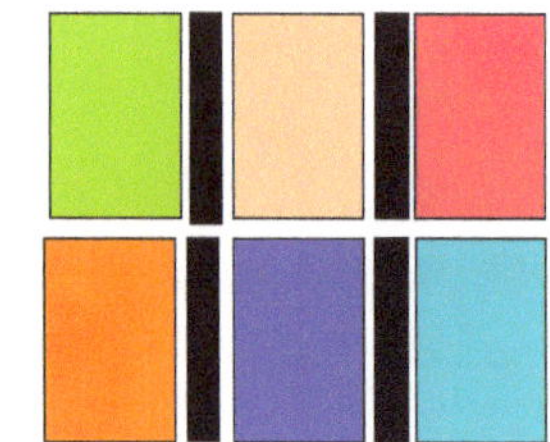

– Cut ten grey arch squares, each 1.75" x 1.75". Press each in half diagonally, matching points. They will later be sewn in the top outer corners of the 10 colorful Row **C** pieces.

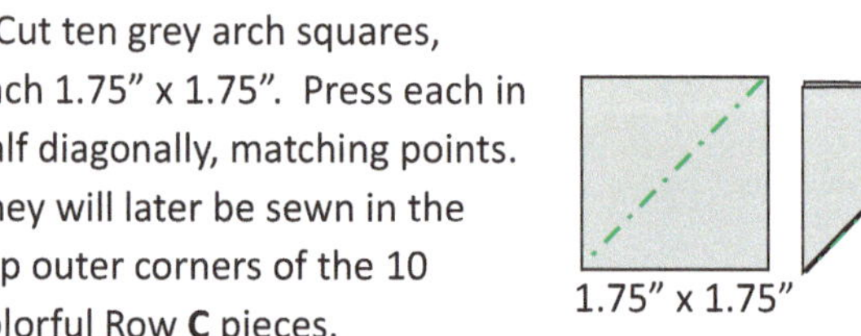

1.75" x 1.75"

Let the Games Begin!

5 Deal out pieces from your row **A**, **B** and **C** stacks. To win this game, avoid placing the same color (or one that's extremely similar) next to or above itself! Lay out black verticals, too. If possible, lay the pieces out on posterboard, or other large surface that you can rotate.

(continued)

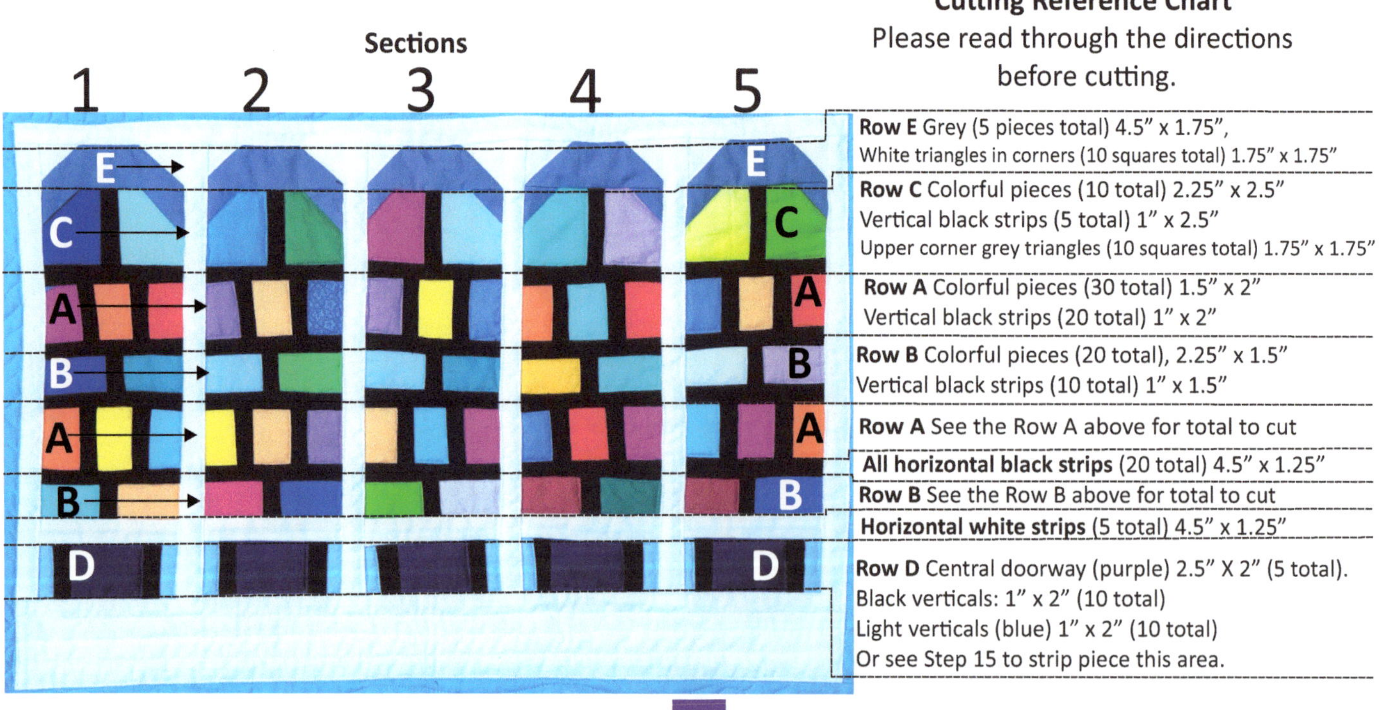

Cutting Reference Chart
Please read through the directions before cutting.

Row E Grey (5 pieces total) 4.5" x 1.75", White triangles in corners (10 squares total) 1.75" x 1.75"	
Row C Colorful pieces (10 total) 2.25" x 2.5" Vertical black strips (5 total) 1" x 2.5" Upper corner grey triangles (10 squares total) 1.75" x 1.75"	
Row A Colorful pieces (30 total) 1.5" x 2" Vertical black strips (20 total) 1" x 2"	
Row B Colorful pieces (20 total), 2.25" x 1.5" Vertical black strips (10 total) 1" x 1.5"	
Row A See the Row A above for total to cut	
All horizontal black strips (20 total) 4.5" x 1.25"	
Row B See the Row B above for total to cut	
Horizontal white strips (5 total) 4.5" x 1.25"	
Row D Central doorway (purple) 2.5" X 2" (5 total). Black verticals: 1" x 2" (10 total) Light verticals (blue) 1" x 2" (10 total) Or see Step 15 to strip piece this area.	

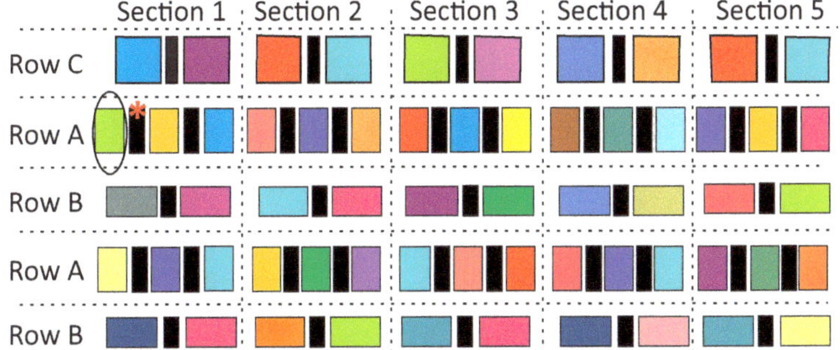

9 Chain sew **B** rows the same way. Join pieces on the far left to the adjacent black strips. Next add the colorful pieces on the right. Press seam allowances behind the black strips. When all rows are assembled, cut apart and place each back in its section.

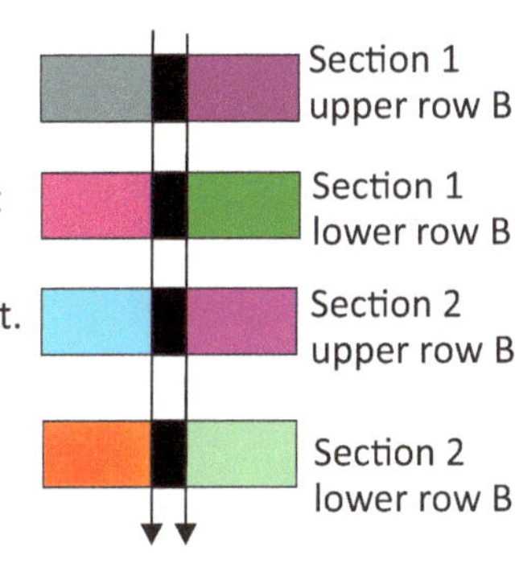

Chain Sew Rows Within Each Section

6 When you like the layout, sew rows together any way you prefer. Here's how I chain sew.

I start on the highest Row A in Section 1, on the upper left of the diagram above, with the bright green piece that's circled. It's also shown in the diagram below.

Flip the black strip next to it, marked with a red asterisk, onto the green piece's right edge. Sew down the edge with the usual 1/4" seam allowance. Don't cut threads!

Pick up the first two pieces of Section 1's LOWER Row A - the first piece is yellow. Flip the adjacent black strip face down on the yellow piece's right edge. Sew.

Don't cut threads! Move to section 2, upper row A, flipping the black strip onto the first pink piece. Sew. Next do the first pieces in the lower row A in section 2. (The first piece is gold).

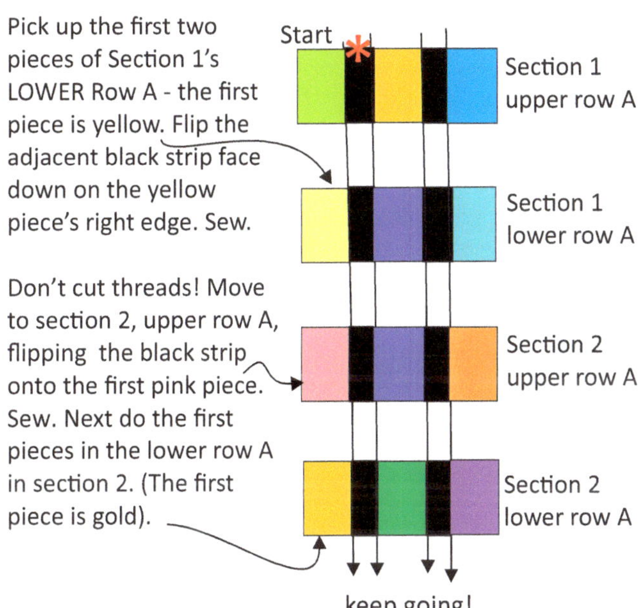

7 Keep going through the sections. When all the first and second pieces in all row A's are together, cut only the last threads. (Don't press yet). Start again at the top of Section 1, upper Row A - this time, flip the third piece in each row (gold in section 1, upper row A) onto to the black strip to its left (with the red asterisk). Do all third pieces like this.

Keep going, adding the fourth and then the fifth pieces on the right to each row.

8 When all 10 row A's are united, cut the last threads, but not the ones between rows. Bring the long chain of strips to the ironing board. Press seam allowances under the black pieces to lift them as in stained glass.

9 At your design surface, cut threads and place each row back in its position.

10 Make sure each **C** piece is oriented correctly, with their longest edge (2.5") vertical. Chain sew the five **C** rows the same way as the **B** rows. Press black strips' seam allowances inward, cut threads, and place back in their sections.

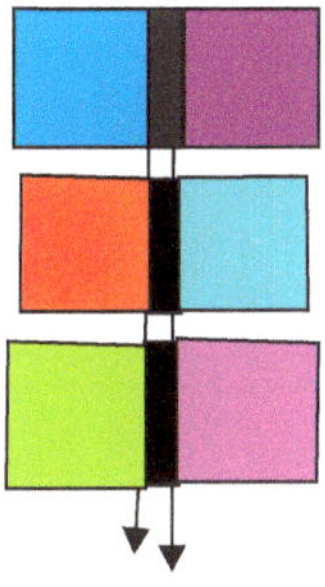

11 Still in the **C** rows, pin a grey square (cut in step 4) in each upper corner of the row. Sew on the diagonal.

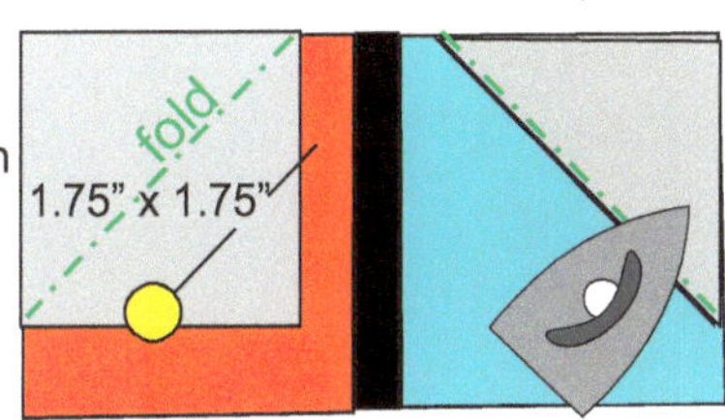

I sew a bit above the crease. Press each grey flap out. To reduce bulk, cut away the back colorful triangle. I leave the extra grey triangle, to help elevate the arches above the windows (but you can trim it away if you prefer).

12 Create Row E pieces:

► Cut 5 rectangles, 4.5" x 1.75", from grey.

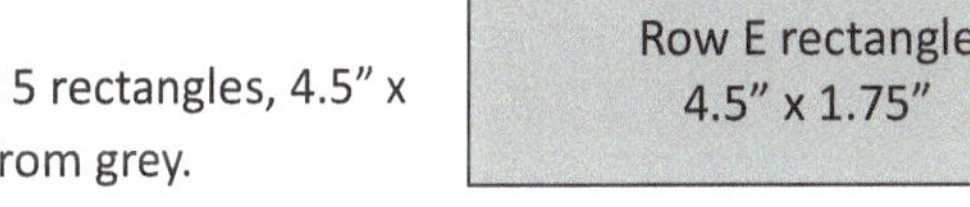

► Cut 10 squares 1.75" x 1.75" from building color. Press in half diagonally, matching points.

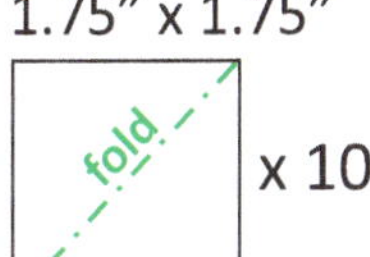

► Pin squares in top corners of each row **E** rectangle. Sew along the crease, and press lower flaps up.

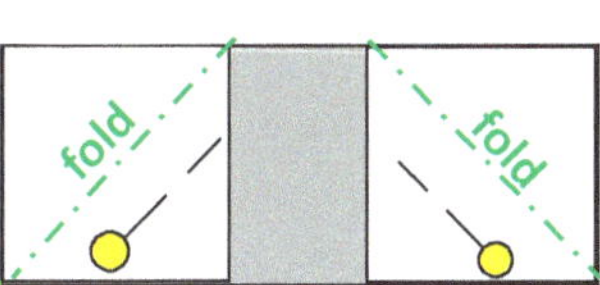

Here's a finished row **E**. I only cut away the extra grey flap on back. I like the lift behind the white area.

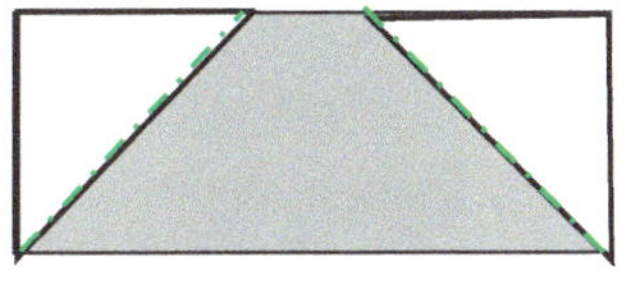

13 Cut 20 horizontal black strips, 4.5" x 1". There are 4 in each section, between rows.

(continued)

14 Cut strips that go over doorways. There's one in each section. Cut all five to 4.5" x 1.25". Use your building color.

4.5" x 1.25"

Create Doorways

15 A door is on bottom of each section. All five are the same, so you can strip piece them. It's okay to repeat a Row **A** color here, but don't repeat a Row **B** color, because **B** is directly above the door.

– Pick a color for the two outer light strips (blue here). Cut two strips 10" x 1".

- Cut two black strips 10" x 1".

– Choose a color for the central doorway (dark purple). Cut one strip 10" x 2.5".

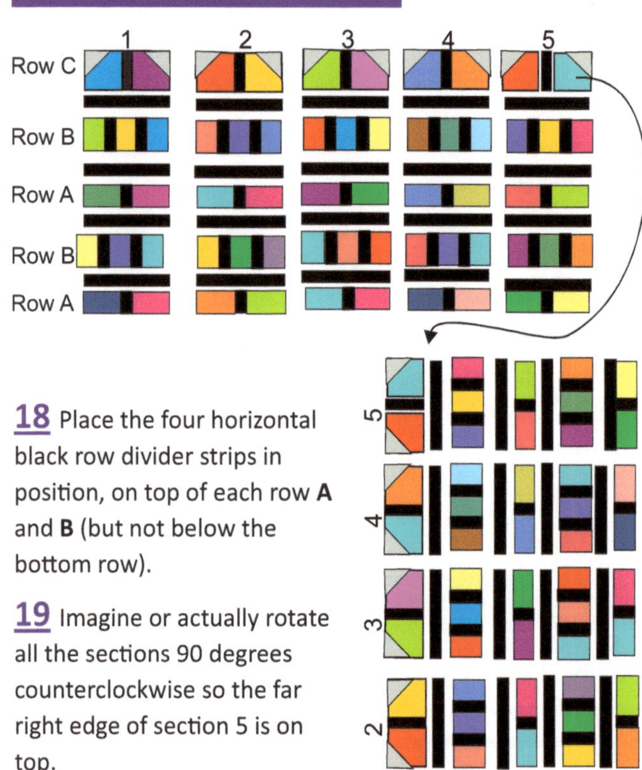

16 Sew strips together as shown above. Press seam allowances under black strips.

17 Subcut the set at 2" intervals, giving you 5 pieces. Set these aside for now - don't put them in the sections yet.

Unite Rows into Sections

18 Place the four horizontal black row divider strips in position, on top of each row **A** and **B** (but not below the bottom row).

19 Imagine or actually rotate all the sections 90 degrees counterclockwise so the far right edge of section 5 is on top.

20 Chain sew the rows together:

▶ Flip Section 5's first black row divider, face down, on what is now the far right edge of row **C**. Stitch down and DON'T cut threads!

▶ Flip section 4's first row divider onto the bottom of its row **C**. Sew.

▶ Continue like this, joining the first two rows of Sections 3, 2 and 1. Cut only after the last thread - leave sections 1-5 attached by the threads.

I find it easier to NOT press between strips. Pressing seam allowances under the narrow black strips would make adding the next-lowest piece tougher. So hold off pressing til you've completed the entire section.

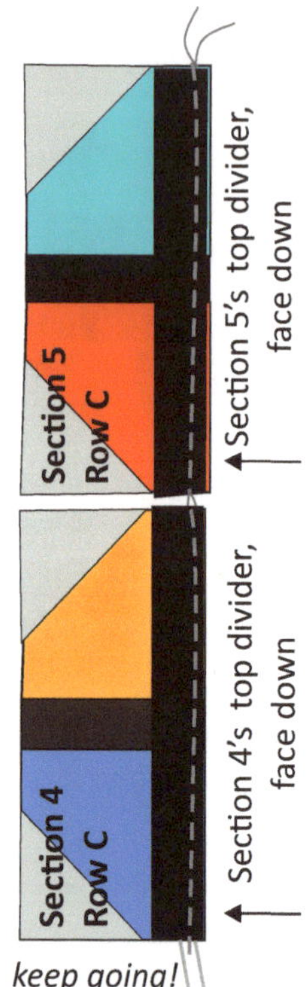

keep going!

21 Start again on top of Section 5 (below). This time, flip its highest row **B**, face down, onto the right edge of the row divider to its left. Pin and sew. Don't cut threads - feed in the top row **B**'s of Section 4, 3, 2 and 1 the same way.

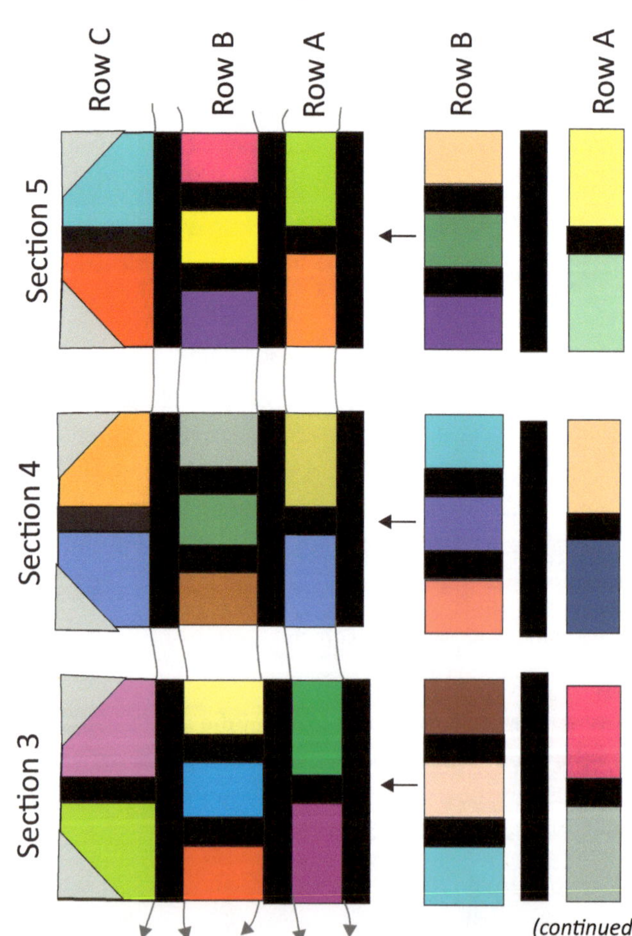

(continued)

22 Keep going to add each row within each section. You'll wind up with a long chain of all five sections, joined by threads. Press seam allowances under the black strips to lift them above the windows. Then, at the design surface, cut threads and lay out sections in order again.

23 Sew each **E** archway to the top of each **C** row.

24 Sew each doorway's top edge to a building color strip.

25 Sew the doorway and white strip unit to the bottom of each section.

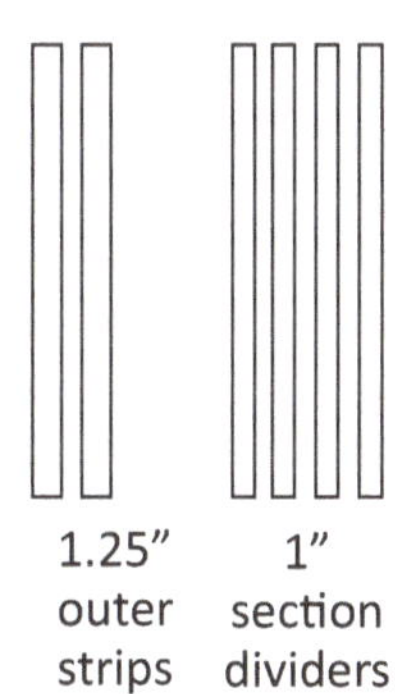

26 Measure section heights. Each should be about 13". If you must trim to make them the same, trim the TOP. Use your average section height for the next step.

27 Cut TWO outer building color strips 1.25" x 13" or your section height. Cut FOUR section dividers from the same building color fabric to 1" x 13" or your section height.

1.25" outer strips

1" section dividers

Align and Unite the Sections

28 Join sections with 1" dividers between them. The biggest challenge is aligning the black row dividers so they look like they flow straight across. Here's the trick I use.

a. Pin a 1" strip to the right edge.

b. Temporarily press seam allowance left, (under section 1), to make sewing easier.

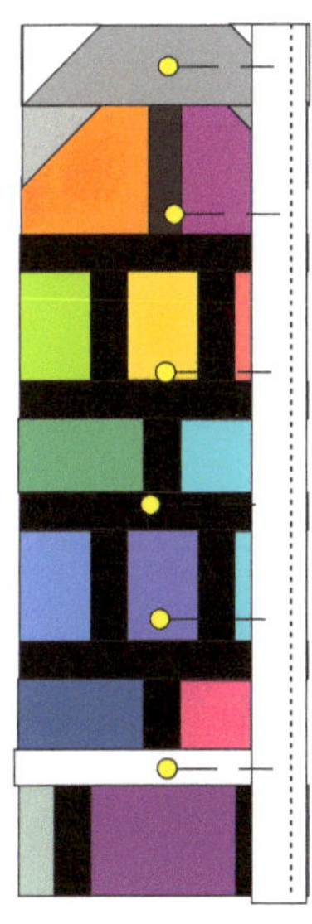

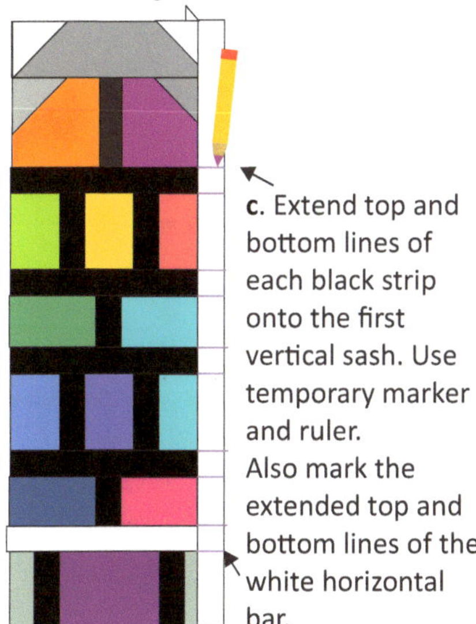

c. Extend top and bottom lines of each black strip onto the first vertical sash. Use temporary marker and ruler.
Also mark the extended top and bottom lines of the white horizontal bar.

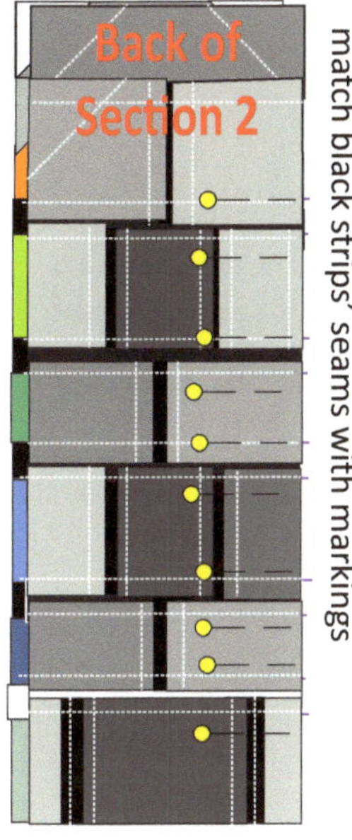

d. Place section 1 on table good side up. Flip section 2, face down (its back is grey here) onto section 1.

Along the right edge, line up each horizontal marking underneath with the seams of Section 2's horizontal black bars on top. Pin above and below each match, as shown.

If the top and bottom corners don't match perfectly, that's not much of a problem. Don't worry about it.

29 Sew down the edge. Press both the vertical sashing strip's long edges INWARD, for a little lift. (Unless you're using a marker that can be permanently set by ironing; in that case, don't press until you've finished joining all 5 sections and removed markings.)

30 As in step 28a, sew a second 1" section divider strip to the right edge of section 2. Press. Draw extended row divider lines as before. Flip Section 4 onto the divider, and match and pin. Repeat until all five sections are joined.

31 If the bottom or top edges aren't in a straight line, trim them straight.

32 Press seam allowances of building color strips inward.

33 Sew the two 1.25" outer strips to the left edge of section 1 and the right edge of section 5. Press seam allowances of colorful areas out under them.

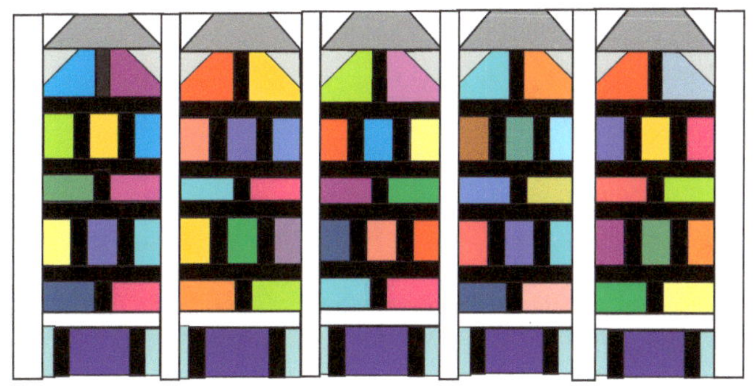

(continued)

<u>**34**</u> Measure the width. It should be about 24". Cut a 1.25" strip to your building's total width. Sew that strip along the top of the building. Press top seam allowance up.

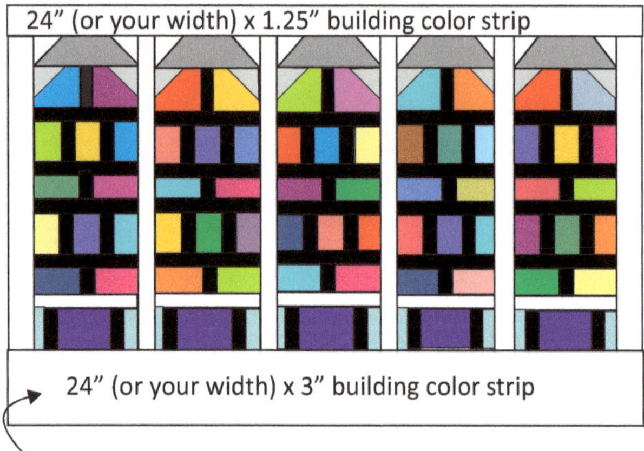

<u>**35**</u> Cut another building color strip, this time to your width x 3" high. Sew it to the bottom. Press seam allowance down.

Finishing Steps

For 'Condensed' quilt: No need to press the bottom edge of the building up. See next steps on p. 71.

For 'Color Block' quilt: Audition background color. In the cover quilt, it's medium blue. Cut size for the background is 25.25" x 22", which is a tight fit. Wait to sew the building to the background until all the background rectangles are pieced together. Or consider PIECING instead of appliquéing the background in place. To do that, cut two background fabric strips to 1.25" strips x the height of your building, and sew them to either side. Measure again and cut to make the total width with background 25.25". Now measure and cut a 4"x 25.25" strip of background fabric, and sew it along the top edge. For the bottom edge, cut a 3"x 25.25" strip. Quilt directions start on p. 76.

Quilting ideas I quilted in the ditch with invisible thread just inside each window. I quilted three echoing half-circles inside each arch.
For the background on the Color Block quilt, I made abstract music, with long wavy lines set 1/2" apart. A flexible curve helped me draw smooth lines. Then I used a stencil to draw circles, which represent musical notes.

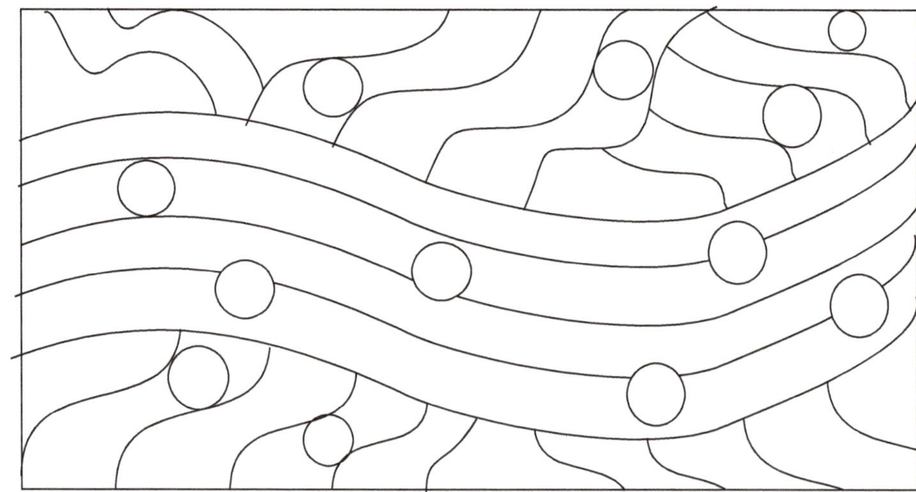

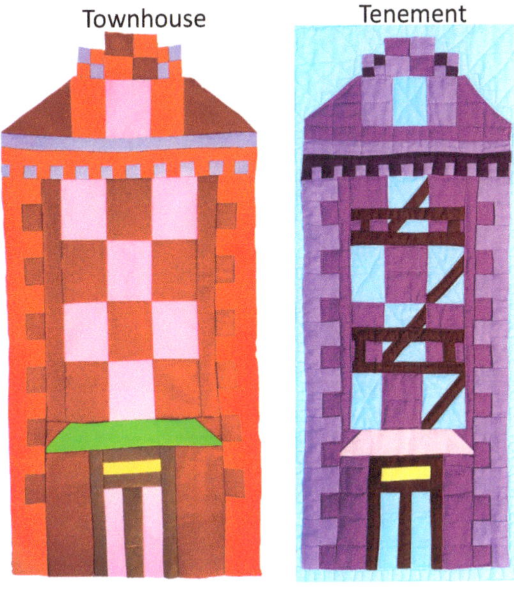

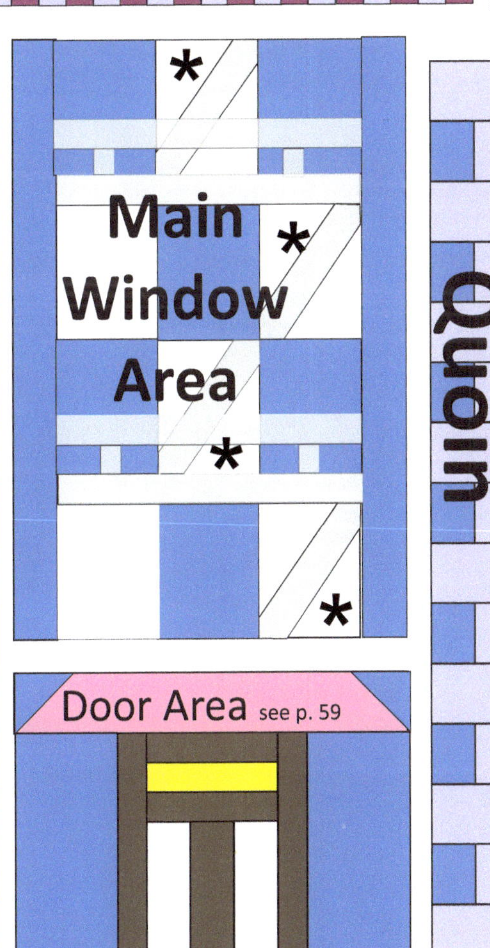

Townhouse or Tenement

Born in 1920s, my Dad and his brother were raised in a rundown Brooklyn tenement. In my memory, it looked like the building on the near left (but it wasn't purple). His mother, an immigrant from Poland abandoned by her husband, sewed purses in a sweatshop. She continued to live in their one-room apartment well into the 1960s, even after Dad moved us to a quiet, green Boston suburb. When we visited her, I envied the vibrant street life, and longed to play on the jungle-gym fire escapes, which, to my frustration, my parents forbade.

The fire escape is optional – leave it off, as on the far left, and you have a fancy Manhattan townhouse! Designing this, I learned that brickwork in building corners has a name – it's a "QUOIN"! Quilters also have a name for this type of piecing: Seminole Patchwork (named after clothing embellishments of Native Americans who lived in Florida, not New York).

In the 'Color Block New York' quilt, this project is interchangeable with the Flatiron building – pick one. They have similar dimensions.

***** Fire escape windows. Directions will take you to p. 64 if you want a fire escape.

Inspired by Townhouses and Tenements

Finished size with fire escape approx. 8.5" x 20.5"
No fire escape approx. 9.5" X 19.5"

Fabric

Main window fabric. Fat-eighth.

Dark main building material. Fat-quarter or quarter-yard.

Light main building material. Fat-quarter or quarter-yard.

Darkest fabric. For door and optional fire escape. Door requires 16" total of 1" strips, plus 3.5" of 1.25" wide strips. Fire escape needs a fat-eighth, fat-quarter, or one 2.5" x 44" strip.

Top trim accent color. Two 11" x 1" strips.

Door's window. A small scrap.

Door's awning. A strip 7.5" x 1.5".

Background rectangle for Color Block quilt only. Cut 10.5" x 22". A fat-quarter is just enough for a background AND windows in this color.

(continued)

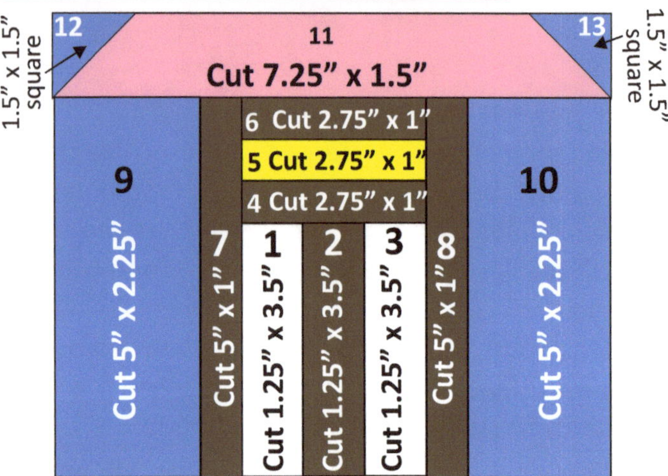

1 Cut door area pieces. There are 5 different fabrics.

From medium-dark building fabric, cut:
– Two strips 5" x 2.25" (pieces 9 and 10).
– Two squares, 1.5" x 1.5" (pieces 12 and 13 in upper corners).

From dark/door fabric, cut:
– One strip 1.25" x 3.5" (center strip 2).
– Two strips 2.75" x 1" (over-the-door pieces 4 and 6).
– Two strips 5" x 1" (side strips 7 and 8).

From main window fabric, cut two strips 1.25" x 3.5" (pieces 1-3).

From door top window fabric, cut one strip 2.75" x 1" (piece 5).

From awning fabric, cut one strip, 7.25" x 1.5 (piece 11).

2 Sew window glass pieces 1 and 3 to both sides of piece 2. Press seam allowances to center.

3 Sew pieces 4 and 6, darkest door color, to top and bottom of strip 5. Press seam allowances outward from piece 5.

4 Sew unit 456 on top of unit 123. Press seam allowances up.

5 Sew dark door strip pieces 7 and 8 to both sides of the unit. Press seam allowances outward.

6 Sew pieces 9 and 10 to both sides of the door. Press seam allowances any way!

7 Press the 1.5" squares in half diagonally.

8 Sew one to each side of the awning/piece 11, stitching on fold lines.

9 Press upwards. Then press the back flaps down to give the awning a lift over the building.

10 Sew strip 11 to the top of the doorway.

Create Main Window Area

11 Cut the six dark and light rectangles in this area:

► No fire escape: Cut all 12 to 2.25" x 2.75". Go to step 12.

► ✱ Yes fire escape: Cut all dark and two light rectangles the same as above (2.25" x 2.75"). Cut four light rectangles to 2.5" x 3". Then complete the box on p. 64. After those steps, you'll be sent back here.

Col. 1	Col. 2	Col. 3
	Fire escape cut: 2.5" x 3" ✱	
		Fire escape cut: 2.5" x 3" ✱
	Fire escape cut: 2.5" x 3" ✱	
		Fire escape cut: 2.5" x 3" ✱

12 Arrange the rectangles as above. Sew together. Here's my chain-sewing approach:

► Start on upper left and flip the top column 2 piece onto the top piece of column 1. Sew.

► Without cutting threads, in the row below, flip column 2 piece onto its column 1 piece. Repeat for rows 3 and 4. Cut only the last threads after sewing off the bottom.

► Start again at the top of column 2. Flip the column 3 pieces on top of the column 2 pieces and sew to the end. Repeat this procedure until all rows are complete.

► Without cutting threads, press seam allowances AWAY from window glass to give the building area a lift.

► Sew horizontal seams, matching and pinning at intersections. I press all three horizontal seam allowances down – but up or down, they'll wind up behind windows. (You can press these seams open if you prefer.)

13 Measure unit's height. With NO fire escape it should be around 9.5". With fire escape, it will be approx. 11".

14 Cut two dark building material strips to 1.25" x measured height. Attach to right and left sides and press seam allowances under the new strips.

15 Sew window unit to the top of the doorway. Press seam allowances down to lift the awning.

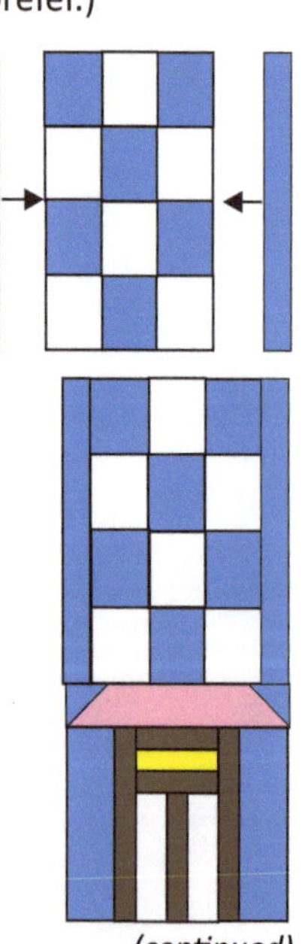

(continued)

16 Cut one light and one dark building strip 1.25" x 22" or 26". If you're starting with yardage longer than a fat-quarter, cut the strips 26".

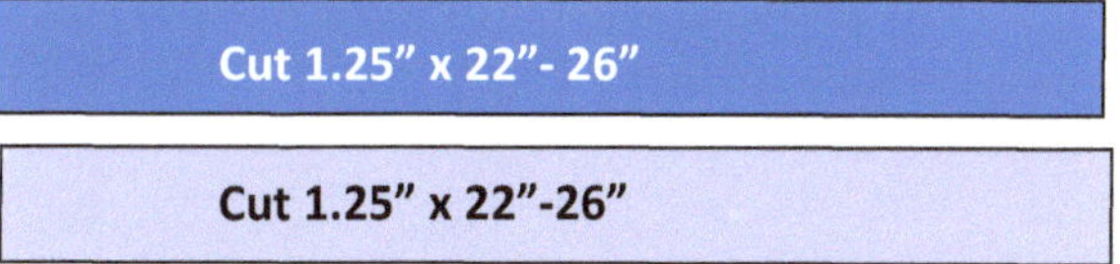

Cut another light building strip, but this one a little wider, 2" x 22". (You don't need to go up to 26".)

17 Sew the narrow strips together, and press seam allowances to the **light** side. (Lighter "bricks" will be on the building's corners, and we want to give them a lift.)

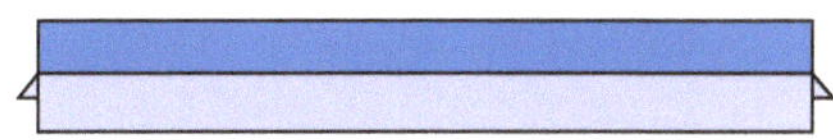

18 Cut the narrow strip unit into at least fourteen 1.5" wide pieces. If you can cut a couple of extras (because you had 26" strips), do so. We'll use them later in the gable.

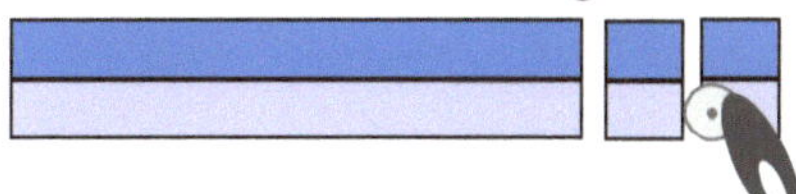

19 Cut the wider light strip apart at 1.5" intervals. Cut fourteen pieces, each 1.5" x 2".

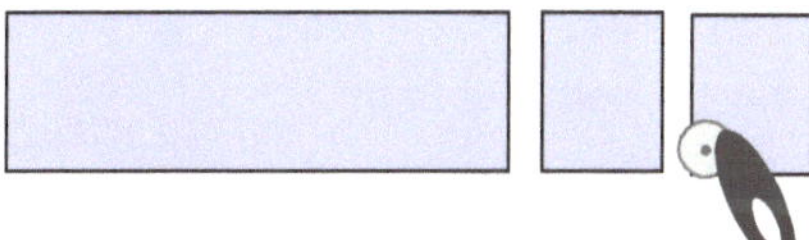

20 Lay out in two rows as below, alternating pairs with one-fabric pieces. These are your two quoins! The difference between the two sides is the position of the dark pieces.

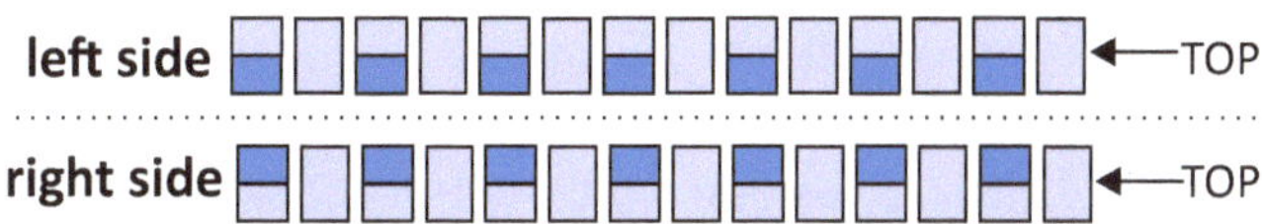

You may have your own method for this situation - go for it. I sew rows separately, to avoid confusing myself (though if I do flip a piece the wrong way, it will be charming!)

21 First let's chain-sew the top row only - the future left quoin. Start by joining pieces in pairs. On the far right, flip piece 1 on top of 2 (checking to make sure 2's dark end is closer to you).

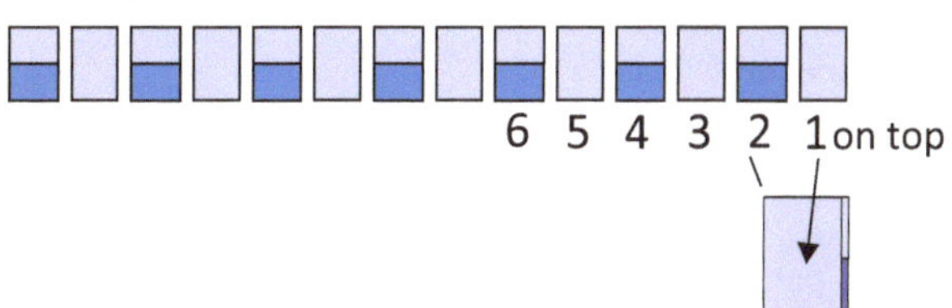

22 Sew the pair together. Don't cut threads, and flip 3 on top of 4, again checking that the dark side of piece 4 is closer to you. Keep going until you have 7 pairs.

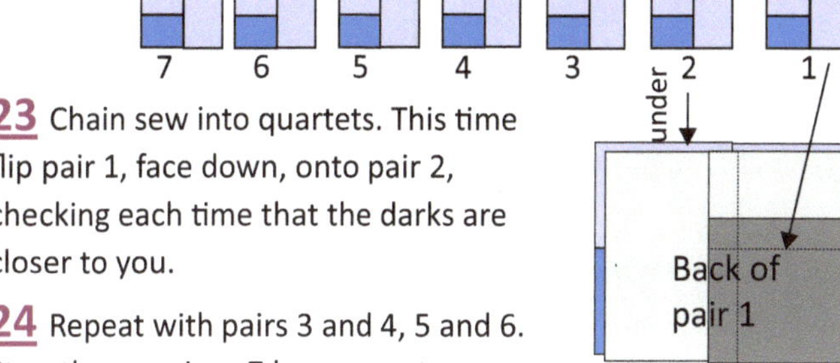

Press now or wait. If you do it now, press seam allowances underneath the lighter pieces to lift those "bricks." Cut apart and lay out again.

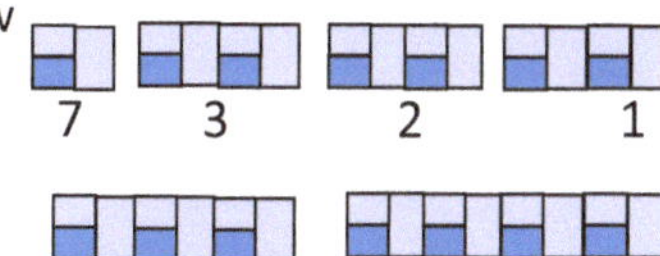

23 Chain sew into quartets. This time flip pair 1, face down, onto pair 2, checking each time that the darks are closer to you.

24 Repeat with pairs 3 and 4, 5 and 6. Stop there – piece 7 has no partner.

25 Cut threads and chain sew to join quartet 1 to 2, and quartet 3 to lonely pair 7.

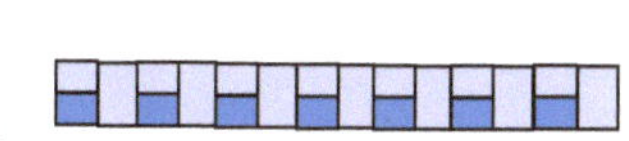

26 Join the two parts.

27 Press seam allowances outward from the 2-color pieces.

28 Do it all over again with the RIGHT quoin. This time, when feeding pieces into the machine, all the darker pieces will be at the *far* end, away from you.

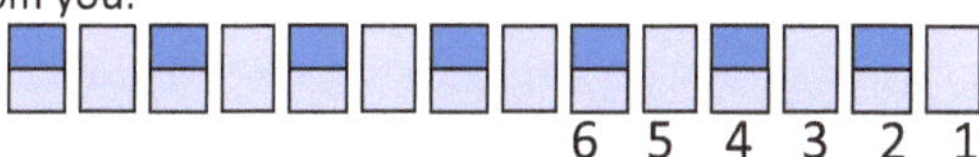

29 Press seam allowances outward from each two-color unit.

30 Place a quoin on each side of the main unit, top edges aligned. On bottom of each quoin, measure how high a "cornerstone" must be to make the strip the same height as your main building.

Cut cornerstones to the 2" quoin width x the height you need PLUS 1/2" for seam allowance.
Yes fire escape: Cut cornerstones ~2" x 2".
No fire escape (shown): Cut cornerstones ~ 1.5" high x 2".

31 Sew cornerstones to the bottom of each quoin strip.

32 Pin and sew quoins to the main building with the back of the quoin facing up, so you can see and maintain seam allowance direction.

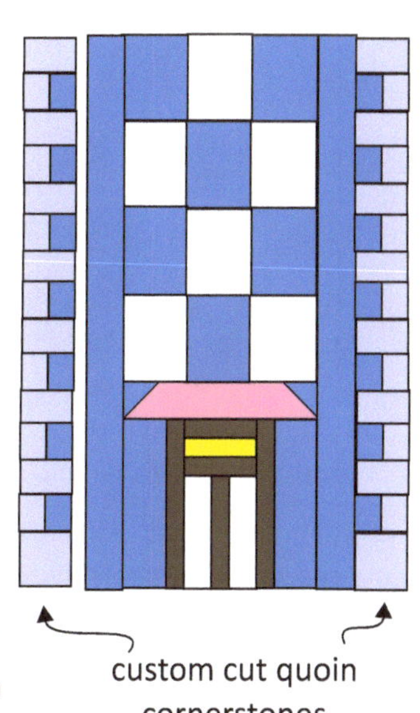

custom cut quoin cornerstones
(say that 5 times fast!)

(continued)

33 Measure the width of your unit so far, with quoins attached. It should be about 10", but use your number.

The top trim area requires four strips. The bottom two create the toothy area. And the top two, A and B are cut to the width of the building.

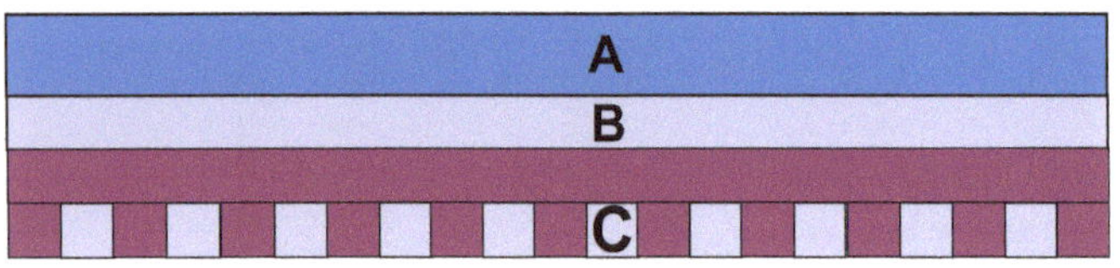

A From dark building fabric cut one piece 10" (or your measured building width) x 1.25".

B From lighter building fabric, cut one piece 10" (or your measured width) x 1".

same

C To piece area C, the checkered strip, cut one more light building strip much longer, to 22" x 1.

C From accent color, cut a strip 22" x 1".

34 The top trim looks like the quoins, but I made it a little differently. Both ways create the same toothy effect.

35 Sew the two 22" pieces together, and press seam allowances under the dark side.

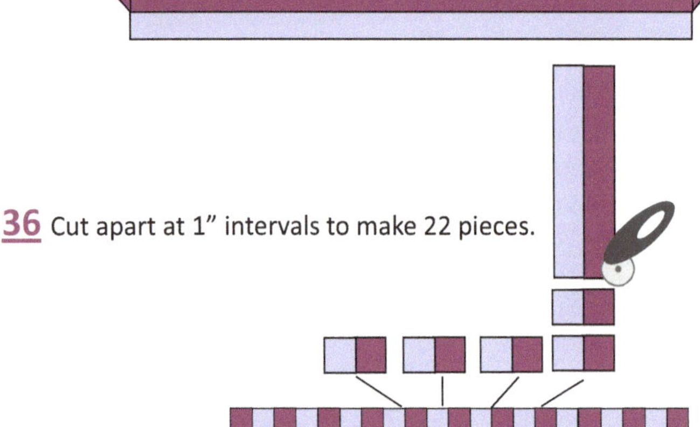

36 Cut apart at 1" intervals to make 22 pieces.

37 Stitch into pairs, then groups of four, eight, etc. When you approach 20 pieces, check length against your townhouse's width. It took me 20 tiny squares to reach 10". You may have to take off a piece, or make a few extra wide seam allowances, to get the right fit.

38 When length is right, sew the two solid strips to the top of the checkerboard strip. The darker "trim" strip goes directly on top of the checkered pieces to create the toothy effect (shown in the diagram on top of this page).

39 Press all seam allowances upward to give this trim an overhang over the top row of windows.

40 Cut 5 pieces:

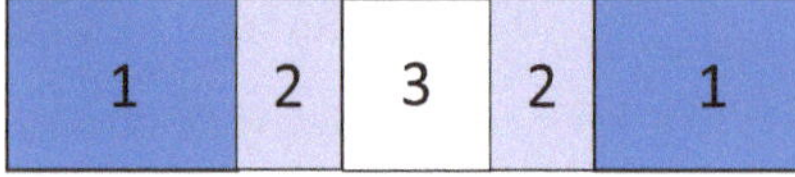

Two pieces 1, dark building fabric, 3.25" x 2.5".

Two pieces 2, light building fabric, 1.75" x 2.5".

One piece 3, window fabric, 2.25" x 2.5".

41 Stitch together. Press all seam allowances outward from central piece 3.

42 Make one mini-4 patch in quoin colors. If you had leftovers (from step 18), use them – sew two pairs together like this. If you need to cut new pieces, cut two lights and two darks each to 1.25" x 1.5" and sew as shown.

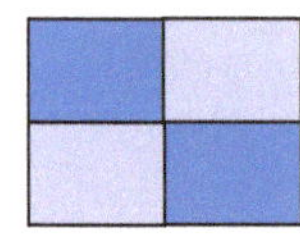

43 Make two more smaller 4-patches from the top trim colors. I used eight leftover 1" squares. For clarity in these diagrams, I'm coloring the darkest orange, and the lightest yellow. (Back sides will be shown in shades of grey.)

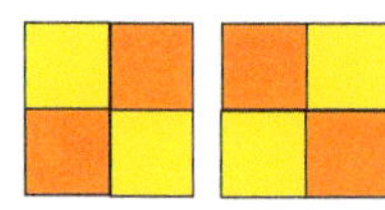

44 At the ironing board, arrange like this. On each shorter unit press top edge 1/4" to the back. A glue dab helps.

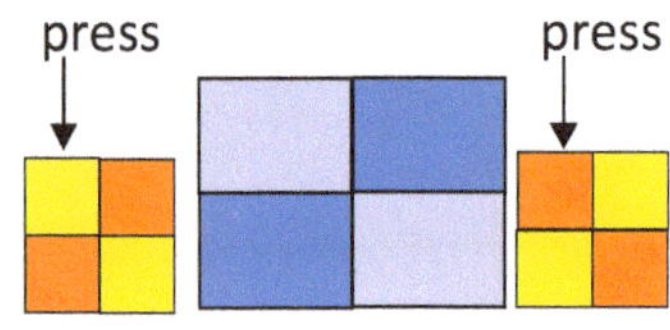

45 Place the right side checkerboard, face down, on the lower right edge of the central checkerboard (which is face up). Align bottom raw edges and right lower corner. Pin.

46 Pull up threads at the dot by the **a**, just below the flap. Backstitch up over the flap, sealing it. Stop at **b**, just before the fold. Sew straight down to the end at **c** - no need to backstitch there, because there's no flap there.

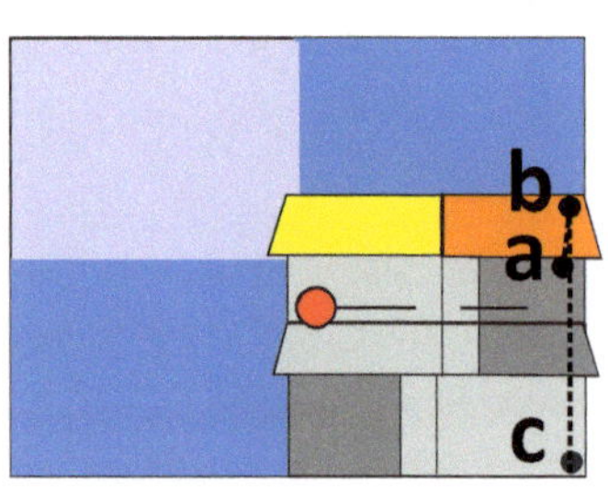

47 Press seam allowances left. Also press the extended seam allowance above the small four-patch 1/4" to the back. A swipe of glue helps hold it in place.

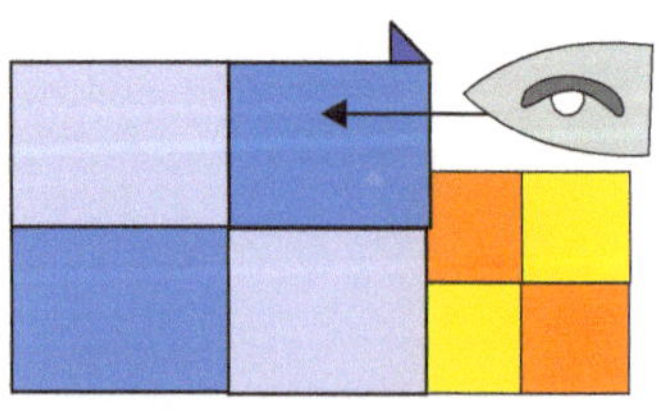

(continued)

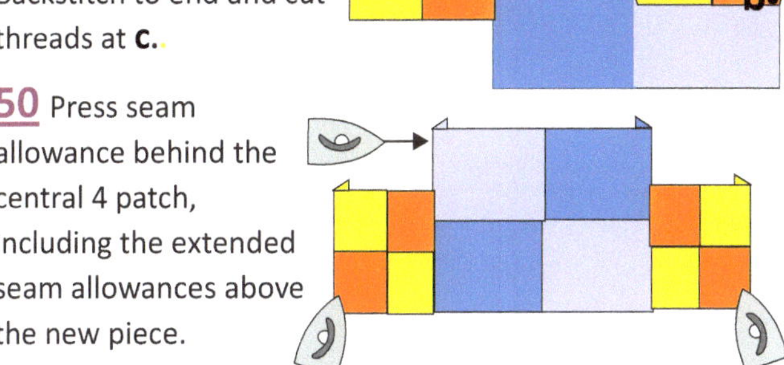

48 We'll do the same on the left side. Flip the second small four-patch, face down, onto the left raw edge of the central checkerboard (the latter is face up). Pin.

49 Rotate unit to put seam on the right. Start at **a**. There's no flap, so no need to backstitch there. Sew to **b**, just before the fold. Backstitch to end and cut threads at **c**.

50 Press seam allowance behind the central 4 patch, including the extended seam allowances above the new piece.

51 Press the two vertical outer edges of the small 4-patches 1/4" inch to the back. They may need glue.

52 Lay out main gable unit from step 41, face up.

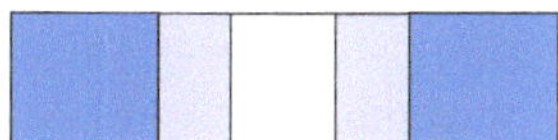

53 Flip checkerboard unit on top of it, face down, and align top raw edges. Center the checkerboard unit (with same amount of fabric sticking out from underneath on right and left). Pin.

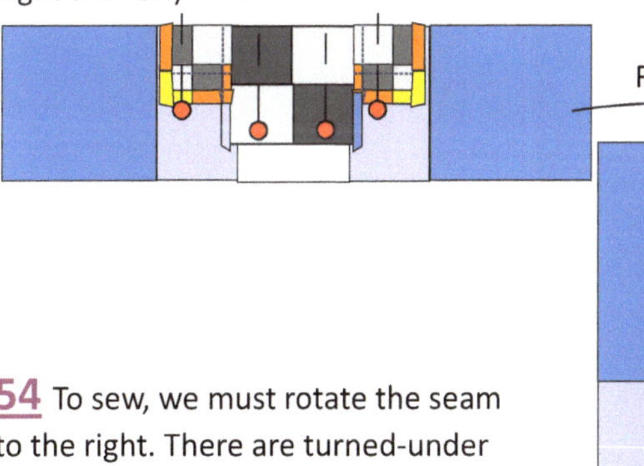

54 To sew, we must rotate the seam to the right. There are turned-under flaps on both ends, so we'll backstitch at both ends.

Pull up threads at **a**. Backstitch to **b**. Sew straight down to **c**, stopping at the fold. Backstitch to **d**. Cut threads.

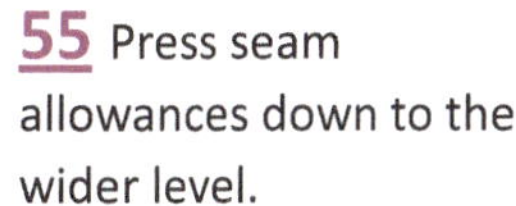
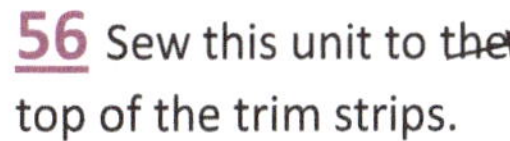
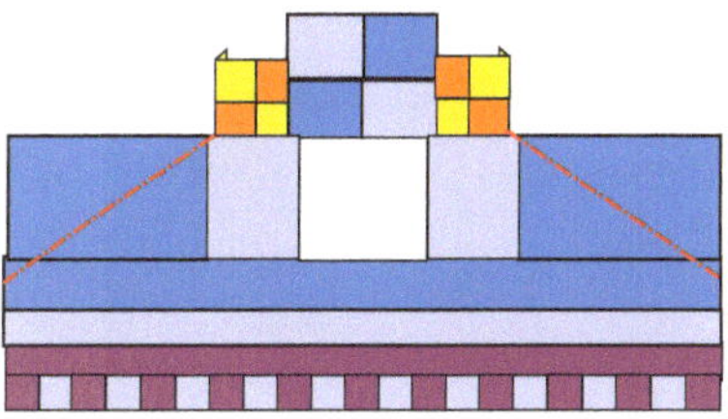

55 Press seam allowances down to the wider level.

56 Sew this unit to the top of the trim strips.

57 Press the two large side rectangles back on the diagonal red lines. Include a little corner of the first strip underneath.

58 The large rectangles' seam allowances will wrap themselves around the bases of the small 4-patches. Trim their back flaps to 1/4". Press back the central 4-patch's top raw edge.

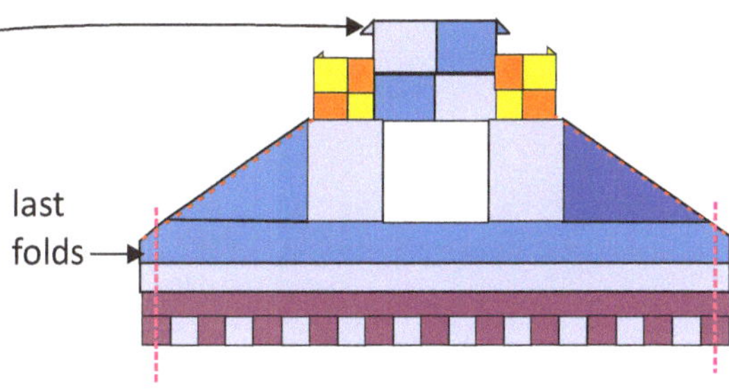

59 Above, the spot where the side meets the diagonal is marked "last folds." Fold here, along magenta lines. At the top, you'll press a flap *on top of* earlier flaps, as you press back the entire extended vertical left, then right sides.

For 'Condensed' quilt: No need to press bottom edges up. See next steps on p. 71.

For 'Color Block' quilt: Press bottom raw edge of building up 1/4". Audition backgrounds – it's light blue in the sample quilt. Cut background 10.5'" X 22". Place building's bottom fold 3/4" above the background's bottom raw edge. **Note:** You may need to turn side edges back a generous 3/8"-1/2" instead of 1/4". If it's still a very tight fit, wait until you've sewn all background pieces together before appliquéing this building in place. Next steps start on p. 76.

Quilting ideas: I stitched in the ditch inside the building. I quilted emanating lines on the background coming from it. In the purple version on p. 59, I quilted in a few horizontal lines suggesting bricks. I quilted "x"s into the full size windows.

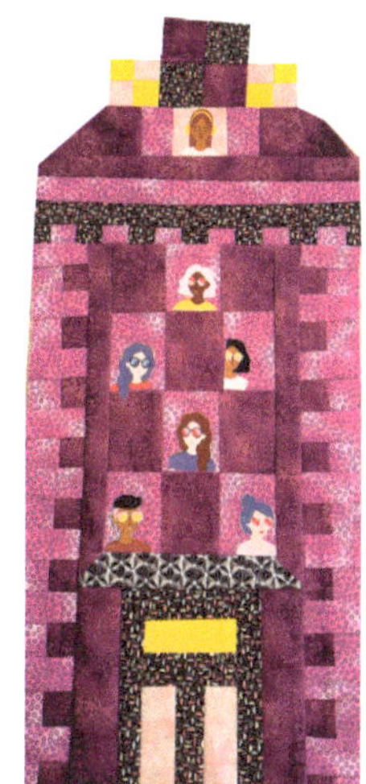

Quilt artist Flora Cohen put people in the windows!

(continued)

Do steps 1 - 11 on p. 60 first. Then do the following.

A Cut about 50" of 1" wide fire escape strips. These needn't be continuous.

B From those cut four 4.5" x 1" strips to become diagonals.

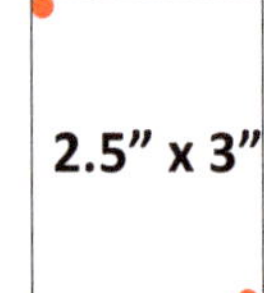

C For the 4 light windows cut extra-large in step 11: Mark a dot in upper left and lower right corners so you don't flip a piece wrong.

D Cut corner to corner, so you have two half-rectangles, numbered here.

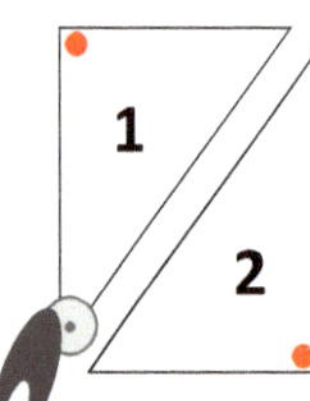

E On each half, press 1/4" under along the diagonal edge. Since it's on the bias, the fold will fight you, but perfection is not mandatory!

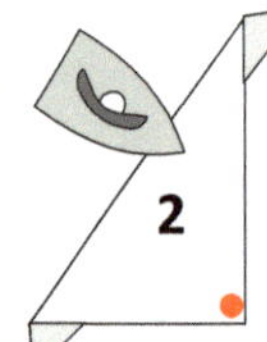

F Center piece 1, face down, along one edge of a 4.5" strip, good sides together. Match and pin top raw edges. Sew along the 1/4" crease.

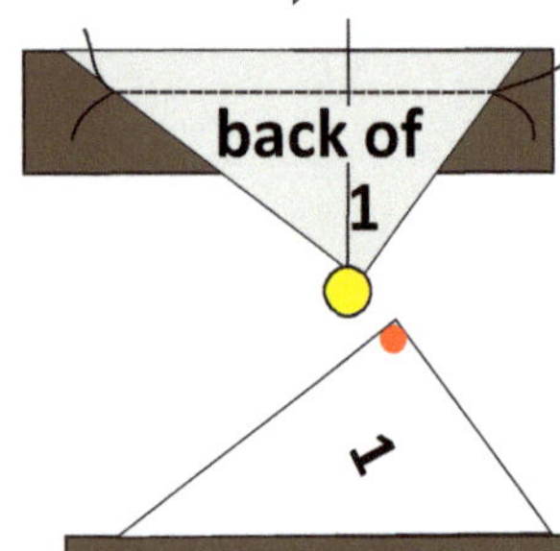

G Open. Press seam allowance down behind the strip.

H Hold second piece over the strip and figure out exactly where it should go to complete the rectangle.

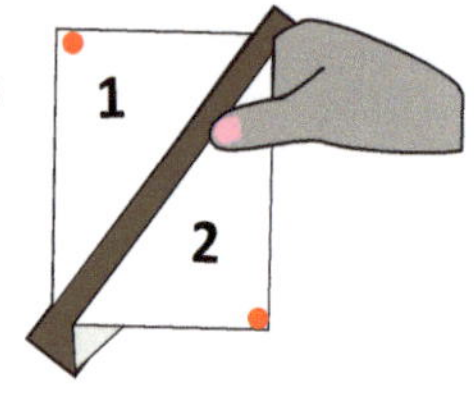

I Holding the two seam allowances in that position, pin the back of piece 2.

J Sew, then press seam allowance under the fire escape strip.

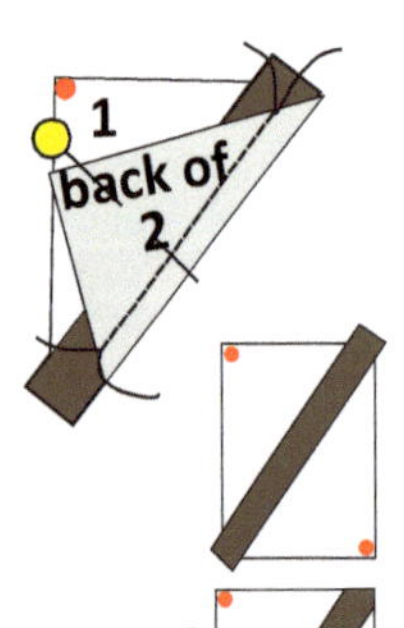

K Do steps C-J for all four windows.

L Use a rotary setup to trim all to 2.25" x 2.75".

M Stitch two of these blocks between two dark building rectangles. Measure both units' width. They should average 7.25" (but if not, use *your* measurement).

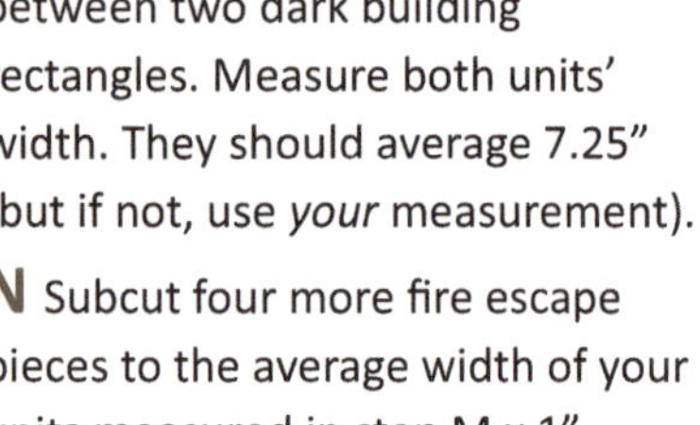
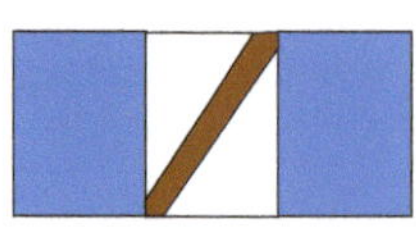

N Subcut four more fire escape pieces to the average width of your units measured in step M x 1".

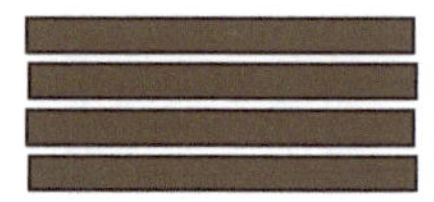

O On one of the units: Cut across 1.25" above the bottom edge.

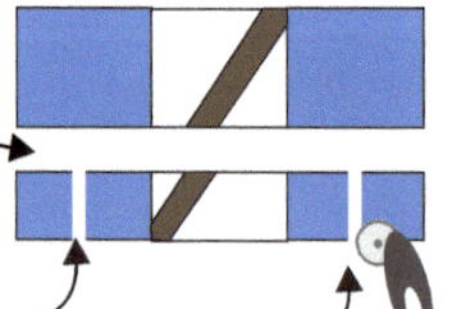

P Make short cuts up the middle of each of the 2 bottom dark rectangles.

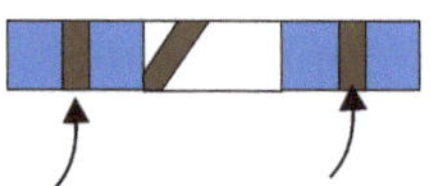

Q From Step A strips, cut four 1.25" x 1" pieces. Sew one into each short side cuts. (You'll use the remaining two in step T below).

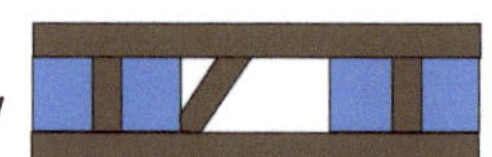

R Sew one of the four fire escape strips cut in N to the unit's top. Sew another to its bottom edge.

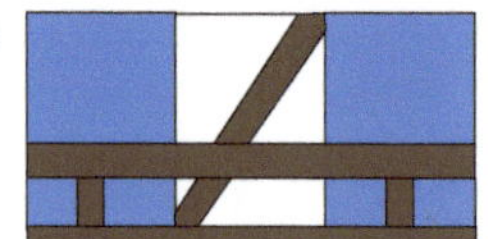

S Sew the top area (cut off in step O) to the highest horizontal fire escape strip. Press all seam allowances to the fire escape.

T Repeat steps O-S with your second unit from Step M.

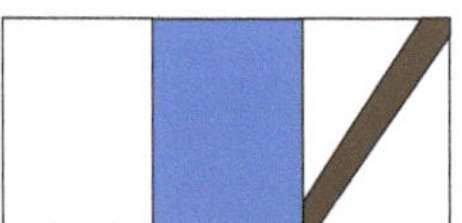

U Use the last two slashed rectangles and a dark and light regular-size rectangles (2.25" x 2.75") to create two rows like this.

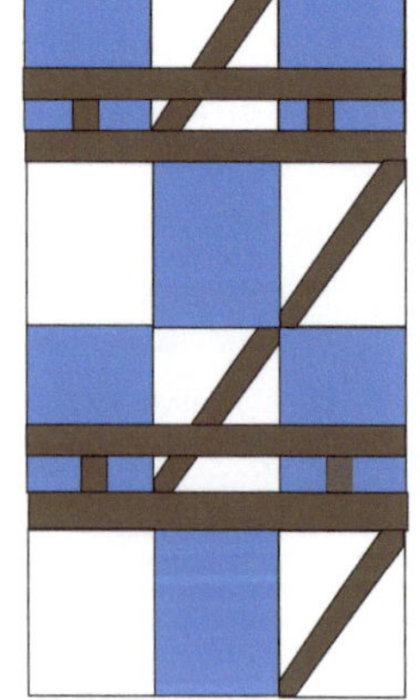

V Stack the four rows, alternating the two different kinds. Sew together. Press seam allowances under the fire escapes when possible. Press remaining seams down.

W Go back to do step 13 on p. 60. Continue from there.

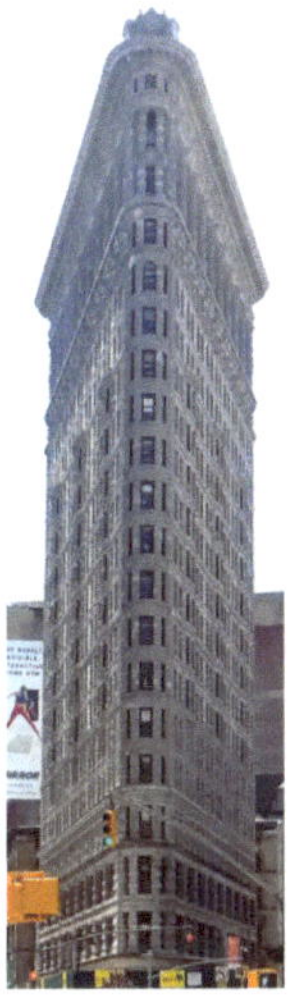

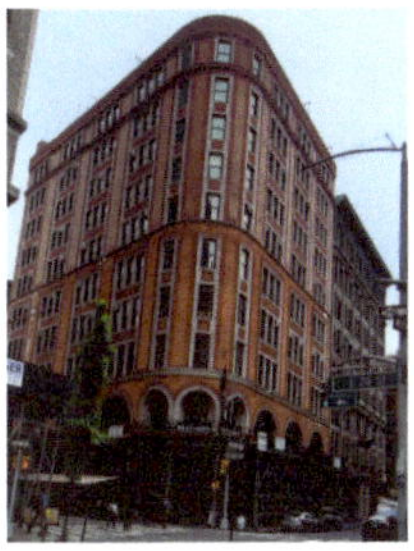

Left, Flatiron. Above, a nearby triangular building (at 20th and Broadway in NYC.)

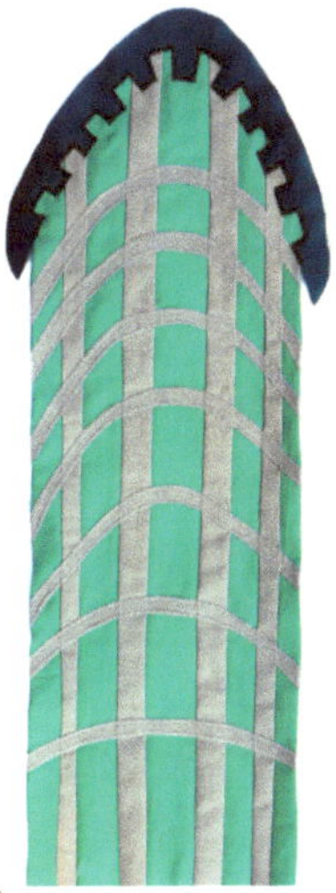

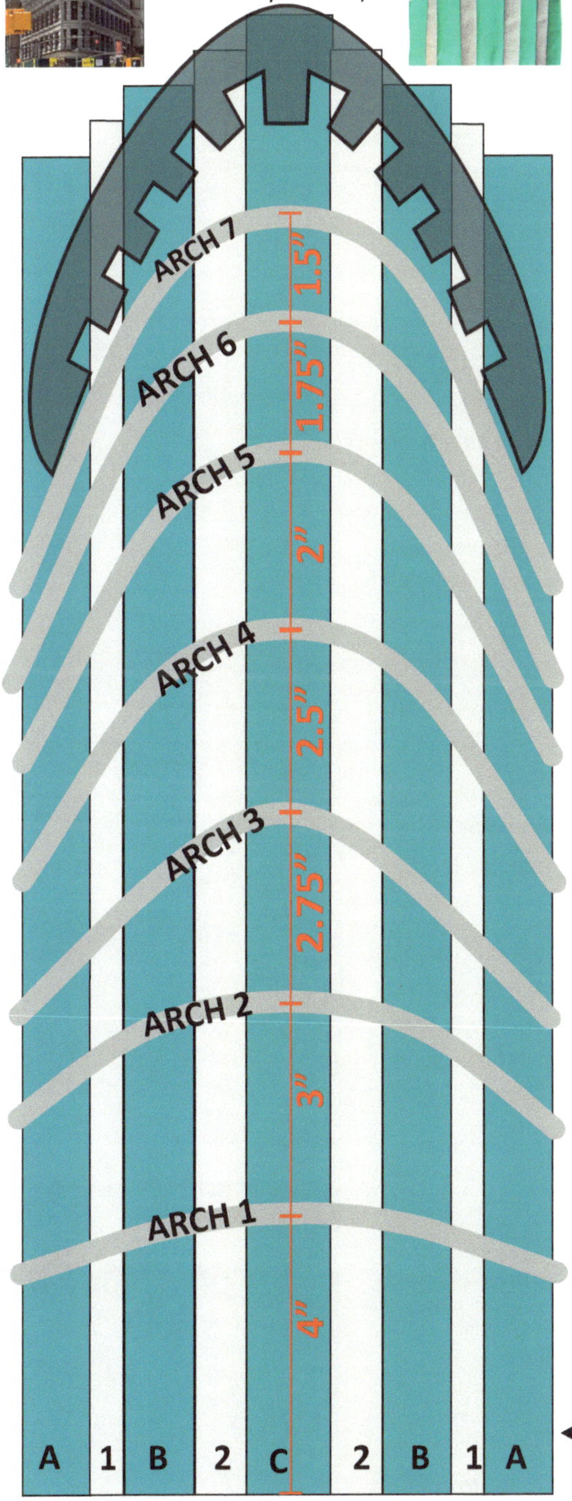

Arch and Roof
Placement Diagram

The Flatiron Building

The 1902 Flatiron Building was built in the elaborate Beaux-Arts style, modeled after French and Italian Renaissance palaces. The shape is a modified triangle, with three main sides and a narrow curved column of windows facing forward. Its name doesn't come from the resemblance to a clothing iron – the district was nicknamed Flatiron before it was built. I wish my iron resembled this gorgeous building! It reminds me of an ornate slice of wedding cake.

There are many, many triangle-ish buildings all over the world – the 2nd photo on the left shows another one – so this approach may be useful for creating a building nearer to you!

Start with pieced vertical stripes, alternating grey and green. Crosswise, the curved grey floor separation arches are done with fusible web. So is the roof's toothy underside. You can do this with just three fabrics (minimum).

This structure is not in my Color Block quilt on p. 76, but it could be - it's about the same size as the "Tenement/Townhouse." Choose one to put in that spot.

Inspired by the Flatiron (and other triangular buildings)

Finished size: Approx. 8" x 20.5"

Fabric

Windows. A fat-quarter or quarter-yard.

Roof. An 8" x 8" piece (or larger).

Light stone verticals. A fat-quarter or quarter-yard.

Arched floor separations. An 8.5" x 11" piece. (Use the same grey as above or a different one. I used the same one.)

Background rectangle 10.5" x 22". For Color Block quilt, p. 76. A fat-quarter or half-yard. This building is not on the Color Block quilt shown in this book.

Other supplies
► Paper backed fusible web, two pieces, about 8.5" x 11" each.
► Appliqué press sheet or parchment paper.

This is not a licensed product. I am not affiliated or associated with any buildings depicted in these quilts.

(continued)

1 Cut strips and lay out as shown below – upside-down! We sew them this way because this end needs to be in a straight line. It creates a half-inch offset at the opposite end.

*SHADING OPTION: For stronger perspective, make the strips on one side darker than the other. The middle piece C can be a middle shade, or the same as either side. If you do this, remember that in this first step because the building is **upside down**, the strips you place on the right will wind up on the left when the building **isn't** upside-down!*

Cutting directions

From green/window color:

Pieces A: cut two, 19.5" x 1.25".

Pieces B: cut two, 20.5" x 1.5".

Piece C: cut one, 21.5" x 1.75".

From grey/building color:

Pieces 1: Cut two, 20" x 1"

Pieces 2: Cut two, 21" x 1.25"

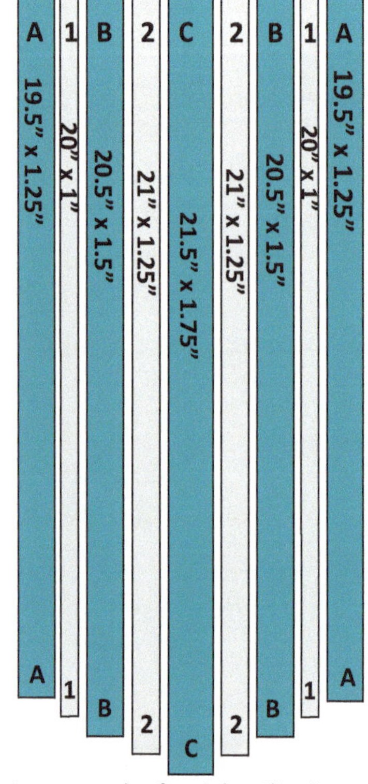

2 Chain sew strips into pairs. I start on the **far right**. Flip the first **A** face down, onto **1**; match top and right edges. Pin and sew to the end of **A**. Without cutting threads, pull first pair back, flip **B** onto **2**, match edges, and stitch.

It's trickier when you reach **C** , because it's longer than the one on bottom, the left **2**. Try to stop where the hidden **2** stops - but if you sew beyond it, no problem – this end will eventually be hidden by the roof or cut off!

Finish the round by sewing the furthest left **B** to its neighbor **1**. There's a leftover piece A. Leave it on the table.

3 Bring everything else to the ironing board – still attached by threads – and do a quick press. I press toward the building material strips (grey), and away from the window strips, to give the building a lift over the windows.

4 Cut threads and again lay strips in order, base up.

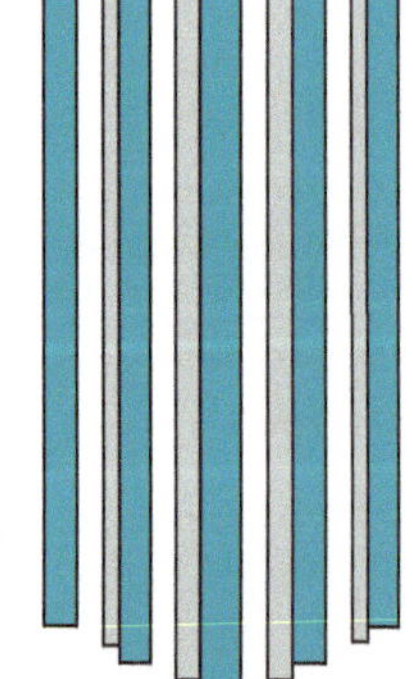

5 Join pairs into two groups of four. Press and cut apart. Join the two groups into one group of 8. Add the last **A** strip to the far side.

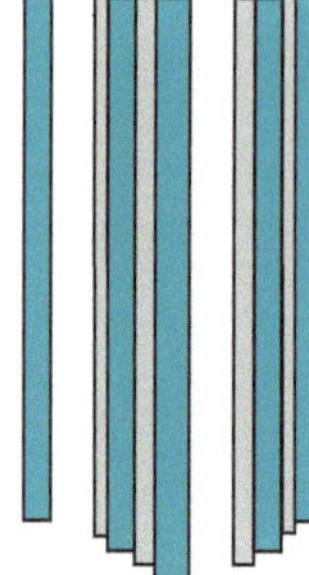

The Fused Elements

7 Trace or print out pp. 69-70. If printing, do the red box size check.

8 For arches: cut paper-backed fusible to approx. 8.5" x 11". Tape printout to a window or light box, and on top, place web, paper side facing you. Trace outline of each arch and write its number on it.

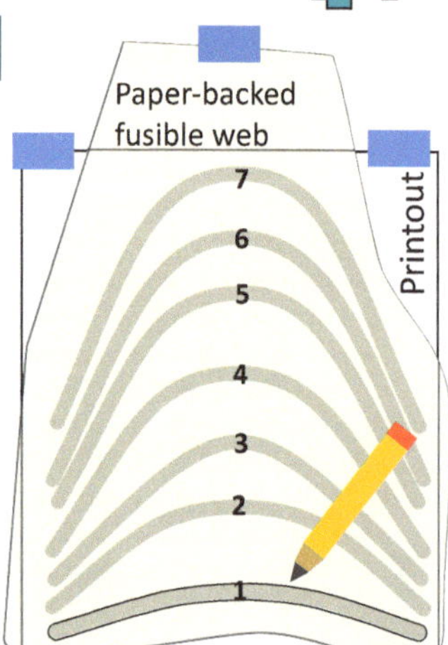

9 You need a similar amount of fusible to cover the roof. Again, tape the printout to a window or light box and trace the outline onto the paper side of the fusible.

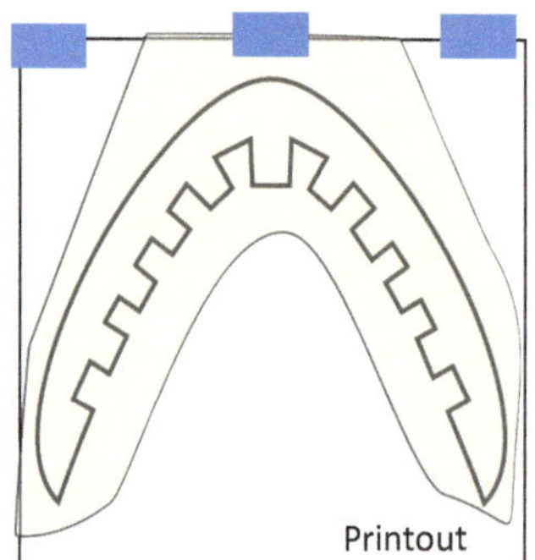

10 Press the fusible arch grouping to the back of building fabric.

11 Cut out each arch through the paper and fabric at the same time. **Don't peel the paper yet!**

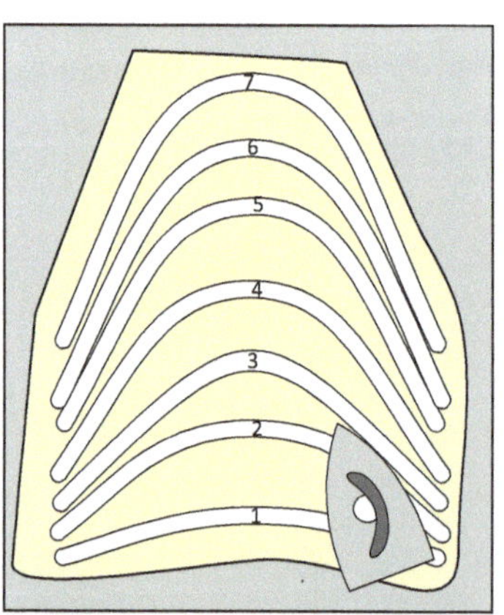

12 Press fusible web roof pattern to the back of roof fabric.

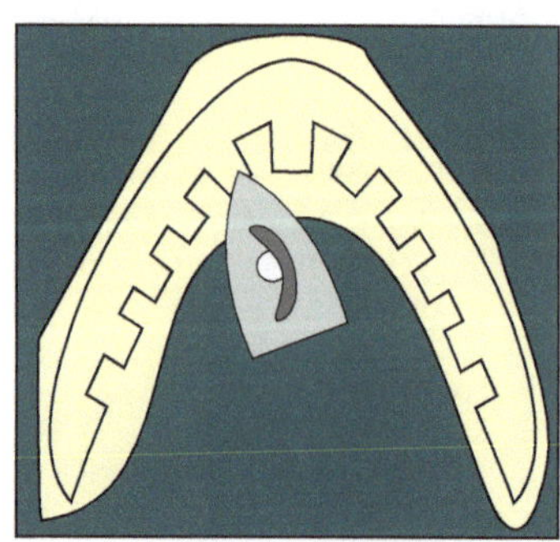

(continued)

13 At the ironing board, lay building on an appliqué press sheet. Follow the red distances in the diagram on p. 65.

14 Start at the center base (piece **C**) and measure 4" up. Peel paper from arch 1 and center it there. Measure 3" up from the middle of arch 1. Peel and lay arch 2 so its middle is on the 3" line. Continue for the distances in the diagram. **Exact measurements are NOT as important as placing arches a bit closer together as they rise!**

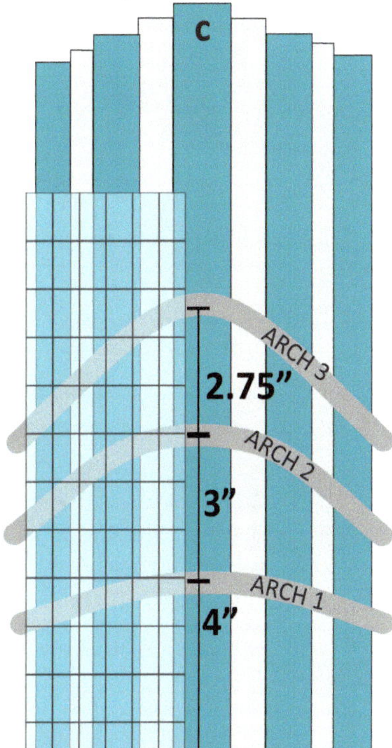

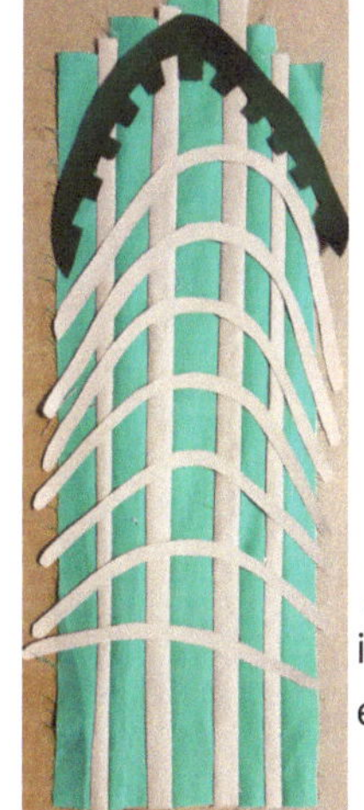

15 Place roof on top, just to get the idea of where it will go. Adjust elements as desired.

16 Remove roof for now and press each arch permanently in position.

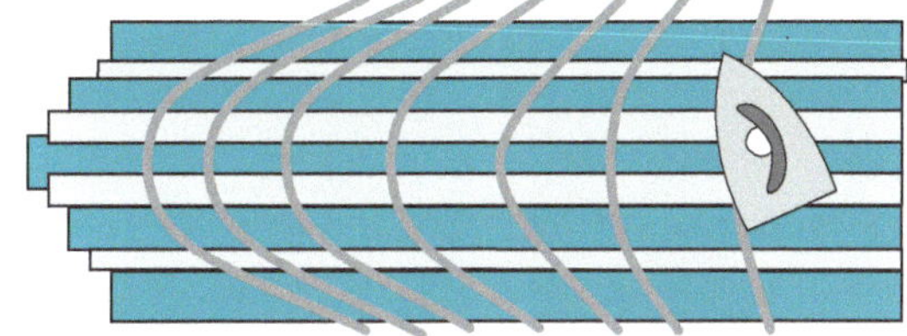

17 Trim excess from arch ends with scissors or a rotary cutter and ruler.

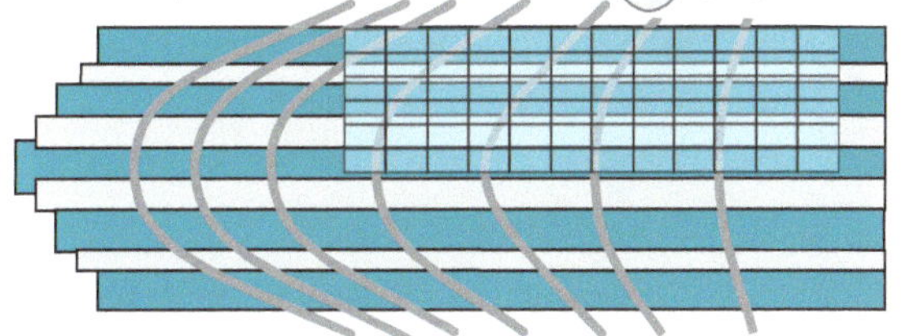

18 Press each long side to the back 1/4" (on red dotted lines). But don't glue the flaps – if you later decide to piece the sides to other buildings, you may want to unfold the lower part.

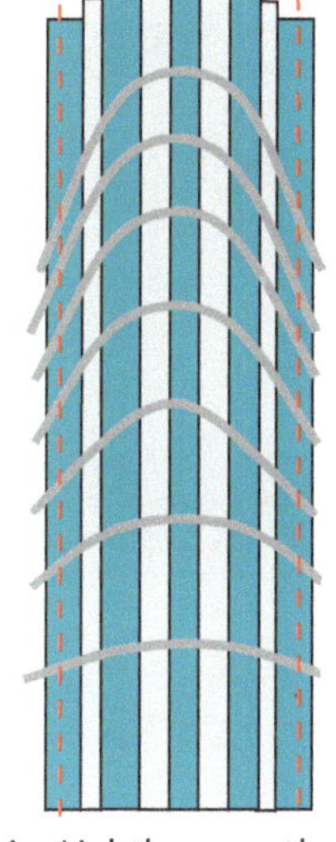

19 Replace the roof again. Lightly press the teeth inside the roof and a bit beyond, but don't press the roof's upper edge.

20 Holding the outer roof arch forward, trim away building strips that show beyond the roof's upper edge. Do a little at a time. In the second photo, all the extra fabric is neatly trimmed. Ideally, a little of the fusible along the top edge should be exposed.

21 Press well on an appliqué press sheet to fuse permanently.

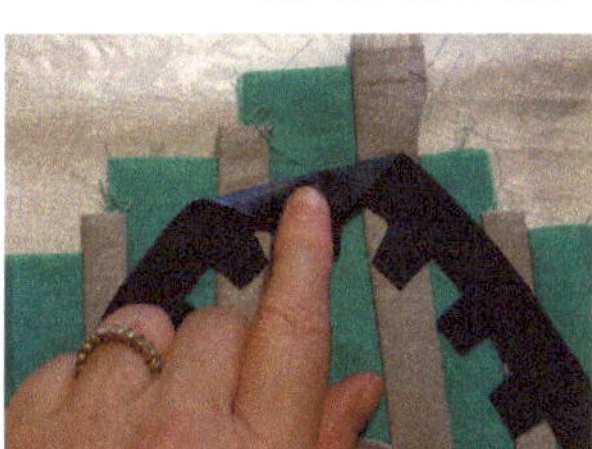

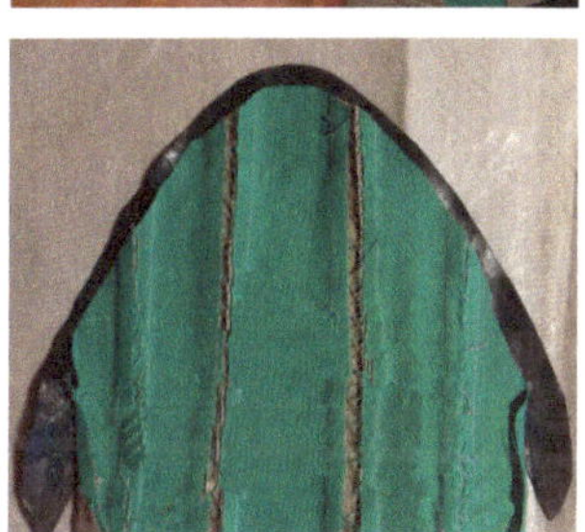

Stitch the Fused Elements

22 Appliqué the arches. (First do a tension test on a sample to see if you need stabilizer - see pp. 5-6.) I used a fairly tight zigzag to cover the raw edges. I used the same grey thread along both top and bottom edges. Alternative: to create a shadowed effect, I could have used dark thread along each arch's bottom edge, and lighter thread along its top edge.

When you stop on an inward curve, your needle should swing **in** and stop **inside** the appliquéd arch. Then lift presser foot and swivel. When you stop on an arch's outward curve, plant the needle OUTSIDE the appliqué and swivel. This principle is explained in more detail on the next page.

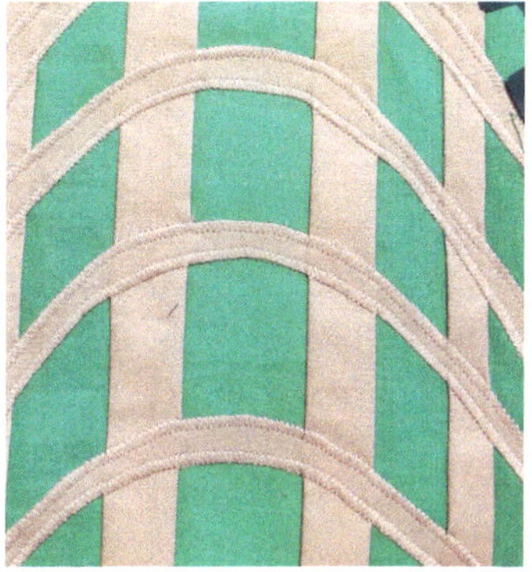

(continued)

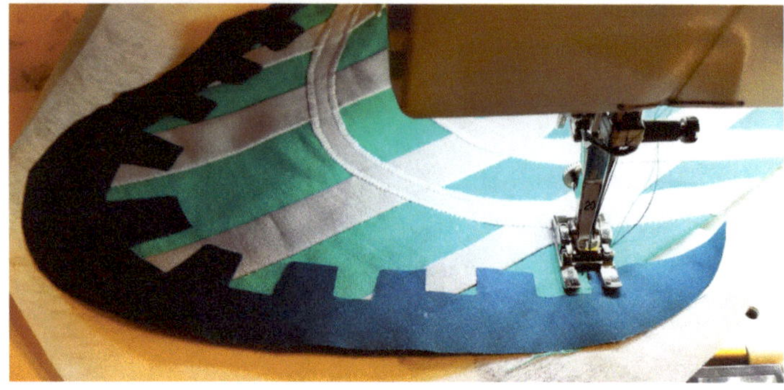

23 Stitch the roof's inner roof edge. Try the suggestions on p. 5-6, doing a tension test, and checking whether you need a stabilizer. I use a relatively tight zigzag here again, to cover the raw edges. I use thread that matches the roof color.

The thread in the diagram below changes with each direction change, but don't try this at home! It's just for clarity, so you can see which stitch lands where!

Start at **1** with a few back-and-forth straight stitches.

Zigzag to **2**, into the yellow dot. I call this convex roof corner an "OUTIE". So I plant the needle OUTSIDE the roof appliqué and into the "background" (which in this case is the building fabric), JUST beyond the roof's corner.

Swivel at **2** and sew towards **3**, one of the roof's concave "INNIEs". Stop with needle down, a smidge INSIDE the "INNIE" corner, IN the blue dot. Stop and swivel towards blue dot **4**.

Sew to **4**, and because it's another of the roof's concave "INNIE" corners, plant needle INSIDE the roof at 4 in the blue dot. Swivel.

Continue like this. All blue points are "innies" — land, plant, and swivel INSIDE them, INSIDE the appliquéd roof. All yellow dots are "outies," so land OUTSIDE the roof (ie on the building). End with a few back-and-forth straight stitches at the opposite end of the roof.

For 'Condensed' quilt: No need to press the bottom edge of the building up. Once you've sewn this building into its row, you can fuse the roof to whatever is behind it. Then use the same stitch as in step 23 to cover the remaining raw edges of the roof. See next steps on p. 71.

For 'Color Block' quilt: Audition backgrounds. My Color Block quilt doesn't have this building, so you're on your own in choosing a background! Place this building in the position of the townhouse/tenement in the sample quilt, on the lower row. Background measures 10.5" x 22". The fit is a little tight, so you may have to fold this building's bottom edge up a bit more. Appliqué all turned edges and bottom in place, then switch to the stitch you used in step 23 to cover remaining raw roof edges.

Quilting Ideas I stitched in the ditch, around all the arches and main building lines, as well as just under the roof.

(continued)

Flatiron Arch Pattern
for arches 1-5
Full size

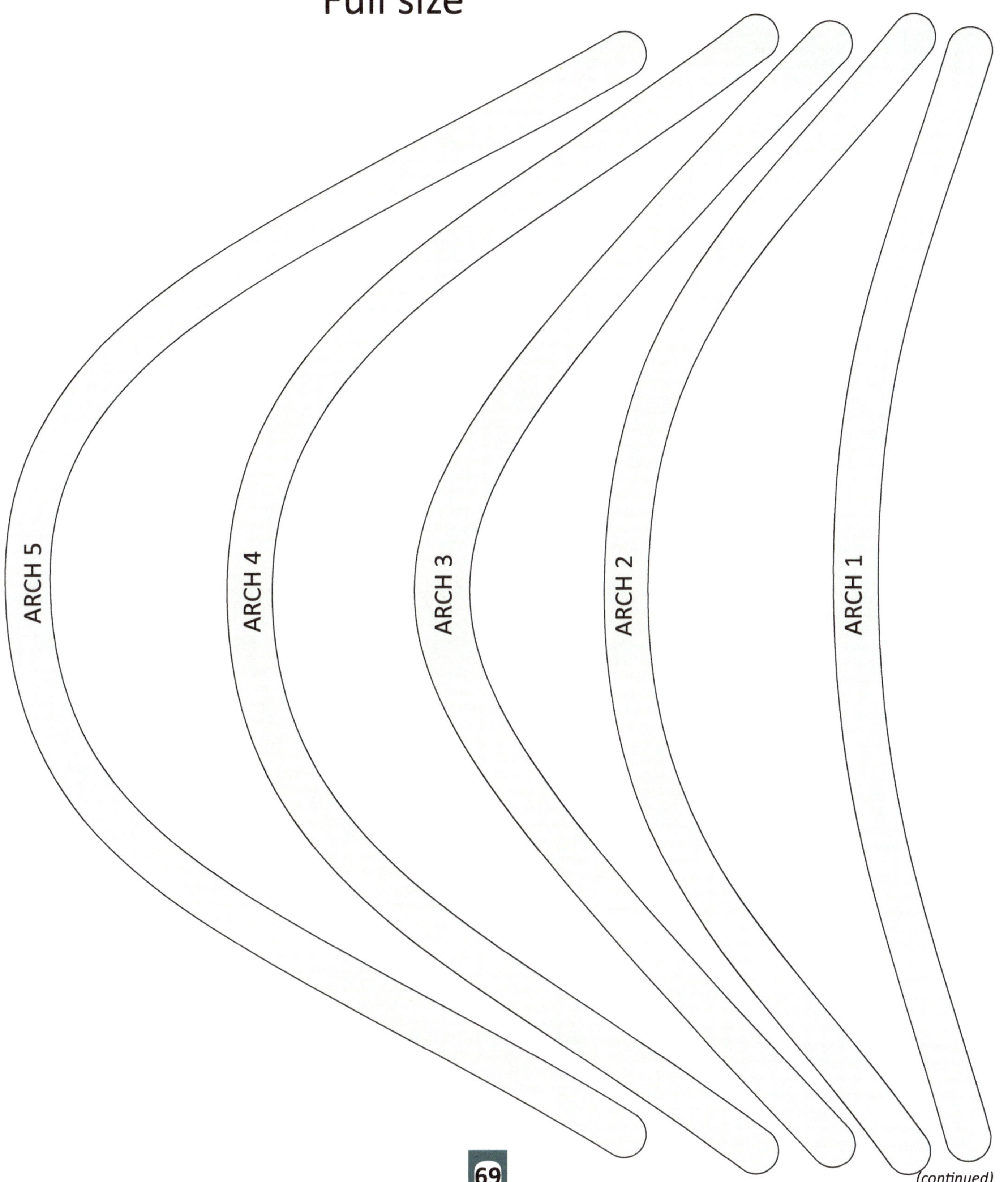

69

(continued)

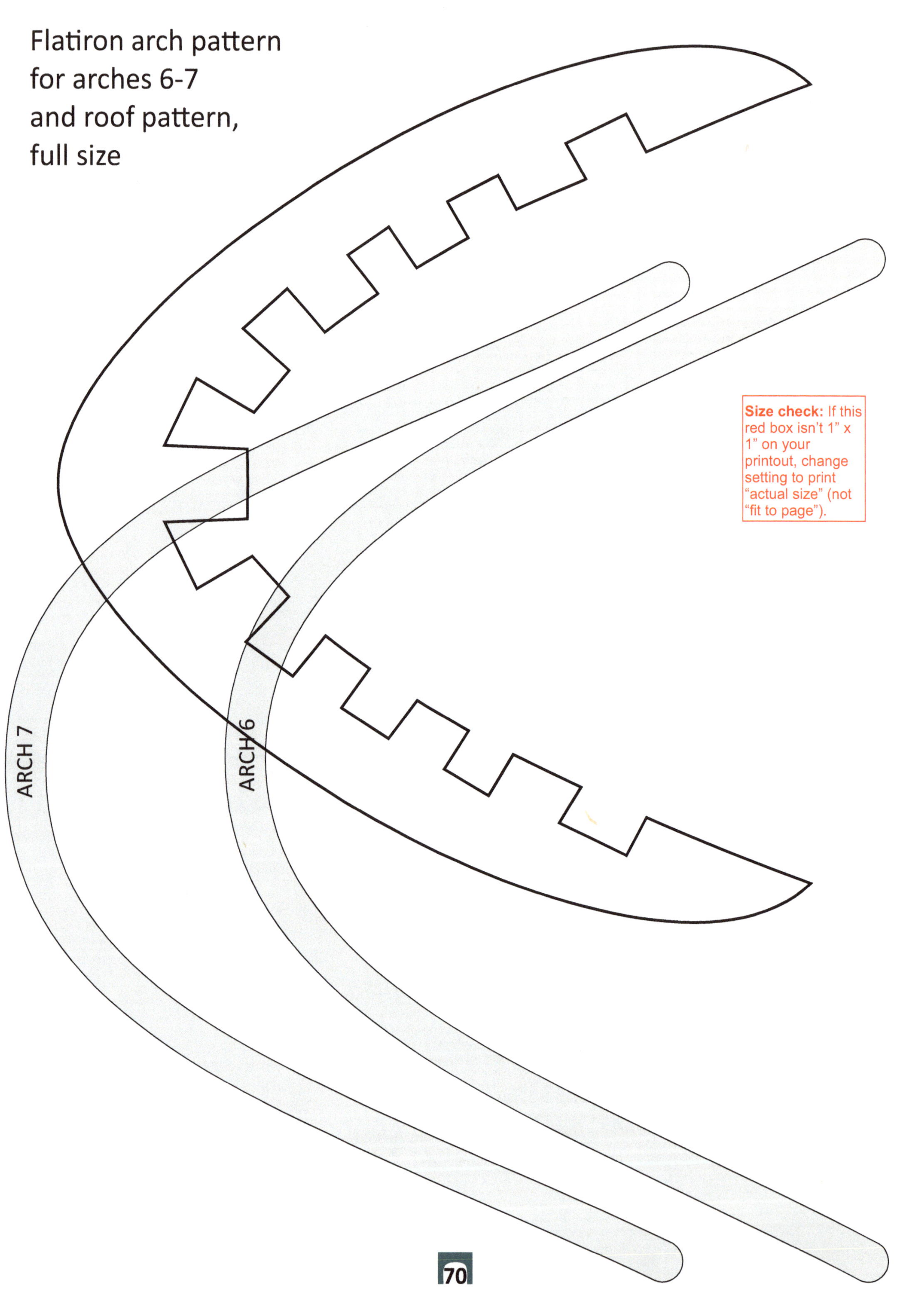

Flatiron arch pattern
for arches 6-7
and roof pattern,
full size
ARCH 7
ARCH 6
Size check: If this red box isn't 1" x 1" on your printout, change setting to print "actual size" (not "fit to page").

Quilt 1: Condensed New York

Do you live in a cramped, New-York-style apartment? This is the quilt for you! It's the smaller of the two in this book, although of course you can add borders as large as you like. You also don't have to stick with this layout – rearrange buildings as desired! See more layout options on p. 81.

Finished size: Approx. 57" x 59" if without borders.

62"x 63" with borders shown.

You will need:

► **All 11 buildings in this book** Finished, with bottom edges NOT turned up.

► **Background/upper sky fabric** 2 yards or 42" x 65". In this example, it's solid black.

► **Colorful borders fabric** Small amounts of many colors.

► **White part of borders, and binding fabric** There's white built-into the left, top and right borders; the same white is used as binding. With straight-of-grain binding, one yard will suffice; for bias binding start with 1.5 yards and cut it first for the binding, before using the rest to piece into the borders.

► **Batting** Because of the black sky, I used black batting. But with any background lighter than black, regular white/off white batting is fine.

– No borders: 61" x 62" of batting.

– Borders shown: 67" x 68" of batting.

► **Backing fabric**

– No borders: 61" x 62"

– Borders shown: 70" x 71"

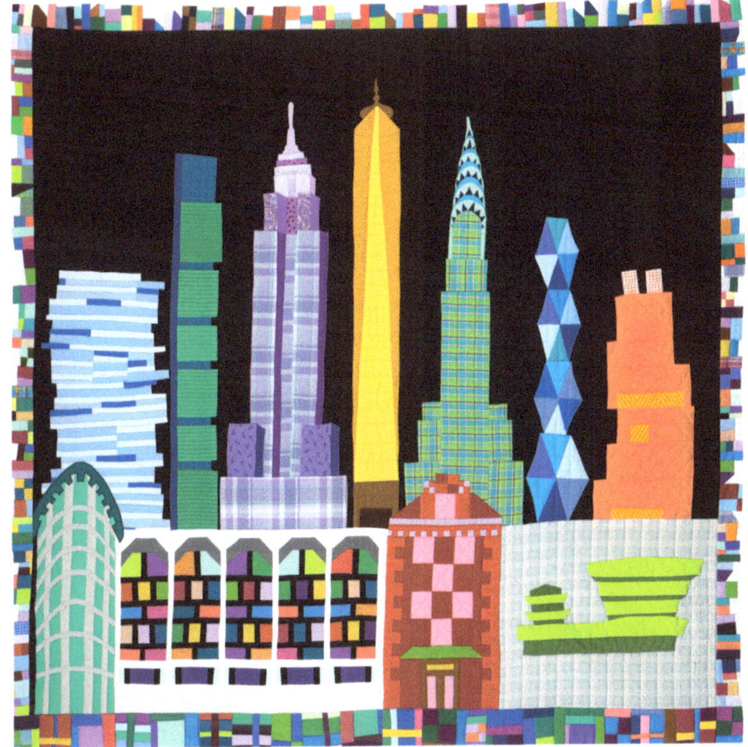

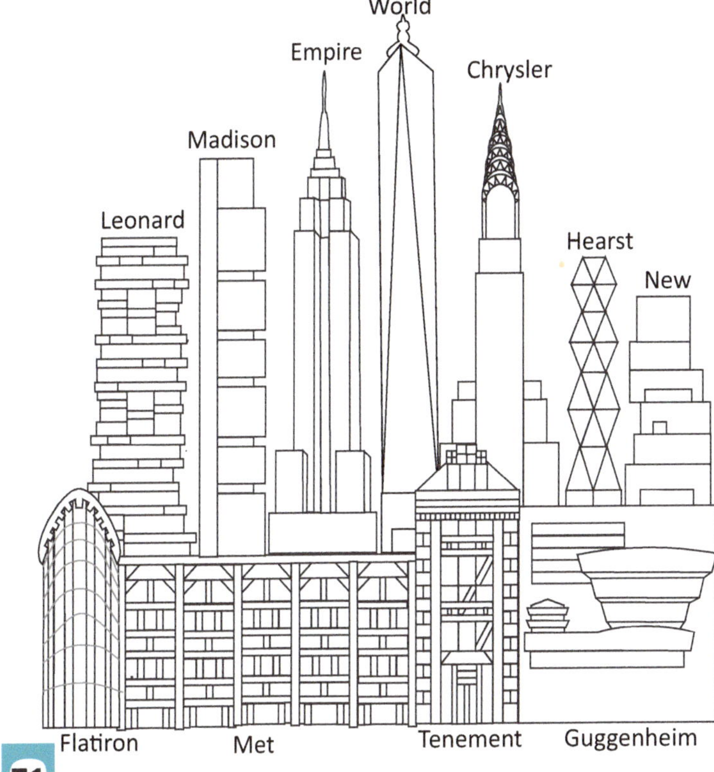

Sew the Bottom Row Together

1 Make all 11 buildings in the book. Appliqué the Guggenheim to the middle of its rectangular "tower" background, finishing it as p. 40.

2 Piece and/or appliqué the bottom row together. Here's my suggested layout. (You can change it, but follow the principles on this page.)

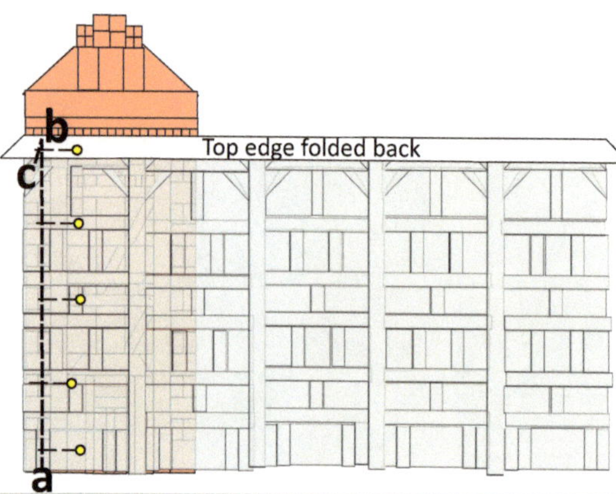

3 Starting in the middle, press the top edge of the Met 1/4" to the back.

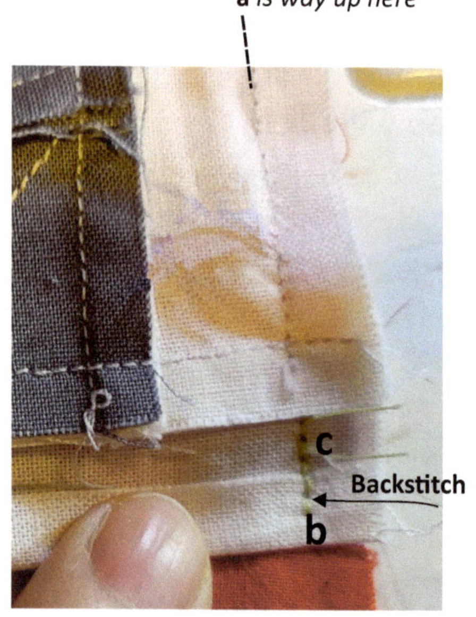

4 Place Met, good side down, on the townhouse, whose good side is up. Match bottom and left raw edges. Pin along the left edge.

5 Rotate everything so you can start sewing from the buildings' base (at **a**). Stitch to **b**, stopping just before reaching the Met's fold. Do a few backstitches to **c**. Cut threads.

a is way up here

6 Press seam allowances under the taller building. The front top now looks something like this.

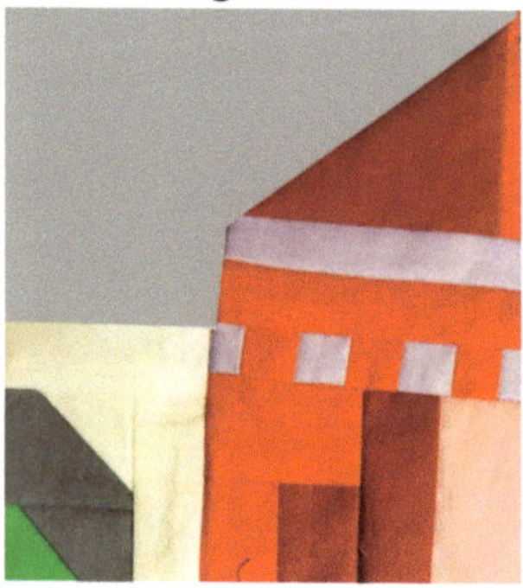

7 Appliqué the right edge of Flatiron onto the Met's left edge. I chose neutral thread to zigzag down Flatiron's lower right edge, starting just **below** its roof (we'll stitch the roof's remaining raw edges later.) I drew a red line on this photo to the left of the appliqué stitching.

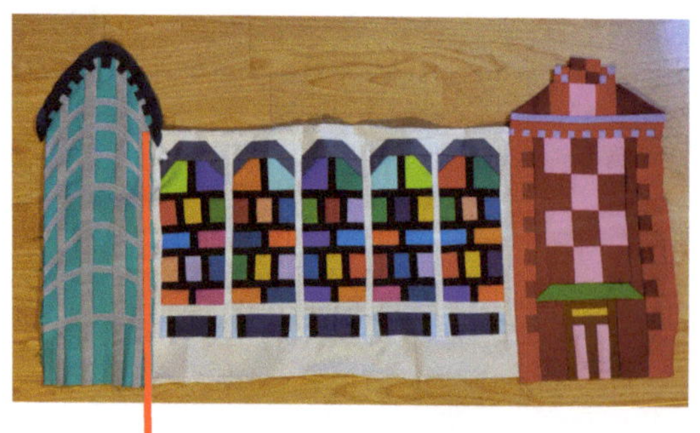

8 Add the Guggenheim. Press its background's top edge 1/4" back. Place it, face down, on the right edge of the townhouse (whose good side is up). Match bottom and right edges and pin as shown. Start sewing at **a**, just below the top flap. Backstitch to **b**, just below the fold. Sew all the way down and off at **c**. Press seam allowances left, under the taller townhouse.

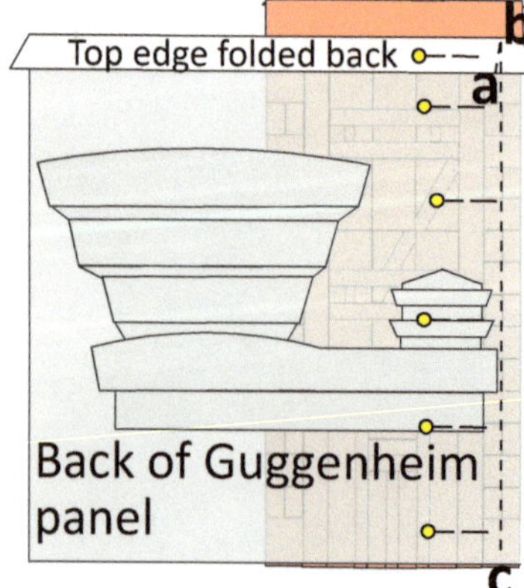

(continued)

<u>9</u> Measure the width of your finished bottom row. My first one came out to 58". Add a 3" safety margin and jot it down.

Audition Skies and Fine Tune Layout

<u>10</u> Audition sky fabric. Ideally, candidates would be at least as wide as the figure you wrote down – but if you don't have that much in your stash, use whatever size you have behind just a few buildings.

I strongly urge you to test 3 or more sky candidates. On a design surface, lay the 7 upper buildings' raw bottom edges along the sky fabric's raw bottom edge. Place front row (transparent in the diagram) with its top edge covering the base of the skyscrapers by at least an inch.

Stand back, take pictures, and ask yourself: Does this fabric enhance the buildings? The answers always surprise me. Over many cityscapes, I've chosen white sky once; navy several times; and whimsical prints. This was my first cityscape with solid black sky, for a sophisticated look that I thought befitted NYC. But prints are SO much fun – geometrics suggest more buildings; flying flowers, apples (Big Apple!) or meatballs make a whimsical statement! You won't know until you try! Once you've picked a favorite, you can hopefully order more of it in the needed quantity.

You're also auditioning the top row arrangement. You may want a different order, especially if you're adding or subtracting buildings. Or you may want their bases to be higher than the sky's bottom edge. So fine-tune your placement.

<u>11</u> Add a sky strip to the lower left to preserve the Flatiron's left roof line. I first marked the tops and bottoms of where I wanted each upper building (black markings in the diagram). Then I removed the buildings. I cut a strip of sky fabric to 3" by the height of the Flatiron (or whatever building's in your lower left corner). I cut that piece off the end of my 61" wide sky fabric because I knew 58" was enough. Sew it to the bottom left edge of the background and press seam allowance down.

<u>12</u> Baste each top row building in position by hand or machine. I don't pin-baste because so many pins, in so many directions, will stab me so many times! I stitch-baste all around them.

<u>13</u> Hand-appliqué or machine appliqué. Information is on pp. 5-6. There's no need to appliqué across the bottoms of the buildings – just sides and top. Do some test samples first, because your stitches might be improved by stabilizer.

For buildings with fusible-backed spires – Empire and Chrysler – once you've appliquéd their turned edges, fuse their spires permanently in position, and switch to a stitch and thread that covers the spires' raw edges and blends with the color better. (Again, test a sample first, explained on p. 6.)

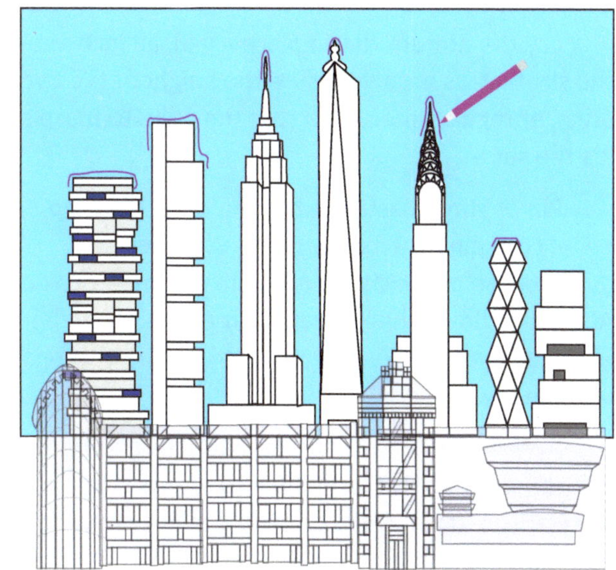

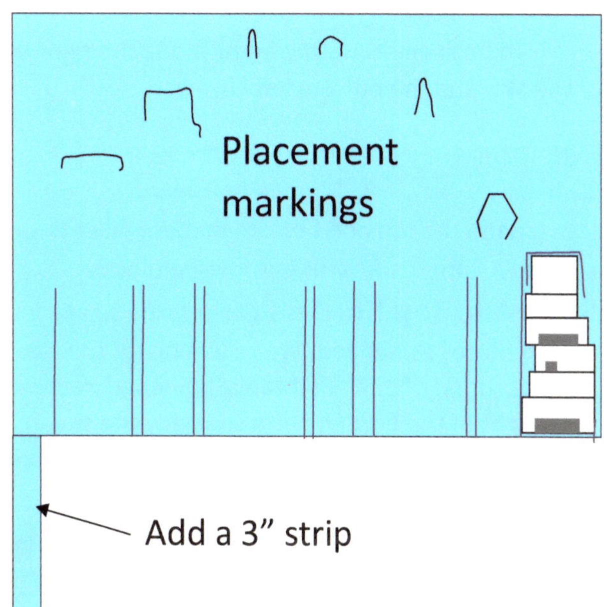

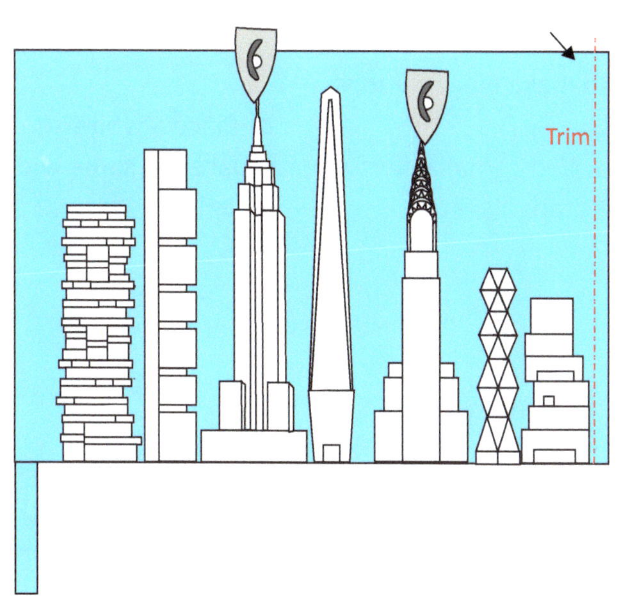

(continued)

14 Lay the bottom row in place again, an inch above the sky fabric's base. Measure the height of the two units, at regular intervals across the quilt, to make sure it's the same.

15 Pin or stitch-baste the bottom row's long top edge. (The pins are mostly pointing in the same direction, so pin-basting isn't quite as dangerous here!) Also baste down the Flatirons' left edge, below the roof. Fuse the Flatiron's roof, covering part of Leonard and the sky.

16 Appliqué with invisible or neutral thread from **A** to **B**, and from **C** to **D**. Then switch to thread that matches the Flatiron's roof, and a stitch you might prefer for raw edges (like a satin stitch). Go over the entire curved raw edge of the roof, including those little unsewn areas just under the roof's sides.

17 Trim back any extra sky fabric along the right edge of the sky, and the bottom left corner.

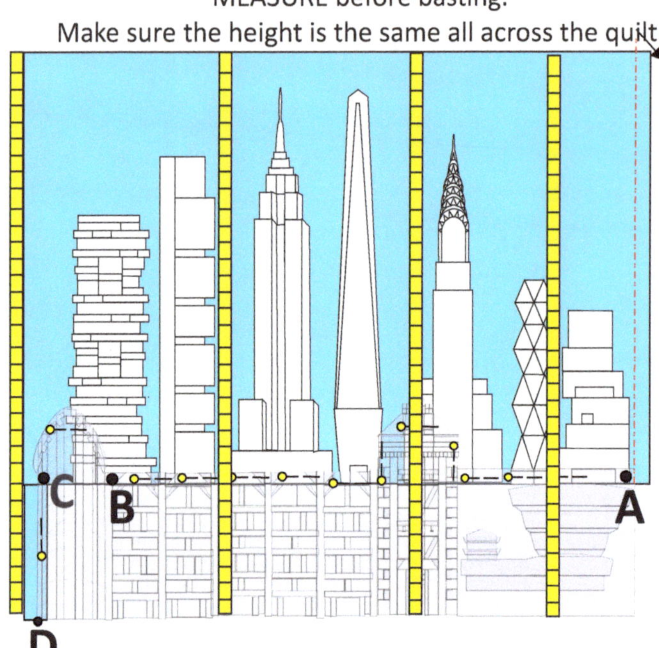

Make the Colorful Borders

18 I made the top and bottom borders taller than the side borders to get this quilt closer to a square. All are made with improvised blocks.

Sides and Top Borders Cut colorful scraps into strips 1-3" wide, plus a long white strip 2" wide. Cut off pieces as needed. We're aiming for the side and top borders to have a width in the neighborhood of 2.5"-3". Many "buildings" received a white sky strip. Some colorful pieces are the full height of the border. I also sewed white squares through their diagonal to colorful strips, to create the appearance of diagonal tops, and/or building sides in perspective, explained below.

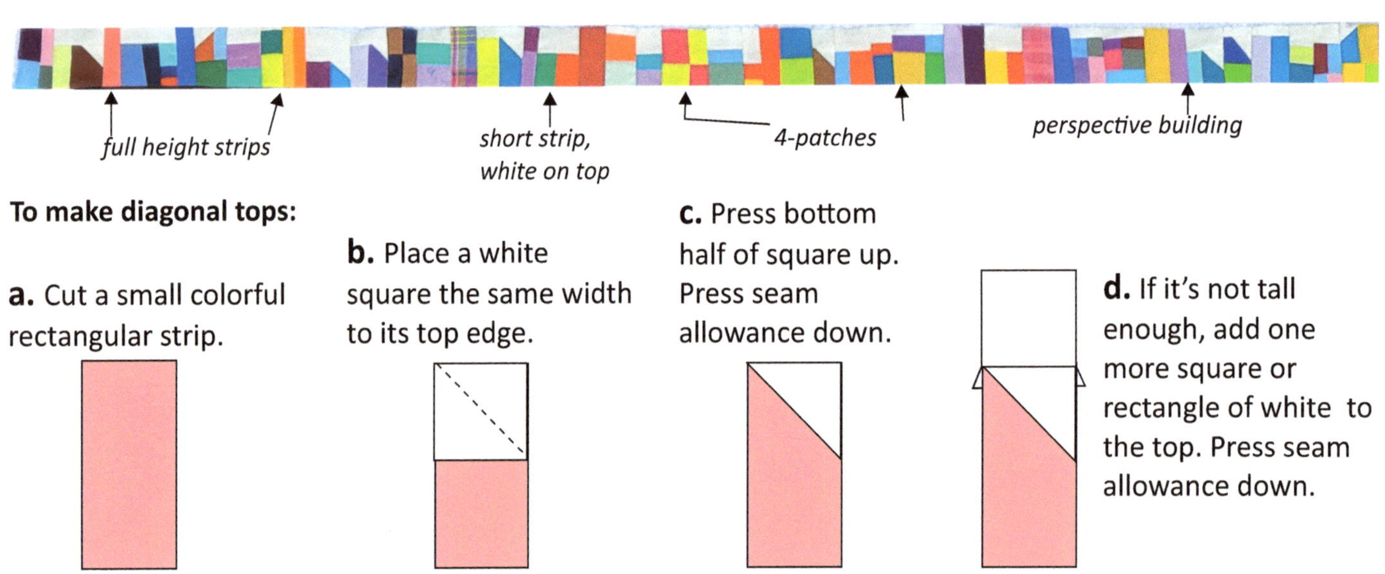

To make diagonal tops:

a. Cut a small colorful rectangular strip.

b. Place a white square the same width to its top edge.

c. Press bottom half of square up. Press seam allowance down.

d. If it's not tall enough, add one more square or rectangle of white to the top. Press seam allowance down.

19 When each border is the length you need for three sides of the quilt, trim the side borders to 2.5" wide and the top border to 2.75". Sew the narrower side borders to the left and right sides of the quilt, and the top border on top.

(continued)

Bottom Border I cut this improv border 3.75" high. There's no white in this border. It's made with four kinds of blocks, most in the neighborhood of 4" wide:

► **"Crosscut stripes"** striped blocks that are cross cut, with a narrow stripe of a different color inserted in the opposite direction.

► **"Window"** blocks with a largish square and a couple logs around them.

► **"Doorways"** with squares resting on the bottom.

► **4-patches** using 2-4 fabrics and additional logs to get the height right.

It's important to do the arranging along the bottom edge of the quilt. You don't want these blocks to accidentally look like extensions of the buildings directly above them. So make sure there's a strong color and/or value contrast with each building they touch. However, if you DO want to make them into a front yard for your lowest buildings, go for it!

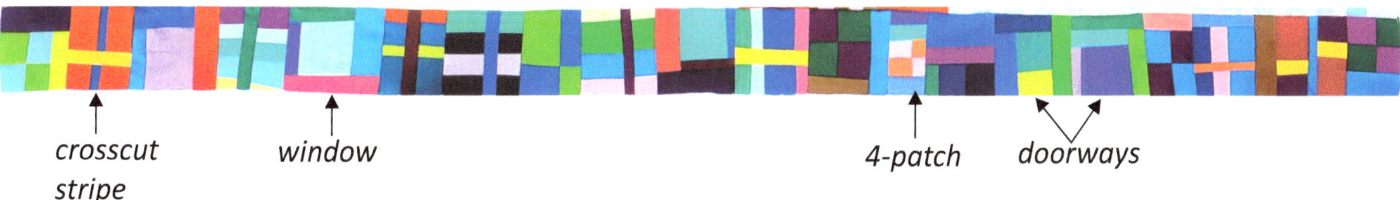

Finish the Top and Quilt It

20 Cut batting and backing a little bigger than your quilt top. Sandwich the layers and baste.

21 Quilt it! I first quilted close around the top edges of all the buildings that are against the sky using thread the same color as the sky.

Next, I quilted in the ditch within each building, following either the construction lines, and/or selected lines of the plaids. I used a different color thread inside each building, to match it. With a multicolored print, used either thin grey thread, or monofilament "invisible" thread.

In some cases, I gave the building texture, like the townhouse's bricks. Suggestions are in the photos and information at the end of each building chapter.

22 I did something simple in my sky for this quilt – a grid of rectangles with one-way diagonals slicing through them. First I marked and sewed the horizontal lines. Then, the verticals. Finally, I marked and sewed the diagonals, connecting corners. I sewed this all in black threads, but could have switched that out. And now I'm contemplating quilted fireworks!
I wound my way through the borders, quilting in the ditch along many (but not all) of the lines with my thin light grey (Deco-Bob) thread. Then I doodled loops and straight-line mazes on the larger strips in the border blocks.

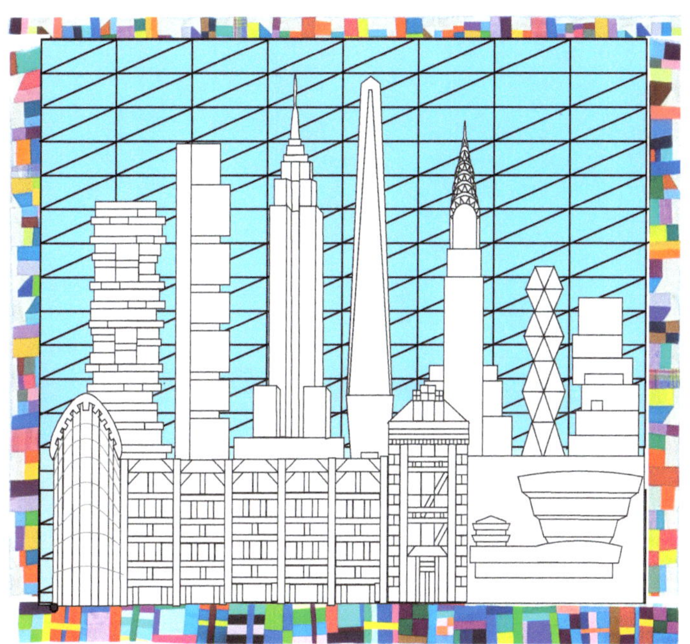

23 The last step was to bind it. I used white bias binding. The white is a deliberate choice - it makes the tiny 'buildings' in the side and top borders look like they're sticking out at uneven heights.

Now send me a picture! I want to see what you made!

"Color Block" Quilt Layout Chart

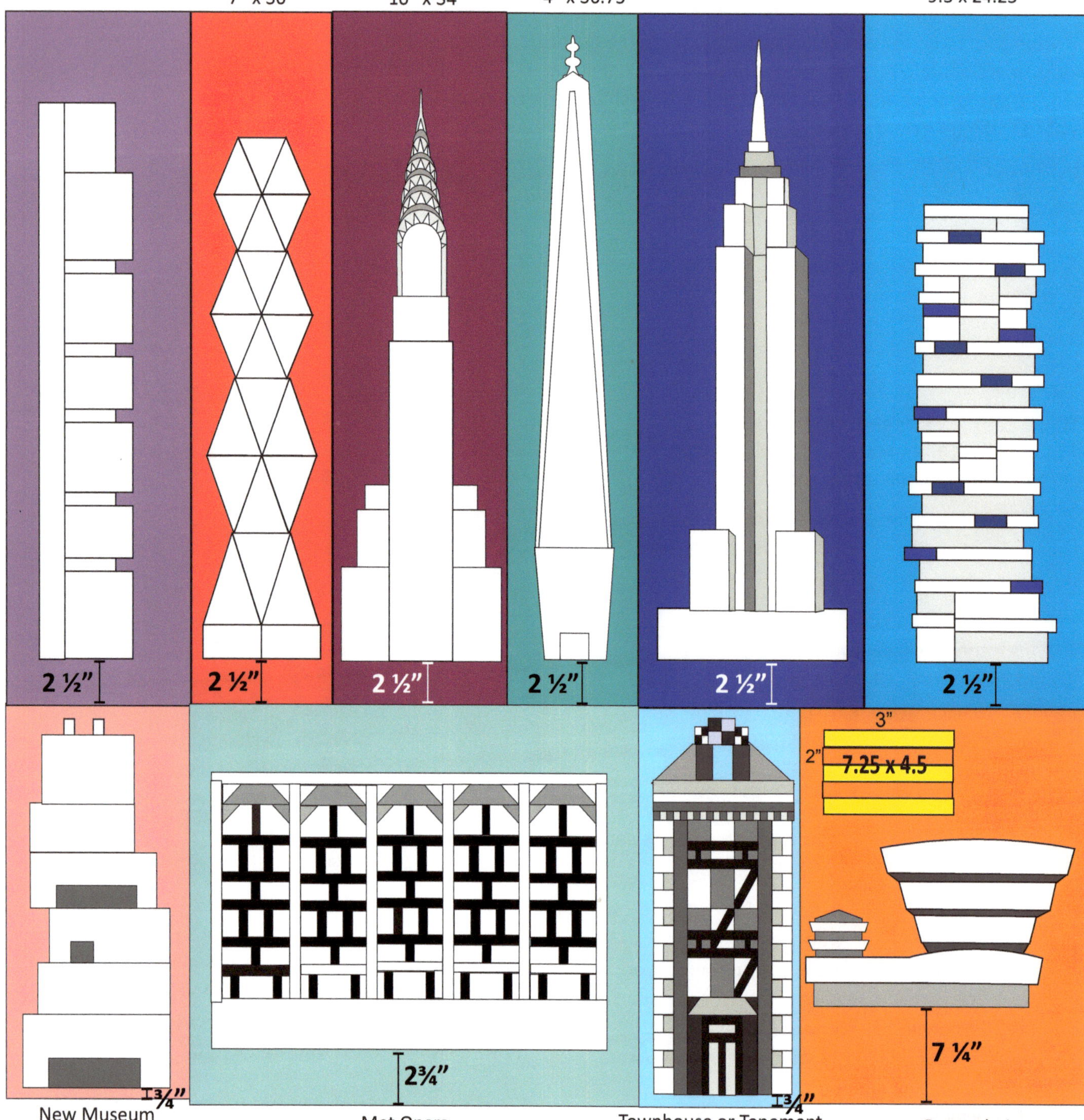

(continued)

Quilt 2: Color Block New York

This quilt will come out a little larger than the previous quilt. If you have plenty of wall space, this may be the version for you!

1 Make 10 buildings. There's no room for the 11th in this design – choose between Tenement/Townhouse or Flatiron for the bottom row, 2nd panel from the right. (See layout diagram on facing page.)

2 Audition backgrounds. My choices may not work for your buildings. Lay each building on a different background, and see what SINGS!

3 Cut background rectangles to sizes in the diagram on the previous page (and in each chapter's supply box). For the six on the quilt's **top row only:** each background is 39.5" high. Four require a third- to a half-yard. Two (Hearst and World Trade) can be a regular quarter-yard. (NONE up here can be a fat-quarter). **Bottom row:** a fat-quarter of each background will work for all except the Met, which needs a half-yard (unless you piece it in position instead of appliqué).

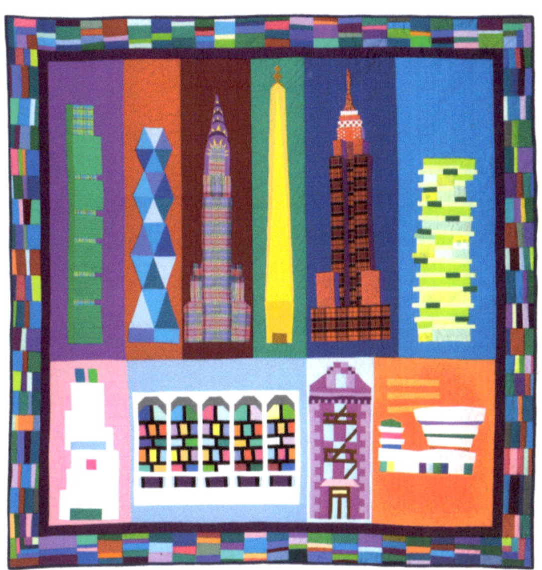

Sew Each Building to its Background

4 All building edges should be turned back (except spires and Flatiron roof), including all bottom edges. Clean up, as in "Tips" on p. 5.

5 Press background fabric. Measure or fold to find the vertical center of top and bottom edges. Pin, mark or crease, as in the diagram on the right.

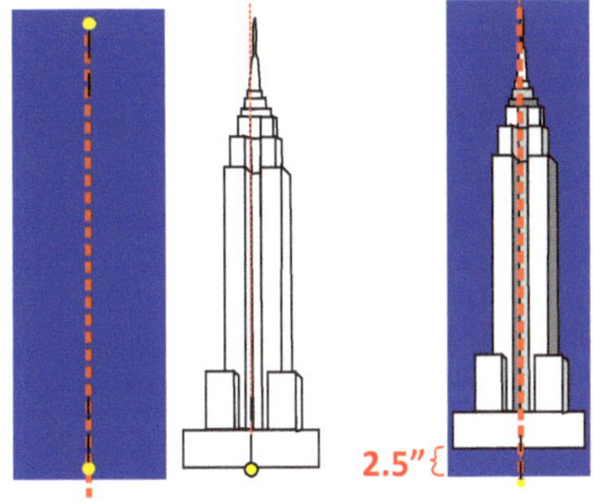

Top Row Place the bottom folded edge of each building 2.5" above the bottom raw edge of the background. This leaves you room to embroider something – the name or height of the building, for example – below it.

Bottom Row The distance from the building's bottom edge to the bottom edge of its background is in the chart on the facing page. (If the building is a tight squeeze, you may prefer to sew the rectangle to its neighbors first, and appliqué the building afterwards.)

6 Pin or stitch-baste each building to its background. If there's a fusible-backed spire or roof (the Flatiron), pin that area in place for now.

7 Make samples to test threads, stitches, tension, and possibly stabilizer. Read pp. 5-6.

8 Use your favorite appliqué stitch on buildings' turned edges. When you reach a raw-edge feature, like a spire, save it til you've done all the regular appliqué. Then you will probably want to change thread color, and switch to a tighter stitch to cover and protect raw edges.

Finished size:
– 61.5" square with no borders
– 63.5" square with just a sashing strip on all sides (cut to 1.75"), but no colorful block borders. (I call this the "inner border"; in the quilt above, it's dark burgundy.)
– 72.25" square with the 1.75" sashing AND colorful block borders, with the latter cut 4.5" wide, shown above.

You need:

► **10 of the 11 buildings in the book**

► **10 assorted background fabrics** Requirements are in each building's supply box, summarized on p. 76.

► **1/2 yard of fabric for inner border** Dark burgundy in the sample quilt, cut 1.75" wide.

► **Backing fabric and batting** With no borders, approx. 70" x 70". With 4.5" borders shown, 80" x 80".

► **Binding fabric:** Just under 300" for the borders version. Start with a yard. If you don't cut it on the bias, a half-yard works.

(continued)

10 **Start with the inner border.** I cut dark burgundy fabric into 1.75" strips - if you're cutting from 44" wide fabric, you'll need to cut and join six pieces to go all the way around the quilt. I sewed these to all four sides of the quilt (I like to do sides first, then top and bottom last).

11 **Make the colorful block borders.** Below is the top border. All four were made the same way. Cut lots of colorful strips 1 - 2.5" wide. I used solids only, but you choose – leftovers from the buildings (prints or solids) help tie everything together. Make blocks 4.5" high and varying widths, from 3-6". Half contain medium and dark colors; half contain at least one light strip. There are about 20 of these blocks per side, plus four 4.5" x 4.5" log cabin blocks, one in each corner, for a total of about 80 blocks. I alternated blocks with and without light strips all around (except corners). Sew borders to central quilt. I sew sides on first, then add top and bottom horizontal strips, which have a partial log cabin block on both ends, as shown below.

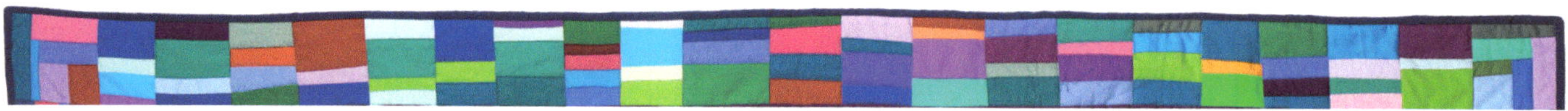

12 Sandwich the quilt and baste it.

13 **Stabilize backgrounds first.** Marked in red on the right. With invisible monofilament, or thread that matches each background color, stitch in the ditch along:
► the horizontal seam between the two rows,
► the vertical line between after the first buildings on the left,
► the vertical line on the right of World Trade.
You can also ditch-stitch the rest of the long seams now – or wait and do it as you fill in each background, when you have a same-color thread loaded in your machine.

14 **Quilt within each building.**
► Ditch-stitch major seams or printed lines (like along stripes).
► Quilt just inside windows, to push them "back".
► See also the suggestions at the end of each building's chapter.

15 **Around Each Building.**
► Outline it first, with background-matching thread, just outside each building, all the way around.
► Fill in remaining backgrounds. I had a lot of fun here. On some backgrounds, I doodled more imaginary skyscrapers – vertical stripes of repeating patterns. On some, I made emanating lines to give the building a glow (World Trade and tenement). See diagrams on next page.
► A much simpler and very "modern" alternative is to do straight line vertical quilting, with or without a walking foot – just lines, up and down, in all the backgrounds.
► While I still had each background-color thread in the machine, I stitched in the ditch along remaining boundaries between color blocks that I didn't sew during the stabilization phase.

16 **Quilt the borders.** I doodled free motion designs in the borders. See those on p. 80.

17 Email me a picture! I can't wait to see what you do with this quilt!

(continued)

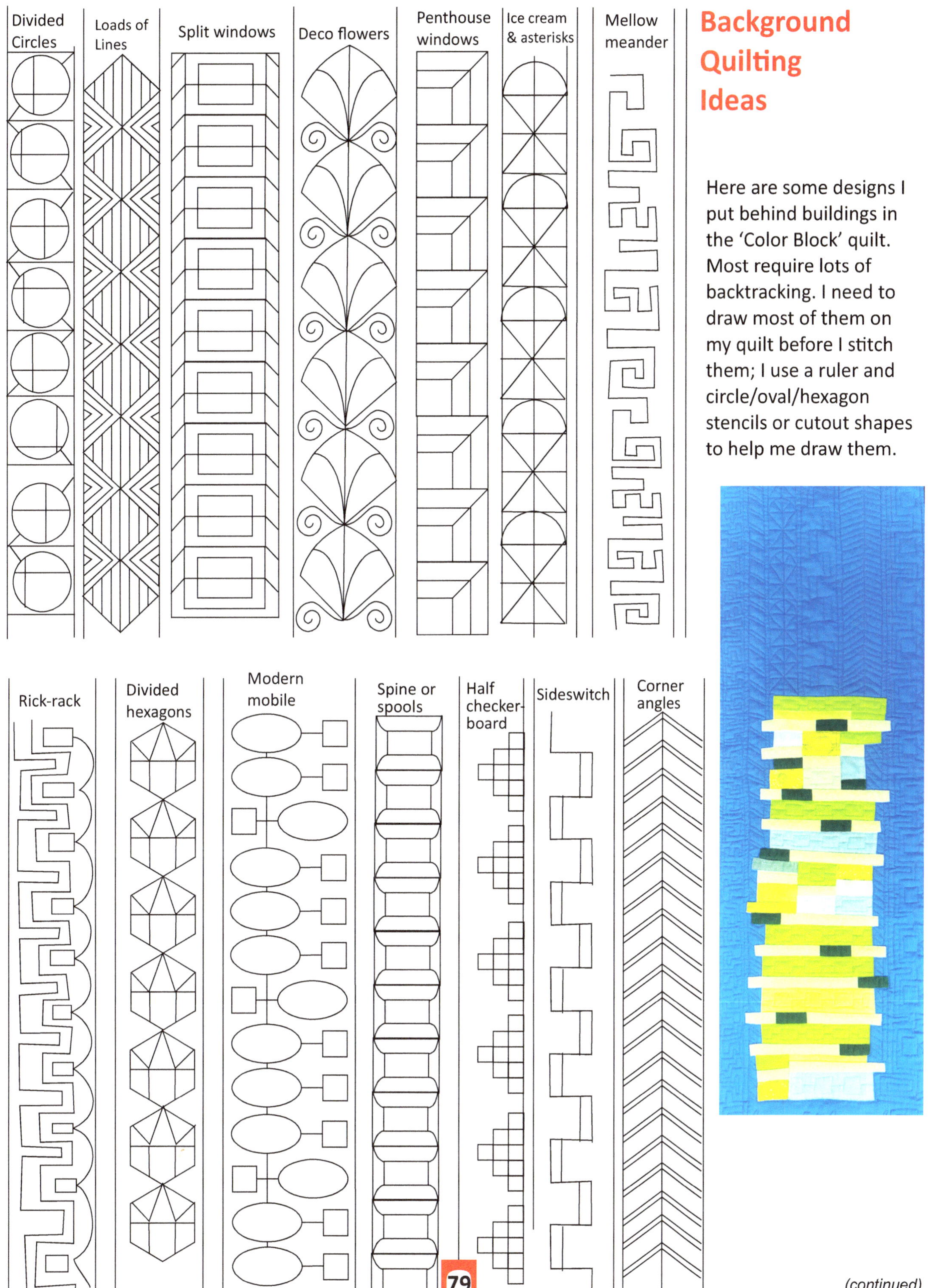

Background Quilting Ideas

Here are some designs I put behind buildings in the 'Color Block' quilt. Most require lots of backtracking. I need to draw most of them on my quilt before I stitch them; I use a ruler and circle/oval/hexagon stencils or cutout shapes to help me draw them.

(continued)

Inner Border NYC-Themed Quilting

The tessellating quilting design along the top inner border (burgundy fabric in the Color Block Quilt) was inspired by the pylons on New York City's innovative "Little Island." They also look a lot like wine glasses, which are even more plentiful than pylons in New York!

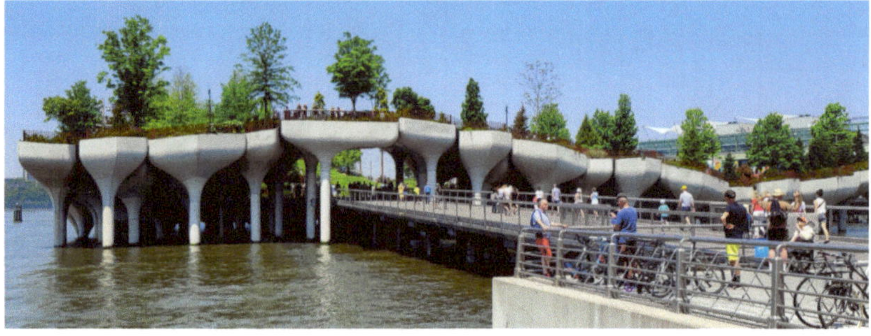

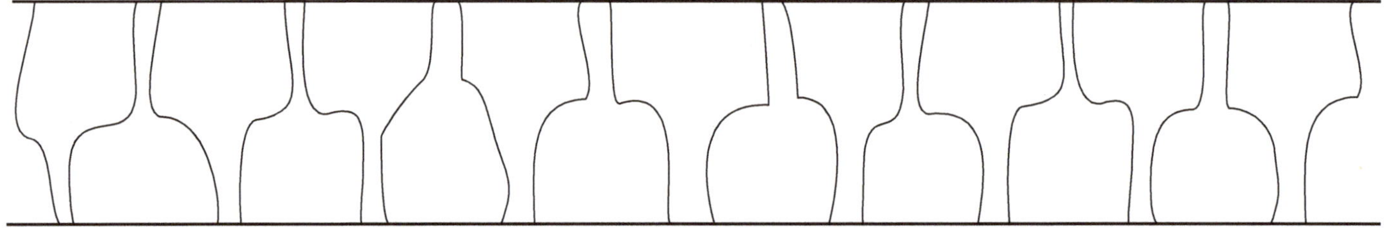

Objects of New York Quilting

The next designs were inspired by my spring of 2022 visit to New York – after a 2-year absence because of Covid. I walked the streets for hours every day, and saw, tasted, dodged, smelled and/or thought about these things, some familiar, some new. I put most of them in the 1.25" high (finished) inside border of the Color Block quilt. (The last six I thought of too late, after that quilt was finished, unfortunately!)

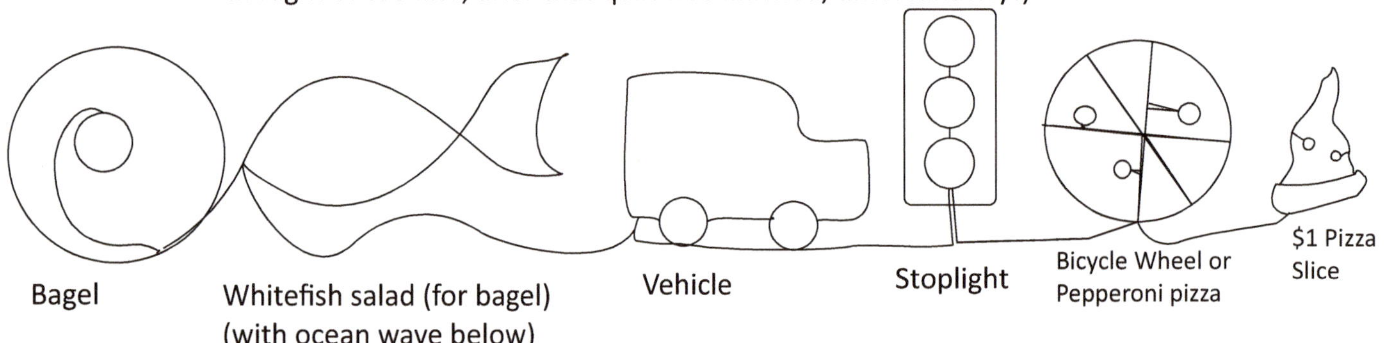

Bagel

Whitefish salad (for bagel)
(with ocean wave below)

Vehicle

Stoplight

Bicycle Wheel or
Pepperoni pizza

$1 Pizza Slice

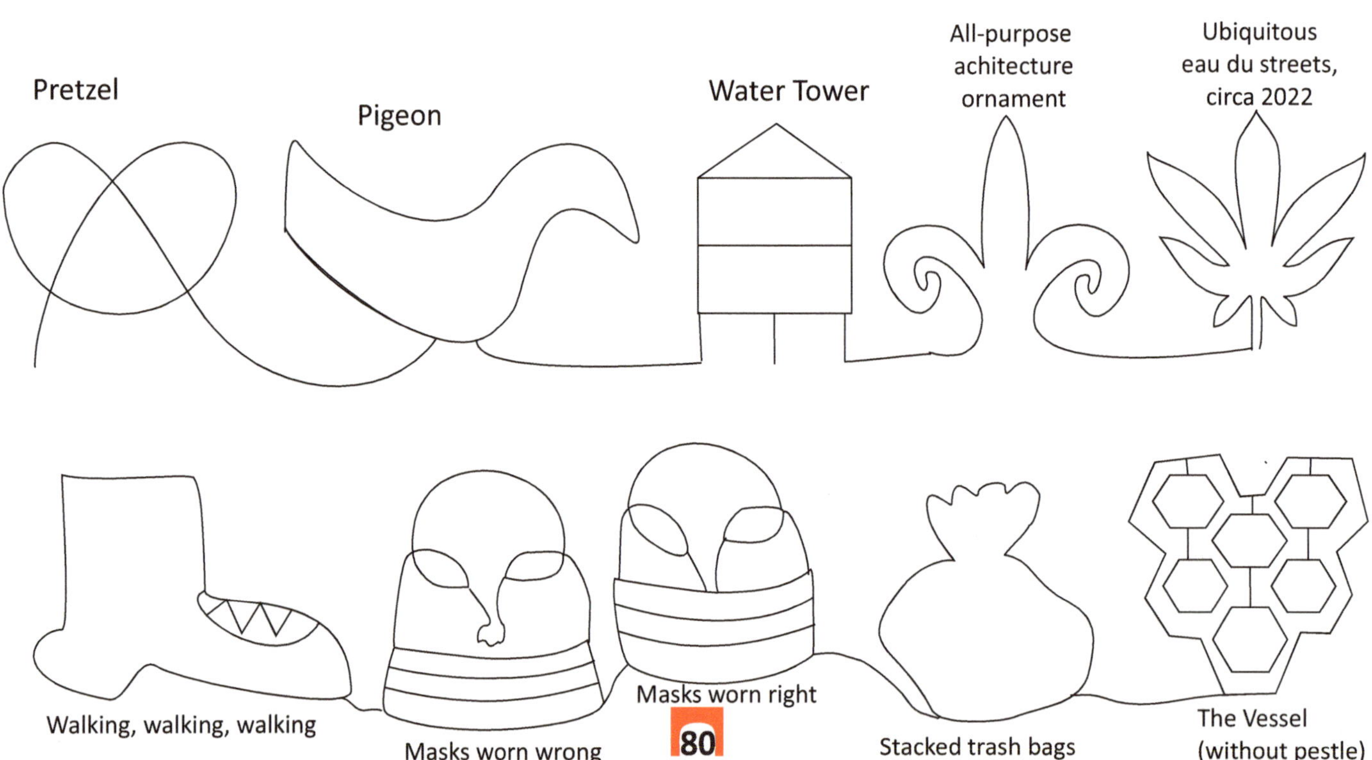

Pretzel

Pigeon

Water Tower

All-purpose achitecture ornament

Ubiquitous eau du streets, circa 2022

Walking, walking, walking

Masks worn wrong

Masks worn right

Stacked trash bags

The Vessel (without pestle)

More Project Ideas

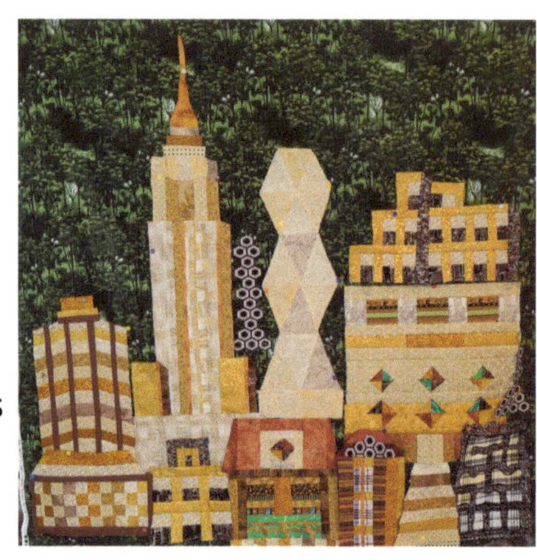

One Building

Make a pillow. Or how about a child's growth chart (left)? Applique a building and a measuring tape along one edge. Start the numbering at 27"/70 cm.

Three-Building Culture Quilt

Right, for the lover of the arts, two museums and an opera house would make a cute wallhanging or pillow.

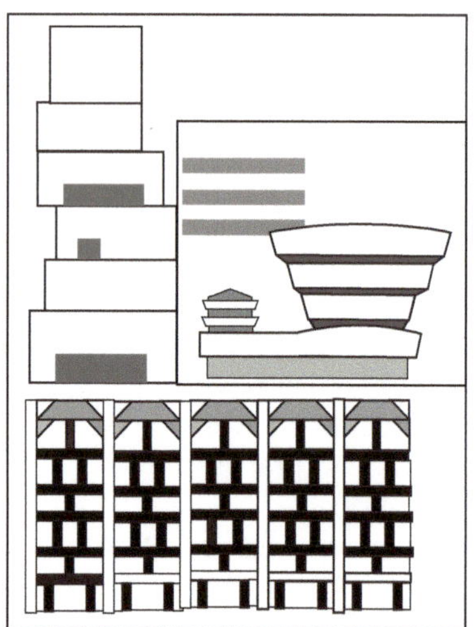

Packed! Right, a small cityscape by quilt artist Flora Cohen, using patterns from a couple of my books as well as her own creations.

Size Matters Layout (May not fit in your New York pied a terre)

This is a G-rated book, so until now I disciplined myself to avoid mention of the potentially Freudian motivations of the robust-egoed developers, architects, billionaires, etc. – mostly men – who willed, financed, bullied, and litigated these buildings into existence or into their possession. Until now! The guys behind the Empire State and Chrysler were especially honest about their passion to make theirs taller! I made relative heights similar to the inspiration buildings, but the proportions aren't exact (56 Leonard in real life is less than half as tall as the World Trade Tower.) A general arrangement by height would look like this. If your wall isn't long enough for a quilt like this, you need not include every one of them!

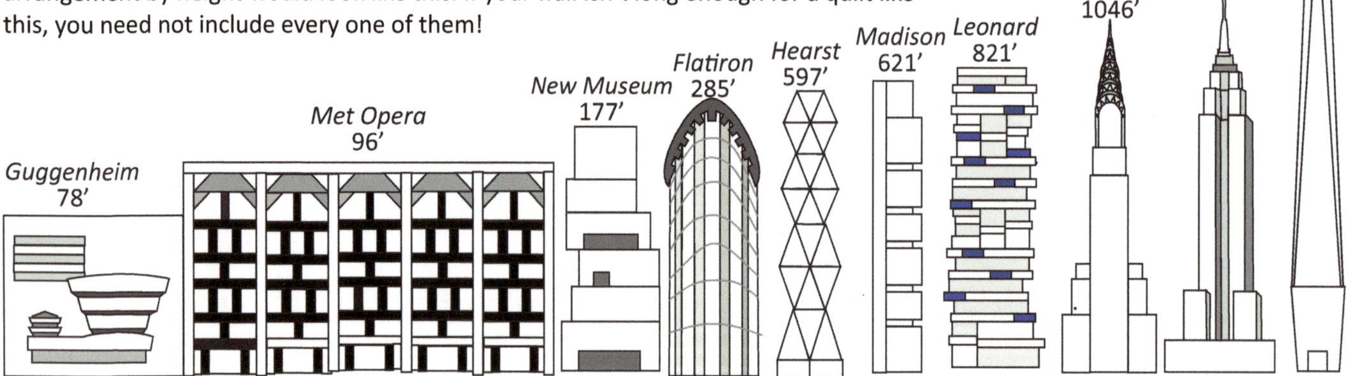

Geographical Layout

If you look at the city from due east of Manhattan, here's how the buildings line up:

World Trade Leonard New Museum Madison Flatiron Empire Chrysler Hearst Met Opera Guggenheim

Index

Recommended Reading & Touring!

Davidson, Justin. *Magnetic City, A Walking Companion to New York*. New York: Spiegel & Grau, 2017. Written by New York Magazine's architecture critic, this is one of the best books I've ever read about anything, not just New York City and architecture. Smart, funny quotable, brilliant insights into the history and socioeconomics of New York's skyscrapers. Even if you never visit New York, you will thoroughly enjoy this book.

Dupré, Judith. *Skyscrapers, A history of the world's most extraordinary buildings*. New York: Black Dog and Leventhal Publishers, Inc., 2013. At 9" x 18", this tome is more than a coffee table book – it's long enough to serve as the actual table. But it's worth the space, with fantastic photography and information about skyscrapers around the world.

Hill, John. *NYC Walks: Guide to New Architecture*. Munich-New York-London: Prestel, Publishing Ltd, 2019. Hill's insightful book will guide you on walking/public transit/driving tours that include most of the buildings in this book, and many, many more! This book fits in a backpack.

Jones, Will. *How to Read Modern Buildings: A crash course in architecture of the modern era*. New York: Rizzoli International Publications, Inc., 2017. This book is small enough to fit in your handbag, and explains almost everything about architecture, with delightful and helpful illustrations.

Bradkin, Cheryl Greider. *Basic Seminole Patchwork*. Concord, CA: C&T Publishing, 1990. My favorite book about a Native American fabric piecing technique that – ironically – is great for portraying urban architecture. (Bradkin's isn't the only quilting book on this subject, it just happens to be the one I own!)

Resources

The Tenement Museum, tenement.org Fascinating resources online and in person, including information about the history of New York's Jewish, African-American, and other ethnic groups who inhabited tenements.

Council on Tall Buildings and Urban Habitats
https://www.ctbuh.org/about
The CTBUH website includes the database formerly known as The Skyscraper Center (skyscrapercenter.com). Search for information about any tall building that interests you, around the world, at https://www.skyscrapercenter.com/buildings.

Help New York's Homeless Here's a list of 8 organizations that serve the homeless and poor. A portion of the sales from this book will go to these organizations.
https://www.timeout.com/newyork/things-to-do/where-to-volunteer-homelessness